*The Written World
and the Unwritten World*

ALSO BY ITALO CALVINO

ITALO CALVINO

The Written World and the Unwritten World
Essays

Translated from the Italian by
ANN GOLDSTEIN

MARINER CLASSICS
New York • Boston

Contents

Contents

Translator's Acknowledgments

I would like to thank, first of all, Giovanna Calvino for giving me the opportunity to work on *The Written World and the Unwritten World*, which has been an education not only in language but in life. I would also like to thank my editors, Pilar Garcia-Brown and Jessica Vestuto, for their stalwart patience. Finally, I would like to thank Enrica Maria Ferrara, professor of Italian at Trinity College Dublin, whose close readings and knowledge of Calvino's works were invaluable.

Reading, Writing, Translating

Good Intentions

The Good Reader looks forward impatiently to his vacation. He has saved a certain amount of reading that interests him for the solitary weeks he'll spend at the beach or in the mountains, and he can already taste the joy of siestas in the shade, the rustling of pages, surrender to the fascination of other worlds exuded by densely printed pages.

As the holidays approach, the Good Reader tours the bookshops, browses, sniffs, has second thoughts, returns the next day to buy; at home he takes down from the shelf volumes whose pages are still uncut and lines them up between the bookends on his desk.

It's the time when the mountain climber dreams of the peak he's getting ready to scale, and the Good Reader, too, chooses which mountain to take on. For example, it could be one of the great nineteenth-century novelists, of whom we can never say we have read their entire oeuvre, or whose mass has always somewhat awed the Good Reader, or whose works, read at different times and at different stages of life, have left fragmentary memories. The Good Reader has decided that this summer he will really, finally, read that author; maybe he won't be able to read everything during the vacation, but he will lay down a base of fundamental readings, and then, during the year, he'll be able to fill in the gaps easily, in a leisurely way. So he acquires the works he intends to read, in the original language if it's one he knows, otherwise in the best translation; he prefers the large volumes of the collected-works editions, but he doesn't dislike paperbacks, which are better for reading on the beach or under the trees or on the bus. He adds some good essays on the chosen author, or maybe a correspondence: there, now he has solid company for his vacation. It can hail the whole time, his holiday companions can turn out to be hateful, the mosquitoes may be intolerable and the food inedible: the vacation will not be wasted, the Good Reader will return enriched by a new imaginative world.

This, obviously, is only the main course, now he has to think of the side dishes. The Good Reader wants to keep up with the latest bookstore offerings; then, there are new publications in his professional field, and it's crucial to take advantage of these days to read them; he also has to choose some books that are different from the ones he's already chosen, to provide variety and the possibility of frequent interruptions, repose, and changes of tone. Now the Good Reader has before him a very detailed reading plan, for all occasions, hours of the day, moods. If he has a house available for his holidays, maybe an old house full of childhood memories, what could be better than to have a book for every room, one for the porch, one for the bedside, one for the chaise longue?

It's the eve of departure. He's chosen so many books he'd need a trunk to transport them. The job of exclusion begins: "This one I won't read anyway, this is too heavy, this isn't urgent," and the mountain of books crumbles, is reduced to half, to a third. Now the Good Reader has reached a selection of essential readings that will lend tone to his vacation. As he packs his suitcases some volumes are left out. Thus the program comes down to a few books, but all substantial; these holidays will represent an important stage in the Good Reader's spiritual evolution.

The days of vacation begin to pass swiftly. The Good Reader finds himself in excellent shape for sports, and stores up energy to get into the ideal physical situation for reading. After lunch, however, he's so drowsy that he sleeps all afternoon. He has to react, and here the company—unusually pleasant this year—helps. The Good Reader forms many friendships, and morning and afternoon is out in the boat or off on a tour, and at night is carousing until late. Reading, of course, requires solitude; the Good Reader thinks up a plan to get away. Cultivating his attraction to a blonde might be the best option. But with the blonde he spends the morning playing tennis, the afternoon at canasta, and the evening dancing. In moments of leisure, she is never silent.

The holiday is over. The Good Reader puts the untouched books back in the suitcase, thinks of autumn, of winter, of the rapid, concentrated quarters of an hour granted to reading before he goes to sleep, before rushing to the office, in the tram, the dentist's waiting room . . .

[1952]

Characters and Names

In my opinion the names of characters are very important. When I'm writing and about to introduce a new character, and I already have a clear idea of what this character is like, I stop to search, even for half an hour at a time, and I can't go on until I've found a name that is the true name, the only name for that character.

A history of literature (or at least of literary taste) could be written based on characters' names. Limiting ourselves to contemporary Italian writers, we can distinguish two principal trends: names that have as little weight as possible, that don't create any sort of barrier between the character and the reader, common, interchangeable baptismal names, like numbers distinguishing one character from another; and names that, even without a precise meaning, have an evocative power, are a kind of phonetic definition of their respective characters and, once applied to them, can no longer be detached, become one with them. Our major contemporary writers can easily be assigned to one category or the other, or to an intermediate system. As for me, I am, in my small way, a supporter of the second tendency; I know very well that there is a constant risk of falling into affectation, into bad taste, into mechanical grotesqueness, but names are a factor like any other in what we are accustomed to call the "style" of a narrative, and they should be chosen along with it, and judged in its overall success.

Someone will object: but the names of people are random, so the names of characters, to be realistic, should be random. I believe, however, that unmotivated names are abstract: in reality one always finds a subtle, impalpable, sometimes contradictory relationship between name and person, such that the person is always what he is plus the name he has, a name that without him would signify nothing but attached to him acquires a special significance. It's this relationship that the writer has to evoke for his characters.

[1952]

The Failure of the Italian Novel

In other literatures the novel had reckless, globe-trotting fathers, and a long, exuberant, and successful life. Here in Italy its father was Alessandro Manzoni: a parent so truly noble that we cannot imagine one more worthy, more diligent and patient in bringing up his only begotten son. He wanted his novel to be a model, and certainly he succeeded. But just as the children of overly staid and virtuous parents often grow melancholy and are unable to treasure the education so assiduously instilled, the offspring of *The Betrothed* encountered a sort of impediment that derived from the not very novelistic temperament of their progenitor. By this I don't mean to diminish in any way that great author and that great book: but only to describe their particular nature. Manzoni was in fact a singular novelist: he had no taste for adventure, he was a moralist without an impulse toward introspection, he was a creator of characters and settings and plagues and lansquenet invasions that were always acutely described and commented on but not fated to become great new modern myths. And he was the maker of a language that was full of art and meaning but lies on things like a layer of paint: a language clear and sensitive like no other but paint nevertheless. And so, lucky him, he was unconcerned with love and its anxieties, whether happy or sad, open or hidden. Not that we'd reproach him for it; rather, today we're bored by eroticism, but, let's admit it, love has always been a great moving force in the novel and elsewhere.

Being in awe of such a father had repercussions from generation to generation, down to those closest to us. It weighed even on the true novelists, like Ippolito Nievo, who got tangled up in the Manzonian moralizing and linguistic traps: he who knew what adventure was, and family history, and social nobility and decadence, and human life and the presence of a woman in the life of a man, and native land, and the transfiguration of memory into a continuous real presence—the generous, the young, the fluvial Nievo.

But in Italy to write novels—then as now—a tradition had to be found, on the plane of great world narrative and on the plane of Italian literature (all of it, not a single genre or school), whose novelistic element lies outside novels, scattered among the early short-story writers and reporters and comics up to Porta and Belli, and among the greatest poets up to Leopardi.* So it was perhaps to the

---

* In the manuscript, the reference to Leopardi the "novelist," which had been suggested by my friend Giulio Bollati, was developed in a passage that I later eliminated in order not to anticipate the subject of an essay that Bollati intended to write. "What sort of father would we have wanted for the Italian novel? An active swordsman like Alfieri or

voices, sounds, and whispers of days and nights in Recanati that other voices responded, other sounds, other whispers from the gardens of Aci Trezza. Advancing in the wake of the French, Verga rediscovered the town as a symbol of Italian reality, redefined the relations of man—idyll and drama—with nature and with history, and in the gaps and intersections between language and dialect, grasped the ideal language of the novel.

Great inventions, which at the time bore little fruit. Descriptive regionalism ruled, a scourge that still afflicts our fiction today. It's not on the ground of taste that I am driven to condemn it but on that of principle. The true novel lives in the dimension of history, not geography: it's human adventure in time, and the places—the places as precise and beloved as possible—are necessary as concrete

---

Foscolo? Or one of those types brimming with plebeian vitality like Porta or Belli? Or a great creator of characters like Rossini or Verdi? Maybe none of these. For me the ideal father of our novel would have been someone who may seem more distant than anyone else from the resources of that genre: Giacomo Leopardi. In Leopardi, in fact, the great elements of the modern novel, those which Manzoni lacked, were alive: the tension of adventure (that Icelander who goes off alone through the forests of Africa, and that night among the corpses in Frederik Ruysch's studio, and the one on Columbus's main deck), the persistent introspective psychological examination, the need to give the names and faces of characters to his own feelings and thoughts and those of the century. And then the language: the path he pointed out was that of maximum effects with minimum means, which has always been the great secret of narrative prose.

"But above all it is typical of Leopardi to enclose the sense of the world within a known place, a town, a setting. And here his seed was quick to bear fruit: voices, sounds, etc." (*Author's note*)

images of time; but to present these places, and local customs, and the "true face" of this or that city or population as the content of the novel is a contradiction in terms.

Thus among the regional realists, or *veristi*, the anti-novel always won out over the novel, and the influence of Manzoni again froze the most pleasurable discoveries of language and place, including those of the best of them: the Genoese Remigio Zena.

But meanwhile more serious national catastrophes were developing in the terrain of the novel: Fogazzaro and Fogazzarismo (which even now has its successors in a provincial-cosmopolitan mode), D'Annunzio and Dannunzianesimo (which, defeated on the cultural level, still re-emerges every so often as a "volunteer" weed), Pirandello and Pirandellism (this misunderstanding about the means of expression, also with its scattered "success"). (And it is telling that the transition from one century to the next was marked not by a novelist but by a narrator in verse, Guido Gozzano.) It's not surprising if the literary generation that followed banished the novel as a spurious and inferior genre. You had to be from a city happily ignorant of the weight of tradition, like Trieste, to write novels with the marvelous literary virginity of Svevo; or from a city in which every stone is poisoned by literature, like Florence, to be able to write *Sorelle Materassi* (*The Materassi Sisters*).

And so we arrive at the problem of today. The new Italian novel originated—it's said—in opposition to the climate of *prosa d'arte* and hermetic poetry. But it was an opposition of themes rather than of content. (And the openness to influences from abroad played out as it had in the eras of Walter Scott and Zola.) The "hermetic man," man on the margins, the man of passive opposition, negative contemplative man, who by now knows everything and is startled only by imperceptible illuminations, is still always the protagonist of the generation of writers associated with the journals *Solaria* and *Letteratura*. A common social climate unites even Moravia's indifferent Michele (although he hadn't taken those paths) and Vittorini's more restless Silvestro, in Sicily (read: of *Conversazione in Sicilia*), and Pavese's prisoner and, later, Corrado, of *La casa in collina* (*The House on the Hill*). And Pratolini's delicate idyll rises on the shores of hermetic lyricism. Again, in these authors, compared with the period of Montalian poetry, there was the problem of relations with the surrounding world. Thus the novel is reborn from this convergence of a lyrical and intellectual vein with the need to be reflected in human stories.

This first period, which lasted until after the war, today is obsolete: no one is writing novels with a lyrical-intellectual protagonist in a working-class setting. Unfortunately, however, there has been a return to, on the one hand, slice-of-life naturalism and, on the other, pure lyricism. The problem today is not to give up either of the two elements—the lyrical intellectual or the objective—but to fuse them into a unified whole and . . . a new unified expressiveness.

(For memoir and nonfiction narratives that are documentary, portraits, discussions of ideas—that is, in the style of Carlo Levi—I would like to claim autonomy with respect to the novel; it's a genre necessary to a literature that sinks its roots into well-worked cultural terrain. A clear formulation of this need would be useful both for a serious connection with reality—more than what is achieved with superficial documentary narrative—and for the possible future life of the novel-novel.)

Can the novel-novel be reborn in Italy, today when great fiction is in crisis elsewhere as well? In Italy, certainly, there are a lot of irons in the fire, with new misunderstandings (dialect that has become precious, regionalism that has become expressionistic, photography back in favor, lack of culture that is thought to be youth, archaic imitation thought to be tradition), but something good, eventually, will come out of it.

One thing has always been missing from the Italian novel, and that is what I most love in foreign literatures: adventure. I know that not too long ago this was the watchword of Bontempelli, who perhaps had an idea of it that was only theoretical, with a streak of the irrational: whereas adventure is the rational test of man over things opposed to him. How could there be an adventure novel in Italy today? If I knew, I wouldn't be here explaining it: I would write it.

[1953]

The Fates of the Novel

We cannot use opposing terms to describe the situation of fiction, as we can with other means of expression. We can speak of objective narrators and lyrical narrators, of intro-spective narrators and symbolic narrators, of instinctive narrators and calculating narrators, but these categories define nothing and no one; all good writers have to be clas-sified not just in a single category but in the intersection of at least two. Each works in his own way; schools don't exist except in the shadowy margins. This is because fiction is the means of expression that is most severely in crisis and has been for the longest time; and also because it has more breath in its body than any other means of expression and can live in crisis indefinitely.

At one point we said: No, it's not in crisis, we'll show you. It was after the war, it seemed to us we had an engine inside, we saw the terms of the crisis of fiction but didn't believe they concerned us. I even claimed that the novel couldn't die: but I was unable to make one hang together. All of it was right, including making mistakes: many good things came of it, but not a new literary civilization.

Now, to convince ourselves of the everlasting power of the novel, we need to read Lukács, let ourselves be gripped by his classic faith in genres, by his clear sense of *epic*. But, having left the nineteenth century, we find his aesthetic ideal to be blurred by a soft patina of boredom: we don't see in it the agitation, the hurry of our lives. Rather, the response, the perfect measure of the new epic is not the developed novel but the lyric style of the short novel, or the crude journalistic novella at which Hemingway excelled.

Someone will object: There is Thomas Mann. Yes, he understood everything, or almost, about our world, but he was leaning out over the last banister of the nineteenth century. We're looking at the world as we fall into the stairwell.

We'd have to write stories like Faulkner's *The Old Man*, the story of a convict during a flood of the Mississippi. It's from 1939, I think, but as it happens I read it only this year, when a translation came out in Italy (a fine translation, by a friend of mine); and since the day I read it I've understood that either we write like that or fiction is condemned to become a minor art form.

(Minor but still useful, maybe. In Russia, for example, in the past couple of years some interesting short novels have been published, about man's behavior, his moral position in the face of both practical problems and problems of conscience that are encountered in daily life; in America, too, if I'm not mistaken, there is a literature of the common dignity of the white-collar worker in the great industrial and bureaucratic complexes. Fiction can also confine itself to this modest yet serious task. But it will do so in a slightly dull way, while cinema, if it responded better to its task, would be the ideal tool for the job.)

The habit of requiring fiction to say this, that, and the other depends on our belief that in telling a story we can say everything, unlike, for example, in poetry or painting. But it's only an indication of the inadequacy of a culture that is unable to forge the tools needed for every function. With this I don't mean to insist on *pure storytelling*; I always prefer the contaminated and impure to what is pure. But telling a story is telling a story; narrative that is concerned with telling a story has its work to do, and its moral, and its way of leaving a mark on the world.

I hope for a time of good books full of new intelligence, like the new energies and machines of production, and I hope that they will guide the renewal the world needs. But I don't think they will be novels; I think that certain flexible genres of eighteenth-century literature—the essay, the travelogue, the utopia, the philosophical or satirical story, the dialogues, the moral tale—have to regain their place as protagonists of literature, of historical intelligence and social battle. The story or novel will have this ideal atmosphere as a premise and as a point of arrival: because it will come from that terrain and will influence it. But it will do so in one way only: by telling a story—by seeking the right way to tell a story today, a way that for every period and society and human being is one and one alone, like calculating a trajectory.

Recently I've become fond of Brecht, not just the plays

but the theoretical writings, which I had unjustly neglected. A Brecht of fiction doesn't exist, unfortunately, and I am continuously tempted to transpose his understanding of theater, to translate it into other terms for fiction. Starting from his first marvelous axiom: That the purpose of theater is to entertain. That, yes, there are in the history of the theater all the religious, aesthetic, ethical, social motivations but on condition of entertaining people. It's the same for fiction. And that is too often forgotten.

[1956]

Questions on Realism

(1) In the light of recent political events in the socialist world, from the "thaw" to the actions in Hungary, how do you think the problem of "realism" should be presented in Italy?

(2) In Italy there is a rising literary tide calling into question the works of writers who are committed to Marxist ideology or at least tied to a particular political attitude of the left, and declaring neorealism—and, even more, that version of neorealism which is explicitly inspired by popular subjects—a failure. Do you think this position has a regressive and backward character or is it something positive and propulsive?

(3) If by subject matter we mean not only the choice of a particular setting but, more essentially, the attitude of the writer and of a generation toward that setting: What kinds of subject matter do you think constitute models that can be artistically realized today, and what works of the postwar period have been realized in that way?

(4) Gramsci declares that literature's inability to "be an epoch" involves not only literature but the entire "life of a particular historical period." Do you think that the "movement" in creation and criticism that we are witnessing is what Gramsci

calls "the dog biting his own tail," or does it contain in itself a precise unfolding?

(5) Do you think that the autobiographical writing of the postwar period, unlike that of the prewar period, which was stylized and strictly personal, documents a change of situations in a definite social process, and can rise to the dignity of political concept and ultimately replace the old political or philosophical essay?

(6) Do you think that representations of eroticism, or anyway fiction's particular insistence on problems of sex, as documenting moral dissolution, rule out the existence of a "general conception of morality" or contain it? In other words, is that dissolution comparable to Alexandrianism, that is, to a long-lasting historical and cultural experience, or is it a way of reacting to an old moral conception that has become pure formalistic hypocrisy and is trying to keep itself alive by force: a phenomenon more restricted in time, comparable, mutatis mutandis, to that of the age of Dante or the Enlightenment?

(7) In relation to the coercion exercised by Catholic conformity in the present time of crisis, and, more specifically, to the intervention of the supreme authorities of the Church, in flagrant contradiction to the spirit and the letter of the Constitution, what are the prospects, do you think, for Italian society and culture, and how do you think writers should intervene to confront and defeat the current impasse?

The literature of the past half century has had two great periods: the avant-garde and *l'engagement*. Both these modes of understanding literature have long been in crisis.

(But to call the literature of the avant-garde dead and gone is also a frequent philistine cliché, which has served to repopulate our literature with dull nineteenth-century mannerisms. On the other hand, in certain literary zones and above all in the figurative arts, there are supporters of a perpetual avant-garde, who are equally annoying. As for *engagée* literature, in ninety cases out of a hundred it's foolish to say it's in crisis, like those who say it's in crisis because of what happened in 1956, for example: those who, in the face of great and terrible historical events, have nothing better to think of than the repercussions of literary tendencies are petty-minded. On the other hand, there are people who don't know how to read a book unless it has an immediate political function, and that's an equally gross limitation.)

The avant-garde writer throws himself body and soul into a regeneration of language, with the energy of someone who believes that he is bringing about man's total regeneration. If you don't believe in that anymore, the avant-garde is finished. Some possibly perfect things can still be achieved, like technical invention (Alain Robbe-Grillet's *La jalousie* is, finally, a story that says something as a story), but, come on, it's not the same. (The strength of the avant-garde still lies in being the daughter of aestheticism; its weakness lies in repeating the characteristics of Romanticism, its grandfather.)

Engagée literature would like to insert the formal and moral revolt of the avant-garde into the political and social revolutionary struggle taking place in the world.

(More than the daughter of the avant-garde it's the sister—Expressionists, Mayakovski, Brecht—but a tendency to resemble naturalism, its uncle, emerges as it ages.) Its great moment was in the thirties, from the repression in China to the Spanish Civil War. In comparison the second postwar period added very little. But the story of *engagée* literature is told not by following its record of events or problems but rather by its work of defining the man of our time (Malraux, Hemingway, Picasso, Sartre, Camus, Vittorini, Pavese). Now, in what today are its reserve troops (Roger Vailland in his latest novel theorizes *désengagement* for his *homme de qualité*), there is a tendency to assert man's right to a dimension that can't immediately be used by history, which, if you think about it, is an assertion of the obvious.

(We'd need a separate discourse on *socialist realism* as it has been defined in the Soviet Union, on what it has in common with *engagée* literature and what is different or even contradictory, and on what it was and what it might become today. But you already know all this, and I will spare you. Then we'd also need a separate discourse on Italian literature, on neorealism, on how much of the avant-garde is in it and how much *engagement*, on its past and future. But you would skip right over it, and I will omit it.)

So now: We can say that the avant-garde has won its battle (or, if we prefer, that it has lost it). Has it won because it has imposed its language, its authors make headlines in the newspapers, its taste dominates from museums to household furnishings, what else can it demand? (Or, if you like, it has lost its battle because the plans for renewal of a kind of mysticism of the avant-garde have ended in nothing other than fashion.) We can also say of *engagement* that, for better or worse, it has won its battle (or, on the other hand, has lost it). It has won not because the biggest social problems have been solved but because it has brought up a generation of readers with an alert political conscience, whether they are Harvard sociologists, political officials, or Marxist union leaders, experts in human relations or in operational research, managers of university research offices, economic historians, intensely ideological literary critics: a somewhat boring, technologically savvy generation, with a lot of general ideas, but all in all a high-level management class, which could be usefully employed either by a functionally structured socialist regime or by a functionally planned capitalism, if they existed. (Or we could also say that *engagée* literature has lost its battle because in the harshest political and social history it hasn't counted for anything: it has had to either give in to political reason or be reduced to the rank of outsider.)

What is the writer like now? He is conscious of the historical process, of the political dimension of everything he writes. (It's not that he has to be; he *is* and can no longer not be.) He has to feel the means of expression as a tool to be invented or reinvented each time while knowing the entire process. (It's not that he feels it instinctively; he always has to force himself, in this sense, in order to give life to forms that are worn out, fungible.) That is, what before was innate inspiration can only be conscience and rational pleasure; what before was voluntary, intellectual intervention is now a priori historical conditioning. What will come out of it? I don't know.

(I realize that I've talked about everything but realism, the theme of your questions. I have to confess that I've hardly ever used the term *realism*, I've always circled around it, and the more I heard it talked about the less I wanted to talk about it myself. I read Lukács, I read Auerbach, with great interest and profit, but especially when it comes to the marginal observations, while the main core still escapes me. And yet it's not that those who express contempt for the concept of realism are more convincing to me—anything but. That's the point I've reached.)

But I would like to say something about your last two questions.

On autobiographical writing. I'm in favor of it. (As a reader more than as an author; it's a terrain where I prefer to see others advance.) I would say not prewar and postwar autobiographical writing but autobiographical writing by a man of the old society and by a man of the new society. The second interests me, those aspects of the man of the new society that can be found today in autobiographical testimony interest me. The literature of Communism, which has staked everything on the novel, in a hundred years may remember not the novels of this era but mainly autobiographical works, diaries, correspondences.

On eroticism. I'm against it. By now, sex can only be written about badly. It seems that only those who write about it with boredom and disgust manage to do it skillfully. Even if one found something good in it, one can't write about it. The Italians, especially, are hopeless at eroticism. My opinion is that it shouldn't be written about for thirty years, since nothing new would be said. Unless the Soviets started writing about it, finally, and then maybe a new literature would emerge.

[1957]

Answers to Nine Questions
on the Novel

Do you think that the novel is in crisis as a literary genre or, rather, as part of the more general crisis in all the arts?

Let's define the terms of the question. What do we mean by *novel*? What do we mean by *crisis*? By *novel* many people mean "nineteenth-century-type novel." In that case there's no need even to talk about a crisis. The nineteenth-century novel had such a full, luxuriant, various, and substantial development that it has done enough for ten centuries. How could it occur to anyone to add anything? Those who would like it if nineteenth-century novels were still being written would do harm to what they say they love.

Recently, the novel was defined by Moravia (in contrast to the short story) as a narrative with an ideological framework. Has there been a crisis in that sense? Yes, but mainly in the ideology behind the novel. The great novel flourished in a time of philosophical systems that sought to embrace the whole universe, a time of all-encompassing conceptions of the world. Today philosophy tends—more or less in all schools—to isolate problems, to work on hypotheses, to offer precise, limited goals; corresponding to that is a different type of story, usually with a single character depicted in an extreme situation, and this is done precisely by the most ideological writers, like Sartre and Camus.

Another way of defining the novel (the historical and sociological way) is to consider it connected to the emergence of books as goods, hence of a commercial literature, of—as is said nowadays—"the culture industry." In fact the first novels that deserve to be called that, Defoe's, appeared on the bookstalls without the name of the author, their intention being to answer to the tastes of the masses, who were eager for "true" stories of adventurous characters. A noble origin: I am not among those who believe that human intelligence is about to die, killed by television. There has always been a culture industry, containing the danger of a general decline of intelligence, but something new and positive always emerges from it. I would say there is no better terrain for the birth of true values than that which has the stink of practical requirements, market demands, consumer production: that's where Shakespeare's tragedies originate, Dostoyevsky's serial novels, and Chaplin's comedies. The process of sublimation of the novel from a product of the market to a system of poetic values took place broadly and in several phases in the course of two centuries. But now it seems that the novel can no longer be renewed: it hasn't been reborn by means of "detective stories" or "science fiction": there are few positive examples of the first type, even fewer of the second.

A definition that is more literary but in a way merely a translation of the previous one is that of the novel as a *gripping* narrative, as a technique for capturing the attention of readers, by having them live in a fictitious world and take part in events with a strong emotional charge, and by forcing them to keep reading because they're curious about "what happens next." That definition has the advantage of also being applicable to the oldest incarnations of the novel: the Hellenistic, the medieval, and then the chivalric, picaresque, *larmoyante*, et cetera . . . The accusation of immorality on the part of religious figures and moralists was aimed at this aspect of the novel; the accusation was not completely unjust, note, and was similar to the one that we often make against movies and television, when we're upset by the forced passivity of the spectator, who, induced to accept everything the screen pours into his head, is unable to give shape to a critical thought. It should be said that, apart from the substantial differences between reading—always "effortful," with pauses, and critical—and sitting like an idiot watching television, this danger of "capturing" the reader already existed in the traditional novel (certainly in lesser novels, but also in masterpieces) and was a reason for its unmatched fascination, not to mention the intangible annoyance provoked in those who don't want to be "captured" by anything or anyone. In the twentieth-century novel the "gripping" element went missing (while remaining characteristic of the type of literature known, precisely, as the thriller) and the participation required of the reader is increasingly a critical participation, a collaboration. Is this a crisis or not? Certainly it's a crisis, but a positive one. Even if the narrative has no purpose other than to create a lyrical atmosphere, that can emerge only with the cooperation of the reader, because the author can only suggest it; even if one merely proposes a game, playing the game assumes a critical act.

And so none of these various definitions of the novel speak to us of something that is necessary or possible to keep alive today. We might be tempted to conclude that continuing to discuss the novel, focusing on that concept, is a waste of time. The important thing is that good books be written, and, in particular, good stories: whether they are novels or not, what does it matter? As the novel had taken on itself functions of many literary genres, so now it redistributes its functions among the lyrical story, the philosophical story, the fantastic pastiche, the travel memoir, or the memoir of encounters with countries and societies, et cetera . . .

Does the possibility of a work that is all these things together no longer exist? Among our recent readings is *Lolita*. This book has the virtue that it can be read on many levels at once: objective realistic story, "story of a soul," lyrical reverie, allegorical poem about America, linguistic entertainment, essayistic digression on a theme-subject, et cetera . . . For that reason *Lolita* is a great book: because it is so many things at once, because it can shift our attention in infinite directions at the same time. I have to recognize (even if it threatens to carry me far from my preferences and orientations as a reader up to now, including those expressed in the other answers to this survey, which should be considered as preceding in time what I'm about to say) that there is a need today for readings that have more than one dimension, a need that is not met by the many works that may be perfect but whose perfection lies precisely in their rigorous one-dimensionality. In contrast to these there are a few contemporary books the reading and rereading of which has given us particular nourishment precisely because we can immerse ourselves in them vertically (that is, perpendicular to the direction of the story), with constant discoveries at every layer or level: the human comedy, the historical picture, the lyrical or visionary, the psychological probe, the allegorical and symbolic (including the most diverse allegories and symbols), the invention of its own autonomous linguistic system, the network of cultural references, et cetera . . . (For instance, regarding books of this type, Denis de Rougemont recently wrote an essay about Musil, Nabokov, and Pasternak, an essay that is one of the hundred keys in which these three books can be read.) And, reflecting on this for a moment, I would be quick to admit that the possibility of reading on several levels is a characteristic of all great novels of all eras: even those which our habit of reading leads us to believe we read as something firmly unitary and one-dimensional.

So at this point it seems to me that I can venture a new definition of what the novel is today (and therefore always): *narrative work that is accessible and significant on many intersecting levels.* Considered in the light of this definition, the novel isn't in crisis. Rather, ours is an era in which no reality can be approached unless it is read in multiple ways. And there is a correspondence between some of the novels that are written or read or reread today and this need for representations of the world through many-dimensional, perhaps composite approximations. The unity of a mythical nucleus, an internal rigor—without which a work of poetry doesn't exist—has to be rediscovered beyond the various lenses of culture, conscience, inspiration, and personal mania that make up the telescope. In other words, novels like the novel—I will name only one of those which come to mind—*Don Quixote*.

There is a lot of talk about the novel-essay. Do you think it will replace the novel of pure representation (or behaviorist)? In other words will Musil replace Hemingway?

The relationship between the culture of a given period and its creative literature is embodied in a given worldview; that is, in the means of expression (behaviorism-Hemingway; logical positivism–Robbe-Grillet, et cetera). It's natural, however, that there is also today a type of fiction that takes as its subject the ideas and complexity of contemporary cultural suggestions, et cetera . . . But there is little point in doing this by reproducing the discussions of intellectuals on these issues. This fiction works best when from cultural, philosophical, scientific suggestions the narrator invents stories, images, fantastic settings that are completely new, as in the stories of Jorge Luis Borges, the greatest contemporary "intellectual" narrator.

The French school of fiction that includes Butor, Robbe-Grillet, Nathalie Sarraute, and others declares that the novel decisively turns its back on psychology. Therefore objects should be made to speak, holding to a purely visual reality. What is your opinion?

The danger of the *nouvelle école* is that it restricts the discourse of literature to the perhaps more rigorous but certainly more limited discourse of the figurative arts. I have nothing against the rejection of psychology, but the trouble is that the *nouvelle école* turns its back on everything except psychology. Robbe-Grillet's *Le voyeur* is a wonderful story until we discover that the whole plot hinges on the fact that the protagonist is a paranoiac. And *La jalousie*, a work of great rigor and effectiveness, is a psychological study, even if expressed in an enumeration of objects rather than introspectively. Robbe-Grillet should follow through with his geometrization, and eliminate every psychological vibration. And Michel Butor should make his form more geometrical, keeping to the closed economy of the story. If *L'emploi du temps* were more concise it would be the perfect novel-labyrinth that it wants to be. And *La modification* would be a fine story if it were reduced to a quarter of its dimensions.

It can't have escaped you that modern novels are increasingly written not in the third but in the first person. And that this first person tends to be the voice of the author (the I of Moll Flanders, just to take an example, was instead equivalent to a third person). Do you think we will ever return to the purely objective, nineteenth-century-type novel? Or do you think that the objective novel is no longer possible?

It depends not on writers but on the direction of the times. When I began to write *I*, fifteen years ago, objective writing seemed to have become natural: you felt like writing the story of all those you met along the road. There are times when stories are in things—the world tends to tell its own story, and the writer becomes a tool. And there are times—like today—when the world in itself seems to have no more drive: in the stories of our neighbor we no longer read a universal story, and the writer can then say of the world only what he knows in relation to himself.

What do you think of socialist realism in fiction?
Revolutionary literature has always been imaginative, satirical, utopian. *Realism* usually contains a sense of distrust in history, an inclination toward the past that is perhaps nobly reactionary, perhaps conservative in the most positive sense of the word. Can there ever be a revolutionary realism? Up to now we haven't had enough convincing examples. Socialist realism in the Soviet Union had a bad beginning, especially because its supposed father was a decadent writer inclined to mysticism, Gorky.

The problem of language in the novel is, first of all, the problem of the relationship of the writer to the reality of his narrative. Do you believe that this language should be transparent, like clear water through which all the objects can be distinguished—in other words do you think that the novelist should let things speak? Or do you think that the novelist should first of all be a writer and even conspicuously a writer?

Language as transparent as clear water is an arduous stylistic ideal, which can be reached only by devoting extreme attention to the writing. In order to "let things speak" you have to be able to write extremely well. All styles can be good; the important thing is not to write in a muddy, blurred, imprecise, random way.

What do you think of the use of dialect in the novel? Do you think that everything can be said in dialect, or at least in a dialectal manner? Or do you think that the only language is the language of the culture and that dialect has very strict limitations?

Dialect can serve as a model for the language of a writer, that is, as a point of reference in determining linguistic choices. Once it's established that under my Italian there is dialect X, I will prefer to choose words, constructions, usages that draw on linguistic climate X, rather than words, constructions, usages that draw on other traditions. This system can serve to give consistency and lucidity to a narrative language, until it becomes a limitation to the faculties of expression; then you can only send it to hell.

Do you believe in the possibility of a national historical novel? Or one that in some way portrays the recent or less recent experiences of Italy? Do you think it's possible, in other words, to reconstruct stories and fates that are not purely individual? And outside of "historical" time?

The historical novel can be an excellent system for talking about one's own times and oneself.

Who are your favorite novelists and why?

I love Stendhal above all because only in him are individual moral tension, historical tension, life force a single thing, a linear novelistic tension. I love Pushkin because he is clarity, irony, and seriousness. I love Hemingway because he is matter-of-fact, understated, will to happiness, sadness. I love Stevenson because he seems to fly. I love Chekhov because he doesn't go farther than where he's going. I love Conrad because he navigates the abyss and doesn't sink into it. I love Tolstoy because at times I seem to be about to understand how he does it and then I don't. I love Manzoni because until a little while ago I hated him. I love Chesterton because he wanted to be the Catholic Voltaire and I wanted to be the Communist Chesterton. I love Flaubert because after him it's unthinkable to do what he did. I love the Poe of "The Gold Bug." I love the Twain of *Huckleberry Finn*. I love the Kipling of *The Jungle Books*. I love Nievo because I've reread him many times with as much pleasure as the first time. I love Jane Austen because I never read her but I'm glad she exists. I love Gogol because he distorts with clarity, meanness, and moderation. I love Dostoyevsky because he distorts with consistency, fury, and lack of moderation. I love Balzac because he's a visionary. I love Kafka because he's a realist. I love Maupassant because he's superficial. I love Mansfield because she's intelligent. I love Fitzgerald because he's unsatisfied. I love Radiguet because we'll never be young again. I love Svevo because we have to grow old. I love . . .

[1959]

Industrial Themes

If factories and workers occupy little space as settings and characters in literary history, we can't forget what an imposing place they have as settings and characters in the history of ideas of the past hundred years. The worker entered the history of culture as a historical-philosophical protagonist, whereas the opposite had been the case before: the hunter, the shepherd, the king, the warrior, the farmer, the merchant, the feudal knight, the skillful artisan, the amorous courtier, the adventurous bourgeois entered the history of culture as a poetic protagonist, in fables, epics, tragedies, eclogues, comedies, epic ballads, sonnets, stories. (And first among these came, even earlier, ritual-religious or narrative-religious, pagan or biblical characters; so it was that, along these lines, Christianity let even the slave, the poor man, the reject enter the history of culture.)

That absolute priority of the standard historical-philosophical definition has so far burdened every attempt at a poetic definition of the worker's life. Mainly, fiction has got involved only to confirm and exemplify what ideologues and politicians already knew. No industrial, workers' city has been portrayed by a novelist more completely, as an image that is also lyrical and evocative of a moral style, than the Turin of Piero Gobetti's writings.

One has the impression that the writer gets more into the heart of things the more he inclines toward the essayistic, in the first person of the commenting intellectual, and the farther he moves from a mimetic-objective representation. (The poetry of Vittorio Sereni and the diary of Ottiero Ottieri in *Menabò* 4 are also examples of this type of approach.)

As soon as the "essayistic" voice of the writer-commentator breaks off, the problem of choosing the linguistic tools begins. Three Italian books on industrial subjects that I've just read (two published and the third about to come out) will help to illustrate the matter: *Una nuvola d'ira* (*A Cloud of Anger*), by Giovanni Arpino; *Memoriale* (*The Memorandum*), by Paolo Volponi; *La vita agra* (*It's a Hard Life*), by Luciano Bianciardi.

Arpino (like many before him) wanted his workers to speak (and think) in a single language, a popular, spoken language that also expressed an ethical-political-cultural awareness. The *engagée* literature of the postwar period (Vittorini, Pavese, and all of us who came after) had tried to introduce this political speech into novels using popular-colloquial and poetic-allusive terms, as if trying to leap over the ditch that separates ideological language, daily language, literary language. This synthesis wasn't a success; and now Arpino stumbles into the same ditch. The assumption that we have reached a cultural and moral harmony that in fact is still far away is the true theme of the story that Arpino tells in *Nuvola d'ira*, and it's one of the most serious themes that a novel can take on today; except today it's clear that one can't take it on using an approach to language that corresponds to that simplification of the problem.

We live in a cultural environment where many languages and levels of awareness intersect. Bianciardi's linguistic assumption in his new book, which starts with parody (like Kerouac, Gadda, Henry Miller) and a playful display of the most various lexical skills, demonstrates the capacity to portray and express a picture and a judgment of a more complex industrial reality (see the pages on the mine disaster, where the accumulation of technical terminology—chemical and mining—culminates in a bare and simple evocation of death), even if here we never move outside the limits of an anarchic private protest.

Volponi's linguistic approach is the most unexpected, given the "industrial theme," and yet it offers the most poetic result. Starting with the imitation of a crude, slightly overexcited style of writing (the memoir of a deranged peasant worker), Volponi arrives at an invented prose interwoven with images and lyrical phraseology, which strives to assimilate the mechanical world into the natural world. Should we consider it a solution, or a delaying expedient? All in all, Volponi's lyrical transfigurative tension turns out to be the most fitting to express the current contradictory and provisional reality: of advanced productive technologies and a backward social-anthropological situation, of glass and steel factories, human relations, and an obscurely biological Italy.

Of course, the choice of an approach to language is not enough; or rather the concept of "language" should be considered in its broadest literary sense, as a method of representation of one's own vision of the world.

Vittorini (*Menabò* 4, 19–20) has explained that the problem has to be considered on the level of the global historical experience initiated by industry (Fortini's polemical essay in this issue, *Menabò* 5, is clearly in agreement on this point), and can't be resolved if it is limited to "themes." No matter what direction they come from—Marxist or neo-capitalist, avant-gardist or traditionalist—the exhortations and the determination to portray particular subjects (the factory, the workers, exploited or satisfied work) or to employ particular forms (inspired by the rationality or irrationality of industrial life, by its labor or its speed) count less and less than what literature elaborates outside the exhortations and the determination, and end up, as always happens, establishing a relationship with those subjects and those forms that wasn't predicted.

On the other hand, the piece by the unionist Bragantin in this *Menabò* 5 is extremely relevant. His "call to ideology" is valid in that it's not an appeal to a corroborative, pleonastic literature but demands a *literary* contribution to the totality of a new image of the world, which socialist ideology has to create in the face of the second Industrial Revolution. Bragantin justly emphasizes that the "question of power" precedes the others; we believe that the sooner we free ourselves from alienation from private profit, the sooner we can pose the problem of alienation "from the object" (on this point: we wish the definition of the problem that Eco gives in his essay were more explicit). But a slight intensification of this call for an ideological contribution would be enough to fall into the demand of burdening literature with some of the tasks that ideology, at this moment still empty and inadequate, should undertake within an essentially scientific sphere. Also, the example that Bragantin uses, Mayakovski, should be understood in the sense of a poetic "plan" that he tried to open in the heart of the political-economic plan of the Leninist era, a new literary field that would enter into a dialectic with the other dimensions of the emerging Soviet society. Today, for us, this literary field enters into a dialectic with socialist culture on the one hand and neo-capitalist culture on the other (that complex of American-Viennese operative and methodological and semantic philosophies that should not necessarily be simply ascribed to capitalism), and does not remain a prisoner of the hesitations of both; that for me is equivalent to saying that the field is already situated at the convergence of various lines that form the starting point of the future socialist perspective.

But how variously this type of literature can be situated in relation to structure and ideology we can see only by following the history of literature beginning with the first Industrial Revolution, and analyzing its situation today: an analysis I attempted in the essay "The Challenge to the Labyrinth" in this same issue of *Menabò* 5.

[1962]

Correspondence with
Angelo Guglielmi Regarding
"The Challenge to the Labyrinth"

Dear Guglielmi,

I read your essay for *Menabò* 6. It's very clear and well argued, and provides a coherent image of the situation. The picture of the situation drawn by the Hegelians and the Lukácsians is similarly endowed with its own logic and coherence, and they reach the same conclusions as you: modern literature and art are the negation of history (of humanism), of rational planning. That they consider the phenomenon negative and you positive doesn't really differentiate you: both of you arrive at a point where the end of literature must be declared. Given that for the Hegelian-Lukácsian all means of expression are contaminated by decadence, it's impossible to see a way out of decadence (which does not mean becoming entrenched, anti-historically, in classic positions). Given that for you the task of art is to unmask the falsity of all meanings and all historical finalities, without substituting new ones, and to reduce any conception of the world to zero, there will come a point when everything reducible to zero has been reduced to zero, and the impulse needed to write will fail, along with the reason and the polemic with the other-than-poetry, *which is always the dialectic condition under which poetry exists.*

I don't doubt that you have good reasons for diagnosing the end of literature, both of you. But I'm not very convinced by them. All reductions to zero interest and cheer me, because then I'll be able to see what comes after zero: that is, how the discourse will resume; that is, how the totality of culture, which has suffered many earthquakes and razings to the ground and has so far lived through them, will manage to overcome this, too (not so big, compared with others); that is, how it will restore truth to old discourses that can be good again.

You want to persuade me, Beckett and Robbe-Grillet to hand, that reality doesn't make sense? I'll gladly follow you to the final results. But I'm glad because I'm already thinking that, since we've reached the limit of this erosion of subjectivity, the next morning I'll be able to start—in this completely objective and asemantic universe—reinventing a prospect of meanings, with the same cheerful attachment to things as prehistoric man, who, with a chaos of shadows and sensations flashing before him, gradually managed to distinguish and define—that is a mammoth, that is my wife, that is a prickly pear—and thus began the irreversible process of history.

Best regards

I.C.

Dear Calvino,

Thank you for your letter and your interest in my essay.

I have nothing to say against your counterarguments, except to make one rather essential point: and that is that I, too, would be interested in a "meaningful" discourse, in a semantic literature, and I, too, think that once the world is reduced to zero we'll have to start from the beginning with a new discourse. What I dispute is whether it's possible today to initiate this new discourse and not end up with a false discourse or, anyway, one that is no longer true. And you yourself offer the proof that this is the danger when in your letter you say that certainly this time, too, "culture . . . will be able to restore truth to old discourses that can be good again." Now the problem isn't whether it's better not to resolve it by turning an already worn garment inside out or by remaking the engine for the car. As long as we act as if the problem were simply one of updating, we will multiply the misunderstandings, introduce new falsehoods, and hence infinitely extend the life (the necessity) of the culture that is reduced to zero or demystifying. The first step toward a new perspective of meanings (for that matter, it isn't literature or only literature that can establish it but, first and foremost, philosophy, morality, politics, etc.) is to free the field of old, no longer vital perspectives; if, instead, we limit ourselves to updating them, all we're doing is camouflaging their negative and falsifying charge.

There are other points in your letter that I have something to say about. For example I don't see how you can say that the difference between my position and that of the Hegelian-Lukácsians is irrelevant, if, owing to that difference, the Hegelian-Lukácsians and I can express diametrically opposed evaluations of cultural positions and specific authors, if owing to that difference I can point to and believe in a current possibility for literature, while the Hegelian-Lukácsians deny it, or, if they do venture a proposal, you realize immediately that it's an invitation to return to the past, to dead forms and thoughts.

What is irrelevant is the fact that there are some coincidences of descriptions (admitting that they exist): common points of style can also be found in a letter from John Profumo to Christine Keeler and a letter from Pascal to his sister.

Kindest regards
A.G.

It's clear that we could continue this discussion for a while without making any progress. Because it's precisely the basic arguments that divide us, the way we regard certain key attitudes of our century's culture. For me, if there's an old story that can be taken up only critically or ironically, it's the failure of rationalism and positivism; I've heard it repeated since I was a boy—it's inherent in the mood of our prewar readings. We grew up in an era in which the only secure "value" was that failure: and idealism, and Bergsonism, and modern physics, and adherence to political reality said only that, always the same tune from all the most venerable bores. (That was what the poetry of the time said, too, but luckily for us in a different way, or in a way that was useful to us, as is often the case with poetry.) We came of age when we understood that there will continue to be failures of reason—maybe one every ten minutes—but the point is to see each time what sort of bridge you can build to get to the other side and go on your way. Only with this attitude will we be able to see as new the things that are new; with the other we'll go on repeating the same tune, like an organ-grinder, and see all cats as gray.

From this it follows that the figure of the ideal reader we assume for literature is very different for Guglielmi and for me.

As ideal readers of literature I think of the only people who count for me, that is, those engaged in plans for the future world (that is, for whom the mutual influence of poetic planning and political or technological or scientific planning et cetera counts) and engaged, more precisely, in a rationalization of the real (which is worth dedicating one-self to precisely because the real is not in itself rational), and I want these people to take advantage of the particular intelligence of the world that literature and only literature can give. Guglielmi's position, on the other hand, assumes the reader who is pleased with the failure of rationality (an inevitable and perhaps necessary moment in every process of rationalization), because he thus finds an alibi, takes a vacation, believes that he can wait in peace for the end of all the old values and, consequently, the revelation of the new. (It's a vain wait, because only in the *continuous* search for values does the crust of the old values crumble—often contrary to the very intentions of the searcher—while the crust of yesterday's values immediately thickens on those who believe they can easily declare themselves free of today's values; and those who think they're on vacation from history right away find that they're spinning on the merry-go-round of an even more antiquated and predictable history.)

Another basic difference is what we look for in literature: some look for something that they didn't know or understand before and some look for confirmation of the ideas they already have. The first is what is commonly called "poetry"; the second is the warming pan of old professors. If I say that Guglielmi's aesthetic resembles that of the Hegelian-Lukácsians (of course they arrive at opposite results; quite a discovery! Otherwise where was the fun in saying they resemble one another?) it's because both are a professors' aesthetic, because both seek in literature illustrations, examples, of a discourse created elsewhere.

(Does the polemic against "professors" belong to the day before yesterday? No: it's a polemic for today, and even more for tomorrow, unless we start warning of the danger of rampant neo-professorialism.)

The general critical discourse I've attempted many times in successive drafts has only this thread: (also) the poetry of the *negative* is always (not only retrievable but) necessary to a *positive* mapping of the world. This is my notion of "engagement," different—it seems to me—from the more widespread notion that Guglielmi associates me with. If he had understood that, it would also have been clear to him that when, at the end of my essay, I spoke of a literature that *challenges the labyrinth* and one that *surrenders to the labyrinth*, I didn't (as elsewhere) categorize authors, putting some on one side and others on the other. I was thinking, rather—as I wrote—of two essences to clarify and distinguish within various authors and various works. All in all, I want Beckett's despair to be useful to those who do not despair. Since the despairing—or rather the obedient citizens of chaos—don't know what to do with it.

I.C.

[1963]

On Translation

Sir,

An opinion expressed by Claudio Gorlier (in *Paragone* 164, pp. 115–16) on the translation of E. M. Forster's *A Passage to India*, published by Einaudi, impels me, as an editor at the publishing house, to write this letter not only to do justice to one of our best translators, Adriana Motti, but to offer some general reflections on the tasks of the critic, starting from the particular point of view of the editorial profession.

Italian publishers bring out foreign books in translations that are sometimes excellent, sometimes pretty good, or inferior, or bad; the reasons for this divide (which can be found even among books from the same publisher) are multiple. Let's say: In the feverish growth of the Italian publishing industry today not all translations manage to be excellent. It's a relatively minor evil as long as we're talking about minor books, but the damage is serious and wasteful when it's a work of literary value. Thus the need for a critic who enters into the merits of the translation is felt today more than ever. It's felt by readers, who want to know how far they can trust the quality of the translator and the seriousness of the editorial brand; it's felt by good translators, who lavish stores of scrupulousness and intelligence, and no one ever says bah!; and it's felt by the editorial staff, who want good results to have the praise they deserve and dilettantish ones to be denounced (every publishing house hopes that a widespread rigorousness would ruin not its own stable but the competition's), and think they have everything to gain if the selection and control of translators happens with the collaboration of critics and in view of the public.

Thus many of us are pleased that this type of criticism is starting to be practiced, and we follow it with interest. And at the same time we urge an absolute technical responsibility. Because if this sense of responsibility is lacking, confusion only increases, provoking in translators a discouragement that is transformed immediately into *pis aller*, and a general lowering of standards. It's not the first time we've heard a good translator say: "Yes, yes, I kill myself to resolve difficulties that no one has ever imagined and no one will notice, and then critic X opens the book at random, casts his eye on a sentence he doesn't like, and, maybe without comparing the text, without asking himself how it could have been resolved otherwise, in two lines dismisses the entire translation." They are right to complain: an author enjoys a multitude of judgments, if he gets the critic who pans him, there will always be the one who defends him; whereas for the work of translators, critical judgments are so rare that they become irrevocable, and if one critic writes that a translation is bad, that judgment enters into circulation and everyone repeats it.

Actually I should have started on this subject not with Gorlier but with Paolo Milano. Paolo Milano should be justly credited as the only critic of the weekly press who almost regularly devotes a part (sometimes a quarter) of his articles to the virtues and defects of the translation. He manages to do it in a broad and illustrative way, despite the space limitations of a weekly, and in a manner that interests the reader and avoids any trace of pedantry. In that sense his criticism is a model that responds to the needs of today. That said, I must add that at various times we have disagreed with his judgments. I'm sorry I don't have on hand a collection of examples from *Espresso,* and I don't want to quote from memory: certainly he has abused translations that didn't deserve it and absolved others that deserved to be condemned.

The art of translation isn't having a good moment (either in Italy or elsewhere; but here let's confine ourselves to Italy, which, in this field, certainly is not the country that has most to complain about). The base for recruitment, that is, young people who know a foreign language well or reasonably well, has certainly expanded; but there are fewer and fewer who, writing in Italian, command the gifts of agility, confidence in lexical choice, syntactic economy, sense of different linguistic registers, intelligence: in short, of style (in the double aspect of understanding the stylistic peculiarities of the author being translated, and being able to offer Italian equivalents in a prose that reads *as if it were thought and written directly in Italian*). These are precisely the gifts in which the singular genius of the translator resides.

Along with the technical gifts, moral gifts are becoming scarcer: that persistence necessary to concentrate on digging for months and months in the same tunnel, with a meticulousness that at any moment might give way, with a faculty of discernment that at any moment might lose its shape, surrender to bad habits, hallucinations, distortions of linguistic memory, and with the nagging thought of perfection that has to become a sort of methodical folly, and has the ineffable sweetness and consuming despair of folly . . .

(The man who is writing this letter has never had the courage to translate a book in his life; he is entrenched behind his lack of those particular moral gifts, his lack, rather, of methodological nervous endurance. But in his career as a tormentor of translators he already suffers enough, for others' sufferings and his own, and for bad translations as well as for good ones.)

(Once upon a time writers used to translate, especially young ones. Today they all seem to have other things to do. And then are we sure that the Italian of writers would be best? The sense of style becomes rarer. We could say that the lesser commitment of young writers to the word and the fact that fewer people have a vocation to translate are facets of the same phenomenon.)

In this situation, in which the true translator should be

encouraged and sustained and appreciated in every way, it's very important that the periodical press and literary reviews judge the translations. But if criticism gets in the habit of panning a translation in two lines, without understanding how the most difficult passages and the characteristics of the style have been resolved, without asking if there were other solutions and what they might be, then it's better to say nothing. (I will mention the most frequent case: the minor error. Certainly the error should be noted. But it's not a sufficient basis on which to judge a translation. Errors lurk even in the pages of the now expert and authoritative translator, whom nobody believes needs editorial revisions, who corrects his own proofs, et cetera, while maybe you don't find one in the beginner's attempt, in which he's sought to straighten out every comma, and which arrives at the printer correct from head to toe . . .)

The critical analysis of a translation should be based on a method, probing broad samples that can serve as decisive touchstones. Above all, it's an exercise we'd like to recommend not only to critics but to all good readers: as everyone knows, we truly read an author only when we translate him, or compare the text with a translation, or when versions in different languages are contrasted. (Another good method for judging: a three-way comparison: text, Italian version, and version in another language.) A technical judgment, rather than one of taste: on this terrain the margins of opinion within which the literary judgment oscillates are much more restricted. If I claim that Adriana Motti's translation is excellent and Gorlier finds only reasons to condemn it, it's not a subjective question or one of point of view. One of us is wrong, he or I.

I will repeat Gorlier's passage, or rather his parenthesis, that refers to the translation:

> (Let's say decent, but no more. In fact this *Passaggio in India* published by Einaudi leaves one a little puzzled, starting with the title, which sounds bad and ambiguous in Italian. And then how is it possible that a good translator uses *affatto* [at all] in the negative sense when only a student at a technical institute would dare such a thing, or writes *cosa* instead of *che cosa* [what], or doesn't know that in the majority of cases "dissolved" means *sciolto* [melted] and not *dissolto* [dissolved]?)

I will address first of all the question of the title, for which the publisher is responsible, not Adriana Motti. We discussed it for months before making the decision. In general, in Italy when you had a title that didn't translate well it would be changed radically; this was the custom until maybe a dozen years ago, but for a while now, fortunately, publishers have been convinced that not to translate a title faithfully is a completely arbitrary decision. However, calling the book *Viaggio in India* [*Journey to India*] would, it seems to me, have done the book a disservice. It's not only the fact that recently in bookstore display windows there have been three or four books with almost the same title, by Italian authors who had been to India and had written a good travel book; it's also that in Italian the title *Viaggio in qualche posto* [*Journey to Wherever*] assumes the genre of the travel book (and isn't the same thing true in English of books with *Travel* in the title?). So? A tour in India? A sojourn in India? These diminished in some way the meaning, they flattened it; they abolished that hint of symbolic vibration that *Passage* seems to me to have. And that *Passaggio* also seems to me to have, a word with so many resonances (don't we say "Life is a passage . . ."?). Gorlier says it sounds bad; and I suppose many would say he's right. For myself I have to say that *passaggio* is a word I like very much, including the locutions derived from it: *di passaggio* (in passing), a beautiful typical Italian term. It sounds ambiguous, Gorlier adds. Precisely: I wanted a word that had an unrestricted range of meanings, a halo of symbolic ambiguity, responding precisely (as Gorlier teaches us very well) to the character of the book. However, I see that everyone says I'm wrong about this, so I have to give in. If the publisher in a future reprinting wants to change the title, we'll fix it. End of self-defense for the title.

Gorlier doesn't find mistakes in the translation. (He uses it extensively for all his citations.) He raises three objections to the translator's Italian, including the choice of the word *dissolto*. On p. 353 (since the incriminating page numbers are not marked we had to skim all 355 pages of the book) Forster writes: "When he had finished, the mirror of the countryside shattered, the meadow dissolved [*dissolto*] into butterflies." Would Gorlier have preferred "the meadow *sciolto* [melted] into butterflies"? I'm sorry: Adriana Motti did very well to use *dissolto*.

I don't like *affatto* in a negative sense, either, but without evoking Gorlier's scholarly outrage. P. 247: "'I fear it's very discouraging for you.' 'Not at all, it doesn't matter to me.'" ("*Affatto, non me ne importa.*") Could she have used *niente affatto* or *per niente?* There would have been the rhyme with *sconvolgente*: the usual humiliation of the translator. Could she have used *per nulla?* Well, she must have had a scruple (excessive) because of that *non* right afterward. The translator writes to me in a letter of complaint: "Also in Riguti-Fanfani (p. 32, Barbera publishers, Florence 1893), the word *affatto* is given in the negative sense with a very mild reproach, which is almost a concession to its use." I am not a devotee of dictionaries: what counts for me is the victory of the harmony and internal logic of the sentence as a whole, even if it happens with a little violence, the rip that the spoken tends to impose on the rule. And the sentence in question, to my ear, sounds good: the *non* of *non importa* fades into *affatto*, consolidates it. The spirit of the Italian is precisely in such things: this is its incomparable richness, and its curse (because it makes Italian literature essentially untranslatable), and its difficulty. (Woe to those who think they can be ungrammatical without an ear and without logic; only those to whom is conceded the arduous Grace of Language are permitted to sin and be saved!)

Cosa? For *che cosa?* And here I lose patience. With all the work that creative literature has done to give written Italian the immediacy of a living language, and with all the ferment of ideas that modern linguistics has generated in every field of culture, making the "linguistic" fact a mobile and organic whole, with its mutual exchanges between spoken and written, its ascents and descents, we were convinced that the cultivators of purist foolishness were confined to the Bouvards and Pecuchets of certain columns in the dailies and weeklies. *Cosa?* For *che cosa?* It's used, and its use is indisputable, because it's shorter, because it eliminates a *che* (the repetition of *che* is the scourge of every writing being), doesn't cause confusion, and, above all, enters into the logic of the simplifications carried out gradually through the centuries in Italian and the other neo-Latin languages.

Before entrusting a translation to someone, we assure ourselves first of all (I think I can speak collectively for the various editorial desks) of the fluency and spontaneity and lack of pedantry and preciousness in the candidate's Italian. What Gorlier censures is therefore precisely what we call "writing well," the *conditio sine qua non* for being a translator.

For being translators. Because one can be a serious scholar and also a critic of clear understanding, and "write badly." (We won't touch the knotty question, which would lead us astray, of writers, even great ones, who "write badly.") "Writing badly," that is, moving uneasily in the language, as if in a jacket that pulls at the elbows, without freedom, without quick reflexes. Can one criticize an art critic for not knowing how to hold a brush? Of course not. So we don't want to reproach the literary scholar

57

who, at the end of the very page where he has given lessons in language, writes *contenuta dal risvolto* ["found on the cover flap"] (a typo? Everything leads us to rule it out), who writes *sensibilizzarsi* and *acutizzarsi*, that is, who is defenseless against the worst—this yes—journalistic and bureaucratic debasements of the language, deprived of the lightning that at the moment of the fall rescues the sinner loved by the gods and flashes before him, in a circle of light, the unique and perfect verb: *acuirsi!* before he falls back into darkness. If his essays are sustained by robust thinking, they will be read and appreciated even if badly written. But he should beware of one temptation: to transfuse that linguistic unease (which is not even a venial sin, it's one of the infinite peculiarities of the individual) into a misplaced love for an abstract, rigid language, which, precisely on account of that rigidity, he imagines that he, too, can possess. Love for the language is another thing entirely and originates in another disposition of the soul, vibrates with another, more acute neurosis.

(This is my official discourse, characterized by tolerance. In secret, in silence I vent my distress when I see the word, the primary substance of every literature, used with such awkwardness and laboriousness and deafness by the new critics, and I wonder what could have driven these youths toward studies that are surely arduous and thankless for them. And in secret I agree with Emilio Cecchi, who, in the *Corriere della Sera* of October 4, 1963, writes: "In a critical essay, the quality of the prose is a guarantee of the truth and vitality of the impressions and ideas that are set forth;

and is an intrinsic part of that truth and vitality." And in secret I go around dreaming that soon, with the kingdom of letters divided between the two opposing factions of traditionalists and innovators, united by an equal insensitivity to the word, I will finally be able to write anonymous works, pursuing an ideal of modern prose to transmit to the generations who may someday understand again . . . So I've gone beyond the limits I had proposed for myself: this was supposed to be a letter from a member of the editorial staff arguing with the critics. I return to the subject.)

Gorlier accuses the publishing houses of neglecting or slowing the appearance in Italy of first-rate Anglo-Saxon writers, while publishing, instead, young, second-rate writers. Among the former he names mostly authors who do have Italian publishers, who are mainly writers with a subtle dedication to style, and for whom it is to be hoped only that the publishers will wait until they have truly good translations to publish them. (It's easy to understand why so many authors haven't been translated: in Italy in the past few years, the capacity for book production and absorption by the market has been increasing; it's natural that in the new climate current books from abroad would have the lion's share and catching up on works left from past decades would proceed more slowly.)

As an example of secondary authors who, on the other hand, have been translated, Gorlier cites James Purdy and Alan Sillitoe. "A Sillitoe punctually makes its appearance." Well. So far, Sillitoe's first book, *Saturday Night and Sunday Morning*, has been translated; it's a good, interesting novel, and not ordinary. Since then, he has published four more books in England (if I haven't lost count), and these have not yet been published here; some will come out in Italy (a couple are excellent, others less good), not excessively *punctual,* but there is no intention of neglecting or underestimating this author.

If Sillitoe is esteemed and translated throughout the world, Purdy is a different story. In America he still hasn't had any success, either critical or popular; he is in a way a discovery of ours. One of the most refined, least indulgent noses in the Italian publishing world (who is now, alas, converted, out of skeptical snobbishness, to mass culture, and has vanished over interplanetary shores) bet on this author among countless American fiction writers, all pretty good, and witty, but lacking any special spark. Purdy is a small discovery that we can be quietly proud of. We haven't yet published *Malcolm,* his most delicate, moonstruck book, but we hope to do so soon.

In short, it seems to me that the task of the editor as Gorlier understands it is to attend to the values sanctioned by the various literatures, to the hierarchies established by age and fame, and transport them here. We, on the other hand, understand it quite differently: what excites and pleases us in editorial work is precisely to offer perspectives that don't coincide with the most obvious. So in following the sources of information and the foreign critics and the publishers' hype, we are always careful not to fall prisoner to others' assessments, to choose on the basis of *our* reasons, and to be sure that our choices will influence the fame of an author internationally. Choosing foreign books is an exchange between two parties; foreign literature gives us an author and we give it our sanction, our confirmation, which is also a "value," precisely as it is the product of a different taste and tradition.

Having reached this point, I have to say: just as a translation shouldn't be judged on the basis of a few isolated lines, an intelligent critic certainly shouldn't be judged by that measure. And Gorlier's reflections on Forster's book are rich and provocative and acute. His criticism of the flap copy of the Einaudi edition seems to me justified, as it in effect flattens the value of the book. The art of the "flap copy" is a difficult one: no one wants to undertake a presentation in twenty lines of an important book that rejects concise definitions (as Gorlier's writing demonstrates); and the pages of the most learned experts rarely have the necessary "concision."

As long as I'm here, I'd like to make a final detour, addressed not to Gorlier, with whom in this case I agree, but to critics in general. Almost as a rule these days critics and reviewers tend to frame their pieces by discussing the "flap copy" or the editorial band (or, among the lazier and more timid, by paraphrasing the flap copy). That is, the publisher, with the flap copy, has a power that seems to me excessive: setting the guidelines for the entire critical discussion. The critic agrees or argues, but doesn't emerge from those themes, those ideas. Someone will say: It's an ordinary pretext for starting to speak. Yes, but the real subject of the review, the book, is, it seems to me, neglected in the end; the real meaning, the real emotion of every critical bullfight, the critic who takes by the horns the bull-book, the bull-author, is lost. Rather than with the author, the critic battles . . . with whom? In the best case with that new institution of our literary life the "editor of the series"; more often, though, with the anonymous "publishing house," that is, the kids of publicity and the press office, who are in general smart and up-to-date, but are led by natural professional bias to simplify and to reduce, in a big way. It seems to me that for readers as well it would be better to teach them to deal with a book by opening it on the first page. I'm almost starting to think it might be instructive to publish books as smooth and skinny as nails, as is done (or used to be) in France.

I apologize for the length of this. We write about literature continuously, while we never discuss what goes on in the editorial kitchen, although it occupies a large part of our time and our anxieties. So I had some things to say. Thank you.

[1963]

Letter from a "Minor" Writer

Dear Fink,

Your review of *Ti con zero* (*T Zero / Time and the Hunter*) in *Paragone* gave me the rare satisfaction of finding an attentive critic, who knows how to *read* (and quote), and who misses nothing on the page. The three parts of the book are described very well, in terms of both the analysis of the individual stories and the brief definitions, like the very beautiful one in the second part. (And thus your stylistic ear makes unexpected discoveries, like the Pavesian assonances in *Cosmicomics*. I would never have thought of it, but your quotation is persuasive.) Yet I don't want you to see the value of the third part only in relation to an argument with other "anti-narrators"; that is, my work—which is autonomous, and naturally it's important to me that this should be recognized—exists in a space that is not chosen by me but is the literary situation in which I increasingly find myself, and which is always posing new problems. Of course, I come from experiences that differ from those which dominate literary discourse today, but the different climate that's been created has made me delve deeper into aspects of my work that were already present, and which I had been more or less obscurely aware of. As for cultural situations one doesn't choose but finds oneself in: for example, you are very right to call "Bassanian" "Gli avanguardisti a Mentone" ("The Avanguardisti in Menton") et cetera, because without Bassani I would never have written those stories, with that particular focus on autobiographical material—let's say on the singularity of the provincial bourgeois experience. Bassani was important for me in emerging from the impasse I'd reached in my early postwar style. (Whereas I wasn't able to grasp Bassani's true value at the time, which even he then lost immediately: the attempt at a Jamesian ghost story about the Italian bourgeoisie.) Then, however (precisely because of the absence of that opening I was just now talking about), I ended up retreating to a zone of minor Italian literature, like *Il Mondo*, made up of moralistic self-importance, easy wisdom, nostalgic lyricism. So those stories of mine (maybe they're more successful than others, but does that matter?) correspond to a regression in me and in the Italian literary climate of those years, and I'm sorry that you remember them so well and cite them twice. So I'm pleased that you find *Ti con zero* "likable"; but the more unlikable a book is (that is, hard to take in, because of our habits of thought and our tastes) the more it counts; the more laborious it is to take in the more it counts. Now, however, I have to explain: Judging this phase of my work in relation and in opposition to the literature of the European avant-garde seems to me irrelevant, because it's clear that I remain a writer of craftsmanlike tradition, I like to make narrative structures that close well, and I have a relationship with the reader based on mutual satisfaction. The avant-garde is a human attitude before it is a literature, and implies a different relationship with the work and the reader (and is judged according to the absolute or heroic nature of this attitude); if someone, let's say, "isn't born to it," that is, doesn't have it as his fundamental vocation, it would be ridiculous to take it up. But here's what I wanted to say: I'm a craftsman but at a time when the avant-garde does this and this other; and even if the two fields don't touch they influence one another (no semantic field can be indifferent to other semantic fields). For example, at the moment I'm reading Heisenbüttel, and he explains to me what I'm doing; I see with interest—and I'd like to accentuate this—an analogy between my position (on the level of craftsmanship) and his (on the level of the avant-garde).

In other words, what's important to me is the participation in a common work, not "the truly outstanding results" that you complain I do not get. What's important is the contribution to that complex thing that is a culture. What are "outstanding" results? Only a *subsequent* cultural situation gives a result outstanding value. And even that result is only a symbol of a whole complex of results, minor, perhaps, but important. I believe that this is a criterion that leads nowhere: let's leave it to the literary weeklies that interview writers about the possibility of writing "masterpieces." I have to say that I have never given a damn about outstanding results. As a young man my aspiration was to become a "minor writer." (Because those who were called "minor" were the ones I liked best and felt closest to.) But it was already a mistaken criterion, because it presupposes that "major" ones exist.

Basically I am convinced that not only do major and minor authors not exist but authors don't exist—or anyway they don't count for much. In my view you're still too concerned with explaining Calvino by means of Calvino, with tracing a history, a continuity of Calvino, and maybe this Calvino has no continuity, he constantly dies and is reborn; what's important is whether in the work he does at a certain moment there is something that can interfere in the present or future work of others, as can happen with anyone who works, merely because, in doing so, he combines and accumulates possibilities.

But I have to say that your search for the real Calvino—although I don't approve of it methodologically—leads to the establishment of a lowest common denominator that I like: *aggressiveness and sharp opposition*. If this comes out even in stories where I tried to be as detached and impersonal as possible, there must be some truth in it and I'm glad. So your essay gave me great satisfaction—as you see also from the passionate argument it roused in me—and I am infinitely grateful to you.

Yours,

Italo Calvino

[1985]

Sitting-Down Literature

G.C.: *The Writer works sitting down (when he is not intelligent or imaginative enough to look for other positions), and being sedentary is a profound evil. An evil for everyone, a universal evil of Western civilization. Tissot, in his immortal* De valetudine litteratorum, *says that all the physical troubles of literary people come from the assiduous hard work of the mind* (mentis assiduus labor) *and the extreme inactivity of the body* (corporis continua requies). *He also speaks of sitting as a sin: a hygienic sin—but a hygienic sin is a true sin, a sin against the body, a tool of the word. Madame de Sévigné writes as an expert to her daughter: "Almost all our ills come from sitting in chairs"* (literally: d'avoir le cul sur la selle: *having our asses in the saddle). Van Swieten imagines that men of letters, because of their sedentariness, are predestined to apoplexy:* frequenter a tali causa oritur apoplexia. *Valensin, a brilliant sexologist and the author of a memorable little book about the prostate (sadly, almost completely unknown in Italy), having listed the troubles that being sedentary causes in the bladder, observes that the modernized Japanese, discovering the chair, at the same time discovered prostatic hyperplasia.*

• • •

Sitting is indeed a bad thing, but riding on horseback was certainly no more hygienic. Literary people and horsemen have in common, among many other things, forcing the body into an unnatural position. Still, it's better to be sitting than to be standing and getting varicose veins. Actually, all man's ills stem from the decision to be a biped, when his nature wanted him to distribute the weight of his body on four limbs. It should be said that by doing this our progenitors developed the ability of the hands, which were freed from the locomotor function, making human history possible. But I think that perfect equilibrium was achieved during the long era of dwelling in trees. Although the hands were needed to hold on to the branches and were not entirely available to learn techniques and skills, the varied structure of supports amid the branches forced the human body into constantly different positions and gave it the opportunity to display constantly new talents. Think of how earthbound civilizations have humiliated the intelligence of the feet, encouraging the victory of an obtuse human offspring whose feet hug the ground with foolish and callous obstinacy, closing off the pathways of natural selection to those endowed with prehensile, versatile, industrious, nimbly digital, nervously tactile, musical feet.

However, the ice ages that drove us out of the trees, condemning us to a life that isn't ours, were an irreversible event. We can't turn back. We have constructed a world for seated bipeds that no longer has anything to do with our body, a world that will be inherited by the organisms best adapted to survive in it. I spend a large part of my life sitting still at a desk, and for me, the shape that would be most comfortable to assume is the snake's. Wrapped in its coils the snake distributes its weight uniformly over its whole body and can transmit every least movement to all its limbs, keeping them exercised even without moving. I realize that a myself-snake, having only the tail available for all the said manual operations, would see some physical-mental capacities connected to the work of the hands diminished, from typewriting to the use of reference books, from counting on the fingers to biting one's nails, et cetera.

So then the perfect shape would be that of the octopus or the giant squid, whose redundancy of limbs with great locomotor-prehensile-positional versatility would become an incentive to new operational talents, new methodologies and habits. In addition to everything else, the octopus is very good at driving a car. It's clear, therefore, that it will be the octopus who takes our place. The world we have constructed is made in its image and semblance: we have worked for the octopus.

[1970]

Art Thefts
(Conversation with Tullio Pericoli)

PERICOLI: The drawings for the show, which I entitled *Stealing from Klee*, originated in a practical necessity: I deliberately suspended my usual mode of working for a while, because I was afraid it was becoming repetitious. I'm referring in particular to the way I start a drawing and proceed to construct it. I felt driven to repeat the same operations, prepare the page in the same way, start from the same mark, almost from the same image, use the same tones.

Why, at this point, did I start working on Klee, conducting something like a lab experiment? Probably because at the very moment when the need—or desire—for change became most evident, I realized that I had to come to terms completely with what I had been, and therefore with certain strategies of my work, and, finally, with Klee: the artist I'd practically lived with for years. It was a cohabitation that irritated me as well. I couldn't pretend to resolve this problem by setting it aside. I had to face it directly. (Maybe I wanted only to fully possess a thing that in reality I wanted to free myself from once and for all.) And the direct contact with Klee helped me break the automatic gestures of my arm and show me how much resistance had accumulated in it.

To truly steal from Klee, I had to track down his discovery, the most advanced and most luminous point of his work, and carry it away with me. Give it a new "metempsychic life" (to use Almansi and Fink's term) on my sheets of paper, in my drawings. So I went looking for where Klee had presumably drawn the first mark of a painting, how he prepared the background, which colors he used first and which later, why a mark was there and not there. And sometimes I managed to find that second anatomy which is the anatomy not of the object but of the painting itself; as if by lifting up the first skin I could glimpse the intersections of the marks that indicated the possible developments.

At this point I understood that I was dealing with a more general problem: what we could call "art thefts." Basically this is a somewhat particular type of theft, which paradoxically enriches both the thief and the one robbed. (Wasn't Cézanne, if I may be allowed the comparison, enriched by the theft perpetrated to his detriment—or rather to his advantage—by Picasso?)

It's here that I had the idea of a conversation with you, who do not appear to be a stranger to the idea of "stealing," and who certainly, it seems to me, conceal, if I may say so, a Klee-like nature. You've spoken of "shapes the world could have taken in its transformations and didn't, for some chance reason or because of a basic incompatibility: shapes thrown away, irretrievable, lost" ("Origin of the Birds"). Like Klee you look for possible and drawable shapes, which don't exist in reality but do exist as possibilities. You use words like *the writable* and *the narratable* (*If on a winter's night a traveler*), you show a shell in the act of its "figuration" (*The Spiral*), you let a story develop from an interdependent combination of images (*The Castle of Crossed Destinies*), and you end the story "A Sign in Space" with "since it was clear that independently of the signs the space didn't exist and had never existed." Likewise the painter's canvas doesn't exist as a space until he draws the first pencil mark.

CALVINO: So let's begin at the beginning. The idea that the artist is the owner of something is a rather late idea. In the beginning the idea of stealing doesn't exist because style is something general, an ideal model. In classical art style is a model to achieve, and everyone is supposed to achieve it. So the criterion of imitating other works is canonical, is prescribed for the artist as it is for the poet. One could say that art originates in other art, just as poetry originates in other poetry, and that is always true; even when you think you're simply letting your own heart speak, or are imitating nature, in fact you are imitating representations, maybe without even realizing it. To me it seems that imitation is always at the start of an artist's apprenticeship, as it is for a writer's. What is the first impulse? One says: I'd like to write a poem or paint a picture or write a story like that particular painting, that particular poem, that particular story. And that is legitimate; to enable the voice to emerge, to exist as an independent poetic personality, one starts by establishing a relationship with a model or with several models. I think that a young person starting any creative activity should have no scruples about imitating, about stealing. The quotation can be conscious or unconscious. Certainly when the writer gives in to his own inspiration reminiscences emerge of other writing, for the painter visual reminiscences of other paintings.

You now propose to come to terms with Klee explicitly, but first, in your tiny and obsessive graphic details, in your musical fugues of signs, in your need to compose different visual materials, you continued to have a dialogue with Klee precisely in what is most original and personal in your work as a painter.

Then there is the conscious quotation, which can be an homage to a beloved author, or a more or less critical or parodic remaking. The example of Klee is of an artist who has great genetic power, who in every picture opens pathways and certainly is there to be stolen from. He's someone who feeds himself to the art of the future. All he does is open pathways that he may not be interested in taking himself, because he is already worried about opening new ones, and so everything he does is a gift to others, whereas he then loses interest.

PERICOLI: If you think of Klee, in fact, it's not one painting or a narrow group of works that comes to mind but a body of work in its totality. Unlike many others.

CALVINO: Unlike many others who can be defined in one painting, or for whom there is a central painting or a group of paintings or one painting per period, Klee has this multitude. In fact, Klee exhibitions—I've seen a lot of them—almost always give me a sense of intoxication, because I don't know where to look. When I find an isolated reproduction or an isolated painting by Klee in a museum, I can concentrate on that, but the overall image of Klee remains this universe of the possibilities of shapes, which are always very recognizable. Klee is so rich, so generous, but at the same time he's never eclectic, he's always himself.

You cited Cézanne-Picasso. In effect we look at Cézanne and at the same time through the developments that cubism gave Cézanne. Picasso is this extraordinary thief, he's the Mercury of the history of painting, who appropriates and comments on and synthesizes the most diverse formal worlds.

PERICOLI: Picasso remade other painters as well, like Cranach, Velázquez, El Greco, but the real theft I think he perpetrated on Cézanne.

CALVINO: Oh yes. On Cézanne, or *arte negra*, or a certain classicism, or certain neoclassical drawings, then there are portraits that are almost like Manet, or even the early thefts from Puvis de Chavannes. He's a man who always knows how to steal. Whereas when he redoes *Las Meninas* it's not that he appropriates Velázquez or when he redoes *Le déjeuner sur l'herbe*. They are like pretexts, reinterpretations of motifs, but he remains more on the outside, on the surface. Who knows: maybe today, after so many years when all the art in the world seemed Picasso-like, we can say that he was more useful in reviving the pictorial tradition that was behind him than he was useful to others. Perhaps it's too soon to say, but today it seems to me that his impulse has remained a little in the shadows.

PERICOLI: I'd like to bring you back to your work and talk about you as a writer-thief, hence of your relationship with the works of others and your relationship with Klee.

CALVINO: I've always been aware of borrowing, of paying homage, and in this case to pay homage to an author means to appropriate something that is his. Starting with the first things I wrote I was proposing encounters between two very different models, for example *Pinocchio* and Faulkner, Hemingway and Ippolito Nievo. It's often what I read in childhood that surfaces. One of these genetic authors is Stevenson. Maybe because Stevenson was, in turn, a writer who remade, who imitated the adventure novel from the point of view of an extremely refined literary person. And just when I began to do things that were more "mine," with *The Cloven Viscount*, Stevenson seemed to show up everywhere, maybe even without my realizing it. Borges also loves Stevenson, and Borges is the typical writer who is always remaking something already written. At the same time, you can get from the works of others the incentive needed in order not to repeat yourself.

You're right that Klee is very important to me. Painting has always been useful as an incentive to reinvent myself, as an ideal of free invention, of remaining oneself while making something new. In this sense Klee seems fundamental.

Then, at a certain point, in the sixties, this business of stealing becomes an important literary theme: remaking, rewriting. A typical example is Michel Tournier, who rewrites Robinson in *Vendredi ou les Limbes du Pacifique*. That's when on a radio show I start retelling *Orlando Furioso* in prose, in my style; in *Invisible Cities* I re-create Marco Polo's *Millions*; then in *The Castle of Crossed Destinies*, I start retelling the stories of Faust, Parsifal, Hamlet, Macbeth, King Lear . . . It's a return to what literature was until the pre-Romantic period and partway into the Romantic. Writers of tragedies were always retelling the same myths, similarly in the arsenal of medieval legends were the Faust stories, the Don Juan stories . . .

The need to invent a story is relatively modern. The ancients went back to what was already there, myth. That same concept of imitation in Aristotle is not so much imitation of nature as imitation of myth, that is, something given that is re-created, reinterpreted.

You are interested now in a particular type of work about other works, and when you use the word *steal* you mean stealing a secret, almost like the theft of an invention. This looking in Klee for a second anatomy, the secret anatomy, the drawing behind the drawing, corresponds, it seems to me, to a curiosity I often feel, even about authors very different from me. I'm eager to understand how they did it, how they constructed a given work. For example, Tolstoy: it's always said of him that he portrays life directly, but what's interesting is to understand the method he's used to construct his story. Whenever I think I've grasped a plan, a design, a strategy in an author like that, I'm happy, as if I'd succeeded in apprehending a hidden secret.

PERICOLI: This activity of the thief or counterfeiter can be carried out in many ways: you can quote, invert the logic, overturn the syntax, upend the plot, change the comic to tragic, invent languages that simulate other ones. Queneau in *Exercices de style* tried ninety-nine possible ways of telling the same story. You translated a novel of Queneau's, *Les fleurs bleues*; I'd like to know what the relationship was between translator and text. Maybe in that case especially you have to find that mechanism, that design you were talking about, to reach the core of the conception.

CALVINO: Translating is the most absolute system of reading. You have to grasp the implications of every word you read. The experience of translating Queneau's *Fleurs bleues* was unusual because very often there was a play on words that I had to replace with another play on words, making sure that the text had the same rhythm, the same lightness, and also the same inner necessity: not just showing that there was a play on words here and I've put in another one. Translation implies a particular intensity of reading: your works on Klee are in essence readings of Klee, the translation and development of something implicit. It seems to me that reading is fundamental to this conversation we're having. Maybe the reading is the theft. There is this thing here, closed, this object, and you're seizing something that's shut up inside it. There's a breaking into, a theft and a break-in, in every true reading. Naturally paintings and literary works are constructed purposely to be stolen, in that sense. Just as a labyrinth is constructed purposely so that you get lost in it, but also so that you'll find your way out.

Being translated is the same type of experience: it's a way of reading oneself. Whenever I discuss my books with a translator, in the languages I know, I'm obliged to go over my work again with another eye. Usually the first impression of reading myself in translation is rather distressing. I see the text impoverished, flattened. Then I'm obliged to try to understand why I wrote that particular sentence in that particular way, and what didn't get into the translation, that is, to reflect on what I've written: that adjective I put here and not here, I used this construction, which is not the most usual, why? Oh, because I intended that. So many things jump out at me . . .

PERICOLI: So then there could be another story, made possible by the new reading, the reading you do of yourself in the translation. In that case you would be confronting the singular possibility of stealing from yourself.

CALVINO: Ah, yes. And at times I realize that I've expressed certain things badly, that I could explicate certain nuances better, that certain of my intentions didn't come through, given that the translator hasn't picked them up.

How do we connect this with our conversation about stealing? When I see right off the bat that the translation hasn't worked, that is, when I see that the translator didn't do a good job of stealing, didn't discover what the secret was, I feel disappointed. That's what it's like.

PERICOLI: But you don't also have doubts that your secret wasn't fascinating enough?

CALVINO: Precisely. Because maybe the secret wasn't there, if it wasn't found. It's good for a secret to stay hidden, but it's also good when it's glimpsed in some way, when the thief understands where it's worth the trouble to break in.

PERICOLI: Now let's talk about copying. Recently in an interview, Eduardo De Filippo recounted that his father had compelled him, as a child, to copy dozens of theater scripts, word for word, and from that had come his love for the theater and the desire to write plays. You, in turn, in your latest book, *If on a winter's night a traveler*, write: "For a moment I seem to understand what must have been the meaning and the fascination of a vocation now inconceivable: that of the copyist. The copyist lived simultaneously in two temporal dimensions, that of reading and that of writing; he could write without the anguish of having the void open before his pen; read without the anguish of having his own act become concrete in some material object."

CALVINO: Apart from the conversation on copying and stealing, there's a preliminary theft here from Borges, who wrote the story of that "Pierre Menard, the author of the *Quixote*": who had written a book that was the same, word for word, as Cervantes's, but it was the work of Pierre Menard and not of Cervantes, because anything said by Pierre Menard had a different meaning, entered into a historical context different from that of Cervantes. Developing this idea, I had the character of the writer [in my book *If on a winter's night a traveler*] copy the beginning of *Crime and Punishment*, to give an impetus to his imagination in crisis; once he's copied the beginning, he's tempted not to stop, to continue to copy. The character of the copyist, which has disappeared from our literary and editorial society, certainly had its fascination. The last famous copyists are Buvard and Pecuchet, who are gripped by that love, by that identification with everything knowable. In my book, in short, I propose, as one of many exercises, taking a given beginning and trying to develop it in another way. After all, one of the canonical processes of the avant-garde is to work on something already written. That's also true for painting.

PERICOLI: Of course. Reynolds, as early as the mid-seventeenth century, in England, had theorized this concept of imitation and borrowed from works by other painters. He adopted theft as a method, habitually and systematically using images and inventions of earlier painters to make his paintings. He was an archaeologist of figurative culture. He would define his style as "historical," probably meaning that in his paintings there is some art history, that a history of images could be read there. He was criticized for these appropriations, which were considered illicit, and in court he defended himself by asserting that a quotation in a new context is still an example of talent and of taste.

CALVINO: It seems to me that this corresponds to an idea of art that is not focused on the personality of the maker but in which every work is our common patrimony. I think that's how it is in many forms of non-European art . . . In Oriental civilization, for example . . . a particular way of representing a divinity, once it has become habitual, is repeated, is introduced into different compositions. This could also be true among us when it comes to artisans' work. A maker of crèches reproduces a given figure of a shepherd or a wise man, just as tradition has handed it down to him, using particular molds . . . But this is also true in the history of poetry. The famous Homeric epithets, the formulas that Homer uses, probably were the common patrimony of the poetic tradition. In a lot of epic and narrative works there are these terms that are part of the tradition.

PERICOLI: And at this point perhaps we should speak of pleasure, the pleasure one gets from stealing, from penetrating someone else's system. Surely every act having to do with stealing—copying, remaking, changing, distorting, quoting, reading with thieving intentions—gives pleasure. Probably at first there's the illusion of being the author of the work that inspires us. And so, as you were just saying, there is the pleasure of rediscovering a pathway and retracing it alone. The pleasure of reliving the moments of the making of a work. Again, our penchant for fiction is satisfied, to appear with a mask, hence not to appear, to hide. To free ourselves from what we don't like about ourselves, entering a body that seems more protective because we're less exposed. Freeing us from "the anguish of having the void that opens up before our pen," from the conflicts tied to creative activity, from the effort to progress in our own search, from the effort to invent. To be able to express oneself while sheltering behind a kind of alibi, with limited responsibility.

CALVINO: Yes, it seems to me that the explanations you've enumerated are legitimate. If we try to summarize them maybe we should see the pleasure of getting involved in an interpersonal work, something that gives us some sense of a natural process that many generations have participated in, and which enables us to emerge from the individual creative struggle that has its satisfactions but is also very stressful. Participating in a collective creation, something that began before us and will presumably continue after us, gives us the impression of a force that passes through us. If we think about it, biological and sexual life is of this type. The act of love is the most individual that exists, but it's also participation in an infinite chain, the repetition of something that we know is at the very center of the course of the living creature.

PERICOLI: Certainly, the history of the figurative arts also appears as a long chain of inextricably joined images. A chain that developed almost independently of human social life, that followed its path as if it possessed an individual existence of its own. And this can be revealed even in a single painting. There's a fresco by Correggio in the church of San Giovanni

Evangelista in Parma, where, around the saint, a circular flight of round angel faces fades slowly into infinity, and the faces of the angels become smaller and smaller until they appear only as tiny brushstrokes, without even dots for the eyes: a simple swarm of tiny brushstrokes. It could be the reading, even if a little schematic, of a path of our art history. The large faces in the foreground allow us to interpret the more distant brushstrokes, which we would be unable to understand if we hadn't already absorbed the images in front. The last stroke of the brush is an angel only because the first large face has declared it.

CALVINO: It's true, every work is legible in its context. But if only the center of that fresco were preserved with those dots, and that's all, maybe that, too, would have value, it would be an abstract fresco.

PERICOLI: But today we can say "abstract" only because there was a path that we know.

CALVINO: Yes, if we abolish the faces of the angels we have to replace them with another path: the dots of Klee's paintings and Kandinsky's triangles and circles.

PERICOLI: This awareness of an almost individual pathway of art seems to begin in the Renaissance and is revealed in the Vasarian concept of the progress of the arts and above all in the theoretical testimonies on painting that Leonardo left us. In fact Leonardo goes so far as to state that the work of the artist shouldn't try to satisfy the patrons but should be made "to please the first painters" who are the only critics of his work.

CALVINO: Painting is something that makes itself, that produces itself through us. But we should be careful not to give to this idea of painting as history, history within painting itself, a sense of final historicism; that is, the idea of the history of painting should be seen as an expansive broadening, rather than as a vertical track toward a point of arrival. The goal we aim for is to paint everything paintable, make explicit the possibilities of painting.

PERICOLI: Certainly there isn't a pictorial truth to achieve.

CALVINO: There isn't progress. For example, for long periods it was believed that progress was truth, the photographic truth, at other times it was the sublime. In fact there is no other goal except to get everything possible out of the pictorial potentialities. This is also valid for literature. And it often leads us to change, to vary, even the criteria we use for evaluation. Such that today, after a long period in which the principal value was stylistic individuality, or personal authenticity, we are attracted by these interpersonal or apersonal procedures, we consider art that acts through us or in spite of us. That's why we talk about stealing and imitating as important operations, while maybe if we found ourselves right in the middle of a classical period, in which all artists and poets tend toward the norm, in reaction we would be led to favor the elements of individual expression.

PERICOLI: So stealing and engaging with the work of other authors seem to you important operations. Then do you think that this type of project, in a given era, is a sign of what is commonly called vitality or is it decadence? Anyway, provisionally accepting this simplistic formula, I think they indicate a period of vitality.

CALVINO: I, too, think it's vitality, but you have to be careful when you're talking about vitality or decadence. Very often the Alexandrian era is spoken of as an era of decadence, but if we recall that much of the culture that sustains us comes from the Alexandrian era, we see that these periods of great cultural accumulation, of the centrifuging of many materials, are like that biological soup where at the beginning of time life got its origin.

PERICOLI: I think that, apart from this, vitality is manifested in the fact that works are not accepted as closed objects, but, goaded by a greater critical spirit, we seek pathways, stages of becoming, stimuli, that generative core we were talking about.

CALVINO: Yes, of course. Every work that contains imitation, quotation, or parody presupposes a choice, a reading, a criticism, favoring certain elements, certain lines as opposed to others, and so it's a critical activity.

PERICOLI: As we conclude this conversation, in which we've talked a lot about stealing, about fathers, and about Klee, it occurs to me to ask myself and to ask you who is Klee the son of, whom did he steal from. Paradoxically I can't find an answer. He seems isolated in a sea of relatives. Some moods come to mind connected to his time, some readings, but they don't materialize into a name.

CALVINO: I would say that Klee belonged to an era in which painting was inspired by anthropology. Just as Picasso and the cubists in general sought out primitive art, *arte negra*, Klee looked at children's drawings. Someone may object that this element is more for show, more superficial than profound, because behind it is an enormous pictorial knowledge, but this pictorial knowledge was applied to an immediacy of representation that resembles children's drawing or prehistoric graffiti.

PERICOLI: You might think that Klee paid more attention to certain graphic solutions, rather than to masks and statues, to certain decorations and stories told in images from primitive art in which the line appears agile, lively—I would say "in the style of Klee."

CALVINO: Yes, perhaps, I think of certain American Indian drawings, and certain motifs, both ornamental and expressive, from Africa, Oceania, pre-Columbian America. Certainly it's the recovery of a primitive force, sinking roots into that more anthropological than historical terrain which produces art.

[1980]

Translating a Text Is the
True Way of Reading It

Novels are like wines in that some travel well and some travel badly.

It's one thing to drink a wine in the place where it's produced and another to drink it thousands of kilometers away.

Traveling well or badly for novels can depend on matters of content or matters of form, that is, of language.

It's usually said that the Italian novels most popular among foreigners are those with a vividly characterized local setting (especially in the south), which describe places the reader can visit, and which celebrate Italian vitality as seen from abroad.

I think this may once have been true but is no longer: First, because a local novel implies a totality of specific knowledge that the foreign reader can't always grasp, and, second, because a certain image of Italy as an "exotic" country is by now far from the reality, and from the interests of the public. In other words, for a book to cross borders there has to be something original about it and something universal, that is, precisely the opposite of a confirmation of well-known images and local details.

And language has the utmost importance, because to keep the reader's attention the voice that speaks to him has to have a certain tone, a certain timbre, a certain liveliness. Current opinion says that a writer who writes in a neutral tone, who causes fewer problems of translation, travels better. But I think that this, too, is a superficial idea, because dull writing can have value only if the sense of dullness that it conveys has a poetic value, that is, if it creates a very personal dullness, otherwise one feels no encouragement to read. Communication has to be established through the writer's particular accent, and this can happen on an everyday, colloquial level, not unlike the liveliest and most brilliant journalism, or it can be a more intense, introverted, complex communication, appropriate to literary expression.

In short, for the translator, the problems to resolve are unending. In texts whose style is more colloquial, a translator who manages to grasp the right tone from the start can continue thanks to this momentum with an assurance that seems—that has to seem—easy. But translating is never easy; sometimes difficulties can be resolved spontaneously, almost unconsciously, by being attuned to the author's tone. But for texts that are more stylistically complex, with different levels of language that correct each other, the difficulties have to be resolved sentence by sentence, following the counterpoint between the author's conscious intentions and his unconscious drives. Translating is an art: the transfer of a literary text, whatever its value, into another language always requires some type of miracle. We all know that poetry is untranslatable by definition; but true literature, including prose, works precisely in the untranslatable margins of every language. Literary translators are those who stake their entire being to translate the untranslatable.

Those who write in a minority language, like Italian, sooner or later come to the bitter conclusion that the possibility of communicating rests on slender threads like spider webs: change merely the sound and order and rhythm of the words and the communication fails. How many times, reading the first draft of a translation of a text of mine that the translator showed me, have I been gripped by a sense of alienation from what I was reading: Was this what I had written? How could I have been so flat and insipid? Then, rereading my text in Italian and comparing it with the translation, I saw that the translation was perhaps very faithful, but in my text a word was used with a hint of ironic intention that the translation did not pick up; a subordinate clause in my text passed rapidly while in the translation it took on an unjustified importance and a disproportionate weight; the meaning of a verb in my text was softened by the syntactical construction of the sentence, while in the translation it sounded like a peremptory statement. In other words the translation communicated something completely different from what I had written.

And these are all things that I hadn't realized while writing, and that I discovered only rereading myself in relation to the translation. Translation is the true way of reading a text; this I believe has been said many times. I can add that, for an author, reflecting on the translation of one's own text, and discussing it with the translator, is the true way of reading oneself, of understanding what one has written and why.

This conference is focused on translations from Italian into English, and I have to clarify two things: First, the drama of translation as I've described it is more powerful the closer the two languages are, while between Italian and English the distance is such that translating means re-creating to some degree, and the smaller the temptation to make a literal transcription, the more likely the translator is to preserve the spirit of a text. The sufferings I described occur more often reading myself in French, where the possibilities of a hidden distortion are constant; not to mention Spanish, which can construct sentences that are almost identical to the Italian but whose spirit is completely the opposite. In English the results can be so different from the Italian that I may not recognize myself at all, but there can also be results that are happy precisely because they arise from the linguistic resources of English.

Second, there are plenty of problems for translations from English into Italian as well—that is, I wouldn't want it to seem that Italian alone is sentenced to being a complicated and untranslatable language. Even the apparent facility, rapidity, practicality of English requires the particular gift that only the true translator has.

From whatever language and into whatever language one translates, one has to not only know the language but have a feeling for the spirit of the language, the spirit of both languages, to know how the two languages can transmit their secret essence. I have the good fortune to be translated by Bill Weaver, who possesses this spirit of language to the highest degree.

I strongly believe that the author should collaborate with the translator. This collaboration, apart from the author's review of the translation, which can happen only in the limited number of languages that the author is competent to judge, arises from the translator's questions for the author. A translator who doesn't have questions can't be a good translator: I feel I can judge the quality of a translator from the type of questions I'm asked.

Then, I also strongly believe in the function of the publisher, in the collaboration between editor and translator. A translation is not something you can simply send off to the printer; the work of the editor is hidden, but when it's there it's effective, and when it's not, as in the overwhelming majority of cases in Italy and as an almost general rule in France, it's a disaster. Naturally it can also happen that the editor ruins the translator's good work; but I think that translators, no matter how good they are, in fact precisely when they are good, need their work to be evaluated sentence by sentence by someone who compares original text and translation and if necessary discusses it with them. Bill Weaver can tell you how important it's been for him to work with a great editor like Helen Wolff, who had an important place in literary publishing first in Weimar Germany, then in the United States. I have to say that the two countries where translations of my books have been successful in the literary world are the United States and France, that is, the two countries where I've had the good luck to have exceptional editors. I've said of Helen Wolff that she has the easier job, because she's dealing with a translator who is also exceptional, Bill Weaver; whereas François Wahl found that he had to redo from beginning to end almost all the translations of my books published in France, by Seuil. With the most recent, I managed to get him to add his name, which in fairness should also appear on the earlier translations.

There are problems that are common to the art of translation from any language, and problems that are specific to the translation of Italian authors. First of all, the fact is that Italian writers always have a problem with their own language. Writing isn't a natural act; it almost never has a relationship with speaking. Foreigners who spend time with Italians will surely have noticed a peculiarity of our conversation: we can't finish sentences—we always leave our sentences in the middle. Maybe Americans are not very sensitive to this, because in the United States people also speak in cutoff, interrupted sentences, exclamations, locutions without precise semantic content. But compared with the French, who are used to starting sentences and finishing them, with the Germans, who always put the verb at the end, and with the English, who usually construct very proper sentences, we can see that the Italians speak a language that tends to vanish continually into nothing, and if we had to transcribe it we would have to make continuous use of ellipsis points. Now, in writing, the sentence has to come to an end, and so writing requires a use of language completely different from that of daily speech. Writers have to compose complete and meaningful sentences, because this writers can't avoid: they always have to say something. Politicians also finish their sentences, but they have the opposite problem, that of speaking in order not to say anything, and you have to recognize that their skill is extraordinary. Intellectuals also can often finish sentences, but they have to construct completely abstract speeches, which never touch on anything real, and which can generate other abstract speeches. Here, then, is the position of Italian writers: they are writers who use the Italian language in a way completely different from the politicians, completely different from the intellectuals, but they can't resort to current everyday speech because it tends to get lost in the inarticulate.

That's why Italian writers always or almost always live in a state of linguistic neurosis. They have to invent the language in which they write, before inventing what they write. In Italy the relationship with the word is essential not only for poets but also for prose writers. More than other great modern literatures, Italian literature had and has poetry as its center of gravity. Like the poets, Italian prose writers pay obsessive attention to the individual word, and to the "verse" contained in their prose. If they don't have this attention at a conscious level, it means that they write as if in a raptus, as in instinctive or automatic poetry.

This problematic sense of language is an essential element of the spirit of our time. Thus Italian literature is a necessary component of great modern literature and deserves to be read and translated. Because Italian writers, contrary to popular opinion, are not euphoric, joyful, sunny. In most cases they have a depressive temperament but with an ironic spirit. Italian writers can teach only this: to confront the depression, the evil of our time, the common condition of humanity in our time, by defending ourselves with irony, with the grotesque transfiguration of the spectacle of the world. There are also writers who seem overflowing with vitality, but it's a vitality that is basically sad, bleak, dominated by a sense of death.

This is why, however difficult it may be to translate Italians, it's worth the trouble to do so: Because we live the universal despair with the greatest joy possible. If the world is increasingly senseless, all we can do is try to give it a style.

[1982]

Literature and Power
(on an Essay by Alberto Asor Rosa)

In the sixties, says Asor Rosa, three prominent groups form in Italian literature, corresponding to three historical perspectives at that moment of transition in our society: reformists, neo-avant-garde, revolutionaries. The reformists believe that reality is knowable and therefore transformable; the avant-garde wants to imitate the process of destruction in order to emerge from it; the revolutionaries reject as deceptive any mixture of literary progressivism and social revolution, in which poets and writers do not have a privileged function or a mandate to carry out.

Between '68 and '77 history becomes confused: reformists and neo-avant-garde are swept away. The revolutionaries remain on the scene, two in number: Franco Fortini and Asor Rosa. A basic disagreement divides them: Fortini, although he denies that literature has any political use, sees as a goal a formal homology: poetry, the metaphor of living life to its full potential, is an end like revolution. Asor

Rosa rejects this "utopia of form" as well: the revolution-ary critic has to know how to say only and always "no."

Events rush headlong. In the last act the two look around: The scene is deserted, politics no longer exists. They approach each other, they understand that they, too, are defeated, they rediscover each other as brothers. The stage lights dim; literature, too, is over. Gusts of cold wind blow through the wings, a dry leaf drifts, a few snowflakes fall. The two wrap themselves in a single cloak and leave as the lights go out. Curtain.

I've tried to simplify Asor Rosa's argument, and I don't think I've betrayed its meaning. Its general outline seems historically accurate, and the position of each actor seems faithfully described. If I've used a caricatured scene it's not to laugh behind the backs of others, given that I, too, am a party to the cause, among the first to be knocked out as a "reformist," and given that I am not insensitive to the hon-ors of war that Asor Rosa grants me as an old adversary. Maybe I'm laughing so as not to release autobiographical sighs myself.

Alberto Asor Rosa has given an openly autobiographical shape to the essay I'm talking about (ninety-five pages in the section "Letteratura e potere" ["Literature and Power"] in the first volume of *Letteratura Italiana,* which he edited for Einaudi), devoted to "Lo stato democratico e i partiti politici" ("The Democratic State and the Political Parties"). The history of forty years of literary debate on the left (es-pecially in and around the Communist Party) comes in to illuminate the antecedents of the positions taken by the author in the sixties (especially the "anti-populist" battle of *Scrittori e popolo*, 1965) and afterward.

Perhaps we should briefly recall the battle that Asor Rosa fought at the time in the ranks of the "workerist" far left against the engaged, realist, resistance, southern, poor, pedagogic, et cetera literature of the left. Not (as often happens in such cases) in the name of a literature that claimed to be even farther left but to say that classist revolutionary politics couldn't and shouldn't have a literature; the last interesting literature from the revolutionary point of view had been the haut-bourgeois literature of the crisis and the formal destructiveness of the avant-garde, both nearly absent in Italy.

The general plan of the operation was clearly formulated and said things that corresponded to evident truths, both for those who shared its illusion of a classist politics seen as an absolute and for those who looked at literature and civic life with a more dispassionate critical eye. In demonstrating the thesis that the false ideology of Italian literature had always been "populism" and hadn't changed throughout the Risorgimento, fascism, and the resistance, the long polemic was often unfair in its details, full of strained interpretations and generalizations, and in its wholesale slaughter didn't stop to distinguish who had had a positive function and who negative, or who had been sincere and who false.

But altogether, I have to say, seeing the battleship *Potemkin* of Italian literature of the left scuttled with flags flying, with officers and crew on deck at attention, was a great sight. I enjoyed it without regret, swimming with all my might to get away from the whirlpool. [Ungaretti's] "Allegria di naufragi" ("Joy of Shipwrecks") is a poem I've always loved, for the title even more than for the poem itself.

No one tried to raise the sunk battleship, and from then on no one wanted to talk about it. Only some post-'68 neophytes introduced themselves as inventors of the umbrella, but without gaining much attention.

Asor Rosa now reworks the fundamental part of his historical excursus, starting with the Second World War and updating it, through the present, that is, almost twenty years after the end of *Scrittori e popolo*. (The new essay ends symbolically on the date 1975 with the death of Pasolini, but the perspective is that of the eighties.) What has changed in his picture? Certainly the failed revolutionary political perspective, and not only that, but something even more important: that is, the idea that politics was the key to everything and that *one* unique, absolute political theory existed.

It's a not insignificant change, and although Asor Rosa's argument seems to proceed for a long stretch on the same track, there are some modifications: the denigrating epithet *populist* is used less frequently, and other problem areas come to light, for example totalitarianism. Asor Rosa today wonders how in the world anti-totalitarian (and, more generically, anti-state, anti-power) polemics had such little weight among "politically engaged" Italian writers. And he cites a single notable exception of an anti-totalitarian writer: Moravia, to whom he devotes an original profile in this light. The other exception that Asor Rosa points out is Carlo Levi, but this is one of the rare cases in which originality of political thought precedes literary expression. However, to develop this argument would require broadening the field of the historical investigation, and discussing areas of Italian literature farther removed from the Communist issues.

To emphasize the continuity of the literary debate in the last years of fascism and immediately after the liberation, Asor Rosa draws up two lists: one of writers who were "politically engaged" before and continue to be afterward, and the other of writers who were "disengaged" before, and remain that way. But many on the list of the "disengaged" have a complex and meaningful political story, even if individual: Brancati (here anti-totalitarianism returns to the foreground), Piovene, Delfini.

In the broad outlines and in the case of the authors and journals that he follows most closely, I would say that Asor Rosa always sees clearly and moves in the right direction, but this accuracy isn't always applied to the details. One could make a list of small but glaring mistakes that seem to be inserted purposely to exercise the reader on the "hunt for errors" and invite him to be wary of what is written.

I will confine myself to some general observations, because this is not the place for a more detailed analysis. The review of the successive phases of the Communist Party's cultural politics in the fifties (and more specifically literary politics: at that time it was the literary critics who were in charge) is full of precise facts, but it seems to me that the forms of unrest inside and outside the party are over-valued: excessive space is given, for example, to the Alle-anza della Cultura, created in view of the elections of 1948 and forgotten right afterward, even though it's true that the participation of Corrado Alvaro was significant. (It's Alvaro himself, in his entirety, who deserves to be reexam-ined in an argument like this.)

This is an overall criticism I have of studies of con-temporary Italian culture: in the study of a movement, a journal, or an author, its counterparts, adversaries, and next-door neighbors should be described first. People talk about *Politecnico* and never mention *Costume*, which was *the* literary review in Milan in 1945–46. Asor Rosa explains very well what Salinari and Trombadori's *Il Contemporaneo* was, in 1954–56, but scarcely mentions Mario Pannunzio's *Il Mondo*, which was its model, graphically as well (indeed, it was immediately dubbed *Piccolo Mondo Contemporaneo*).

In a study of cultural politics of those years one can't neglect *Il Mondo*, a success that has few precedents in our history, since for some fifteen years it managed to gather around itself all non-Catholic, non-Marxist Italian culture. I think that so far what has been studied is the political relevance of *Il Mondo* as a voice of liberal culture in the years when the Christian Democratic Party occupied all the spaces of power, but it would be valuable to study its *literary program*, which also existed. (It wasn't, certainly, in-novative on a formal plane but gave special attention to custom, to Italian morality and psychology, even at the simplest level, observed with bitter irony and also with a certain self-importance.) It was a program that had an influence on Italian fiction; without it we would have a hard time placing today's important writers—for example, Leonardo Sciascia (whom Asor Rosa barely mentions).

To complete the picture of the fifties, a similar study should be made of the scientific interests, literary contents, and ideas of the first series of *Nuovi Argomenti*, which, if you look at it now, seems to have a wealth of material.

And we cannot underestimate the fact that at the same time a link to prewar Florence was reforged with *Paragone*, which again had the canonical role, vacant for years, of a purely literary review.

(Meanwhile government politics bet on this link, without blame or praise, despite knowing very little about the existence of a literature. That was the case in particular with RAI* and the few other opportunities that enabled impoverished literary people to earn some money in those not yet "affluent" times.)

And it should also be said that at the same time the United States, with a view to the Cold War, financed the Congress for Cultural Freedom, a program that gave voice and space to intellectuals and had a journal in every country. All this ended with the revolt of the Americans' bad conscience, but as a fact of cultural politics it can't be dismissed with simplistic formulas: it should be studied

---

* Radiotelevisione Italiana, the national public broadcasting company of Italy (*Translator's note*)

historically, with a comparison of the journals in various countries. My impression is that the Italian one, *Tempo presente*, was the best and least instrumental, thanks especially to Nicola Chiaromonte and especially during the period when Elémire Zolla and J. R. Wilcock were the editors.

Thus I've approached the heart of the problem step by step: the discussion of *Letteratura e potere* in those years should include relations with real power, not only with the power dreamed of by the opposition, and also with the economic power that in those paleo-Marxist times many considered the only effective power (let's not forget that Olivetti and to a degree Pirelli had some relationship with literary people).

But a "style" also had to be chosen, and what's interesting about Asor Rosa's argument is that it's limited to the authors and journals that were important to him at the time, from his workers' perspective, and about which there is a lot to say even today. Because his characteristic feature, even in the sixties, was this: he declared, provocatively, that true literature was only "that one," but then he continued to concern himself with "this one," where he could be critical and drive out the ideological worms that in his view were corroding it.

In the same way, when the current anti-metaphysical trend (such as he expresses in the methodological introduction to the volume) should lead him to contemplate other dimensions, other points of reference, and other genealogies, he sets up the first part of *Letteratura Italiana* with a volume entitled *Il letterato e le istituzioni* (*Literature and Insti-*

tutions); where by *institutions* he doesn't mean the line, the rhyme, the stanza, as the reader might reasonably expect, but literally the institutions of public life, those for which we pay tithes, taxes, and bribes), and will follow it with one entitled *Produzione e consumo* (*Production and Consumption*), centered mainly on "Classi e collocazione sociale dei letterati" ("Class and Social Placement of Literary People"), before he finally gets to the third volume and *Le forme del testo* (*Forms of the Text*).

This is to say that if in interviews and presentations Asor Rosa promises "Enough with De Sanctis!" and Furio Diaz takes him at his word and is outraged (*Repubblica*, December 28), and sends him back to read the texts (ibid., January 4), and the other protests, "But why do you have it in for historicism?" (ibid., January 9), what they're arguing about is merely intentions, and what exists so far in reality is some chapters of literary and civic history, which I believe are very solid (and each one deserves a specialized review).

On the other hand, there are also those who (me, to go no farther) respond to Asor Rosa's intentions to change his method with an "If only!" veined with skepticism. If only we would once and for all rid ourselves of this condemnation as Italians to seek in literature the reasons for the disasters of politics and the dreams of a politics that is not disastrous. We've all known for a while that this is the worst approach to understanding anything about political history or about literature, but so it is, we continue to circle around it.

Rather, it might be interesting, in this very Italian dimension of literature that is called the "ethical-political" or "moral and civic," to look for changes in terminology and concepts. While once we used to write the history of ideals or types of consciousness (including class consciousness), now the emphasis is placed on centers of political power (the court, city government, religious orders, the constitutional state, the parties) and cultural organizations (academies, universities, foundations). Which could be a step forward, in the sense of concreteness, in order to understand how minds obsessed with power function; but we must always remember that the powers of literature are something else, are indirect, act only over the long term, and influence areas that escape the grip of the visible powers (and for that reason can be in some cases more durable).

That politics is now identified with the wretched reality of power that is an end in itself, and with the stratagems to acquire and maintain it, is Machiavelli's truth applied to the lowest, as the TV news and the front pages confirm for us daily. And it's good that we no longer have illusions that things can be different. But in the forty years studied by Asor Rosa there were periods, not so short, when we were still fighting for ideas, ideas of how to live and ascribe values, ideas of public and private morality, of taste and style and language, of images of how we were and how we could be: and literature and politics were aspects of that picture.

The game of power existed, naturally, in those moments, too, maybe on the same terms as today, even if it was quantifiable in figures with fewer zeros, but there were people (scattered around) who believed that the essential questions were different. And there was also the die-hard dream of a positive power that could be installed and opposed to the long series of evil powers: while today we know, or should all know, that the only thing we can do is try to limit the damage of the power of others.

By this I don't mean that periods of idealism (whether it's just or absurd) should be studied in terms of idealistic history, but perhaps by resorting more to the methods of the history of mentalities, of sensibility, of the forms of daily life, of psychology, of religiosity (especially for laypeople), of superstitions and prejudices, of the collective imagination. That would then bring the general historical discourse close to the study of literary forms, of texts in verse and prose seen from within, of the concrete and precise acts that the *work* of poets and writers consists in.

[1983]

The Last Fires

Twenty years is already a "historical" distance, and any consideration of a literary movement of twenty years ago takes the form if not of a theoretical judgment at least of an assessment in relation to the before and the after. And immediately we find ourselves having to choose between two opposing ways of defining Gruppo 63: (a) as the first break in continuity in our tradition, upsetting an image of literature and literary society which until then had been essentially unified by criteria of value, meanings, and exclusions, and that even though it came together again later was no longer the same; (b) as the last time poets and writers gathered around a common program or banner of a movement or a journal, a last attempt to give a collective meaning to the expression of a generation or an era, to separate, and define, and distinguish itself from others in the way it understood literary work, which had happened regularly in the history of our culture of the past two hundred years and which after Gruppo 63 did not happen again.

Good reasons exist for both theses. It's true that, contrary to the system of co-optation that traditionally governed the renewal of literature (we began to consider ourselves writers from the moment the older writers considered us such), Gruppo 63 launches a frontal attack against the "literature of the fifties" seen as a bloc (some authors rather than others were used as scapegoats, with definitions that flatten the intimism of the "literature of memory" into the sentimentality of the romance novel) and establishes itself as a separate and autonomous body. But it's also true that this separateness and autonomy is a fact of organization, of a cultural and behavioral code collectively established and accepted, and young people who want to adhere to it have to give up any expressive eclecticism or compromise with the usual styles, carry out radical operations on the formal plane, and in public readings subject their work to the group's extremely harsh criticism.

That is, the practice instituted is completely new with respect to our habits (thesis a) but is (thesis b) animated by an esprit de corps and by a confidence in its own literary rationale that has direct precedents in the historical avant-gardes but was not repeated afterward. Just as the clear division that is assumed between the two poles of the "establishment" and the "avant-garde" was the last attempt to draw a general map of literature, however rigid and simplified, and to assign each of the components an ideological valence and a historical role, even with all the illusions and strained polemical interpretations. Whereas in the years that follow the five years 1963 to 1967 (I think the activity of the Gruppo and the journal *Quindici* spans that period) nothing similar was attempted.

It seems to me that the only obvious literary grouping of the past fifteen years, that is, the appearance of a new generation of poets in public readings, culminating in June of '79 with the Castelporziano Festival, lacked a comprehensive critical consciousness. The need for individual expression and for communication with an audience was very much on display, but not a plan for a general context where this encounter could take place, that is, a new, renewed idea of literature.

The "historical" argument that could be made today, starting from Gruppo 63, seems to me to be this, on the deficiencies of the "after," which is much more important than any call for evaluation based on the usual questions: How many important works did the neo-avant-garde create? What remains of them? To which there are two responses. One is to note that the legacy of the historic avant-garde movements consists mainly of archives of uncollected texts, curious documents, rare little magazines and publications, which restore to us a certain potential for the energy of that era. The second is to examine a list of books from the past twenty years that are considered meaningful—books by any author, formerly belonging to the neo-avant-garde or not—to see which of them might contain any trace of the seismic movements that took place in the world of literary forms (in Italy and elsewhere in Europe) in the early sixties. An examination of that sort could offer surprises, accounting for the indirect effects that are literature's most significant.

My particular angle, which is certainly related to this

way of seeing, is that of an outside observer, who, although to all intents and purposes he belongs to the vilified "literature of the fifties," realized that many, more stimulating things were happening on the world literature scene that we were cut off from owing to the special angle of our critical discourse, and so he was naturally curious about what could emerge from an abrupt reshuffling of the cards in the deck. Encouraged in this by an alliance with Elio Vittorini, who, despite the fact that among his bête-noirs was the "terrorism of the avant-gardes," was always ready to seize the vibrations of the new and as early as 1962 opened *Il Menabò* to the writers who became the founders of Gruppo 63.

Those who, like me, entered the literary world at another moment that was said to be a rupture, 1945, had been able to follow along year by year as that impulse settled into a formula that was as dignified as possible but certainly not new or sensational, arising from the confluence of the best literary civilization of our thirties (that of the review *Solaria*) and the "moral and civic" tradition of idealist and Gramscian historicism. That was our "literature of the fifties"; but by the end of the decade that cultural frame had become very narrow, given the burgeoning of information about foreign cultures, and given that, with the end of the Cold War, something had changed in the preeminence of politics over every other subject, characteristic of the atmosphere of that epoch, and infusing it first with moral tension but then also with prudence, diplomacy, rounding off of edges. It can therefore be said that all the preconditions for a rupture were present, and that literature was the first to record the change of mindset that was in the air.

A historical picture of the birth of the Italian neo-avant-garde should also recognize some more or less direct antecedents: the Milanese review *Il Verri*, founded by [Luciano] Anceschi, which explored everything that was excluded from the above picture and from which the Novissimi poets emerged, who were later among the founders of Gruppo 63; some university milieus, close to the figurative arts or to modern music; and some arenas for guerrilla actions and raids, like [Giambattista] Vicari's *Il Caffè* for satire and the grotesque.

But it's more interesting, I think, to look at the history of what followed, or what failed to follow, which has to do with the hegemony of politics in Italian culture, or rather: of political language over every other dimension of language. It's been said many times that the neo-avant-garde was in crisis because the milieus that were supposed to provide its potential audience were taken up in the years around '68 by a consuming politicization, to the exclusion of any other language. But even before, or rather starting in '63, Gruppo 63 had felt accused (by the elders at the time) of being the "literature of neocapitalism," and had begun to feel the need to show that it wasn't true, as if arguments like that could ever make sense. In short, the poverty and groundlessness of the political discourse, with its false rigor, had yet again dominated the potential and polyphony and grip of the literary discourse.

Naturally this is a bed of roses compared with the French

experience, parallel at the start and then increasingly divergent, down to the last somersaults of [Philippe] Sollers and *Tel Quel* (now *L'infini*). It, too, was politicized, but only superficially, as much in the Maoist phase as in that of the Stars and Stripes, and now in the arms of the good Lord. But behind it was something that, however one may judge it, can't be put in the same category, and it's a culture that still includes some "masters."

This sense of new continents of knowledge emerging no longer exists anywhere today, and still less among us. The conditions for giving birth to a new avant-garde movement can exist only amid dissatisfaction with what is; that sentiment certainly can't be lacking. Literature has been fragmenting (not only in Italy); each of us thinks of the little or much we can do, and we are increasingly uninterested in situating it in a context, an attitude that seems prevalent especially among the youngest. It's as if no one could any longer imagine an argument that would connect and contrast works, structures, tendencies, at the moment of invention, deriving a general meaning from the totality of individual creations. And it's here that the avant-garde, pre-avant-garde, and post-avant-garde have not had heirs.

[1983]

Gian Carlo Ferretti,
Bestseller Italian-Style

Ferretti's book could have been many things, and maybe that's what I'd like to talk about. It could have been an explanation of what the hell *bestseller* means, what those lists published by the papers signify; but then I'd have to cite absolute figures on the print run and the copies sold, because if we limited ourself to rankings by percentages, ascertained in a sampling of bookstores, we still wouldn't know if that book is in first place because that week among all the other books that don't sell it sold a few more copies, or if it really is successful and to what degree.

It could have been a comparative study of what the success of a book means in the United States (where the term *bestseller* originated), what in France, in Germany, in Italy (and in the USSR, which is said to be the only country where immediate, often dramatic relations are established between the strategy of the number of copies printed and the market response, with the public lining up at the book-stores the day a given book is distributed).

It could have been a reflection on the difficulties that publishers encounter in predicting success and lack of success, and how attempts to force choices end up in fiasco; on how predictions that are too cautious have sometimes proved wrong, and how very often predictions that are too optimistic have filled the remainder bins with unsold books. Every publisher has a vast supply of easy-to-come-by anecdotes on the subject, which can be used to demolish every myth of managerial planning, as well as to try to draft some empirical rule.

It could have been a very serious discourse on the shelf life of a title in the bookstore, the difference between the bestseller whose impact is gone in a season and the book that quietly continues its course over the years, and how from that derive different editorial and distribution politics. Among these would be the problem of the relationship between new works and reprintings and relative costs and fixed capital, the problem of the low-cost series that can be low-cost only with high print runs, whereas print runs tend to be low, the problem of bookstores that have room only for the new (which has been the case abroad for many years and is today in Italy as well). This is the fundamental crux of the problems of publishing and bookstores all over the world. (It's also the crux of cultural problems: the relationship that exists in a given culture between the ideal library based on the long term and books that are more closely connected to current events, to the tenor of the present, to immediate needs and moods.)

Or, leaving the sociological approach in the background, it could have been a shrewd critic on a group of novels that Ferretti wants to criticize: Pontiggia, Calvino, Eco, Fruttero-Lucentini, and some others, and that would be a type of criticism that we very much feel the lack of, an article not on a single book or author but one that makes connections between different works within the general outline of a literary context. But what are these possible common elements? If we put success in the foreground, then we're back at the beginning; we'd need exact figures (which would be evaluated differently, however, for those who are writing their first novel and for those who've had an audience for many years), and we'd probably see that every book is a case by itself. A less external element that Ferretti insists on is "planning," "engineering"; but can it really be a bad thing for writers to try to understand what they're doing with their work by thinking about it, studying it, rationalizing it? (Of course, there are also those who rely on the unconscious overflow of the treasures of their soul, but what can we who lack the certainty of being the chosen by grace do, except laboriously seek a justification for our lives by applying ourselves to a difficult task?)

Another possible common element: An intention to conquer the "market." Then you'd have to explain—with the market motivation taken for granted—why, rather than sticking to the most secure system of following the tested recipes, one's own or others', someone wants to try new ways, which would also be an experiment with the public, an attempt at an encounter between a new work and a public to some degree new. But what is this if not what every literary project needs, and without which a literature doesn't live?

To speak of the "market" when admittedly it's a "micro-market" and is unpredictable, refractory to any "marketing," when all we can say is that it's not mass and not elite, may seem concrete, but in fact it makes everything more abstract. Better to see if every individual book has a literary justification; and then, maybe, if it's had a particular success, study the reasons on this basis.

So if there are elements common to the various novels, they should be sought on the literary plane: whether of form (elaborate and "closed" constructions, as it's put: that's a theme I'd very much like to see dealt with, as we moved from a poetics that seemed to be a deconstruction of the work to its opposite) or of content (in what is portrayed or in the philosophical sense). But there are plenty of interesting things to say about those novels (let's leave aside Calvino, the only one who can't complain, because Ferretti devotes to him a profound and complex analysis). It's striking how political and social themes, which once were the principal nourishment of criticism on the left, are never touched on now, as if it were improper to name them in conversation; not even the fact that in a detective novel (Fruttero-Lucentini) the murderer turns out to be the owner of Fiat was judged worthy of comment by a sociological critique intent on defining the ineffable properties of the "product" and the "market."

As for a general philosophical interpretation, three of the novels considered by Ferretti (Pontiggia, Eco, Calvino) were discussed in an essay that came out last year (Leonardo Lattarulo, *La ricerca narrativa tra logica e misticismo* [*Narrative Study Between Logic and Mysticism*], [Rome: Edizioni Carte Segrete, 1982]); although I don't share the theoretical assumptions (the crisis of totality, Lukács, Goldmann) on the basis of which Lattarulo aims at his unfortunate authors broadsides more lethal than Ferretti's, I have to say that it's a coherent critical argument and as such stimulates reflection and discussion.

Why, instead, does Ferretti's essay leave us unsatisfied? In my view, because one never knows "where" he's coming from. By now, a political label isn't enough to define anyone, and even less the disapproving tone of a moral censor. Ferretti never tells us what the positive models are for the concepts he habitually uses in a negative way, that is, both "high-quality novel" and "novel with a broad audience"; he doesn't say if he thinks that an optimal overlapping of the two terms is possible and to be hoped for (I, for one, think so), or if any contact between "quality" and audience presupposes corruption, or if "quality" for him is in itself a negative term because elitist. The moralistic condemnation that indifferently strikes authors because they are too elite or because they are too readable, publishing because it's too industrial or not industrial enough, can be sure of having countless arguments on its side but it's as if it had none. First he'd have to see clearly into himself: what he wants, what is the scale of values he believes in, in particular literature's relationship to the few and to the many, to feeling and to conjectures, to archetypes and to costs and prices, and what place to give Rainer Maria Rilke and what to Sherlock Holmes.

Someone may have all kinds of good reasons for not knowing which fish to catch; but then let him give up being a moralist; let him speak to us directly of his uncertainty and so help us decide. An uncertain moralist doesn't help anyone; he doesn't even help Fortini, who is always waiting for someone to give him a hand. Instead, to show how it's done, he must yet again brandish his Minos's tail and coil it around the souls of us sinners to establish which hell we are destined for, without ever being sure which god has assigned him that ungrateful task forever.

[1983]

The Written World and
the Unwritten World

I belong to that portion of humanity—a minority on the planetary scale but a majority I think among my public—that spends a large part of its waking hours in a special world, a world made up of horizontal lines where the words follow one another one at a time, where every sentence and every paragraph occupies its set place: a world that can be very rich, maybe even richer than the nonwritten one, but that requires me to make a special adjustment to situate myself in it. When I leave the written world to find my place in the other, in what we usually call *the* world, made up of three dimensions and five senses, populated by billions of our kind, that to me is equivalent every time to repeating the trauma of birth, giving the shape of intelligible reality to a set of confused sensations, and choosing a strategy for confronting the unexpected without being destroyed.

This new birth is always accompanied by special rites that signify the entrance into a different life: for example, the rite of putting on my glasses, since I'm nearsighted and read without glasses, while for the farsighted majority the opposite rite is imposed, that is, of taking off the glasses used for reading.

Every rite of passage corresponds to a change in mental attitude. When I read, every sentence has to be readily understood, at least in its literal meaning, and has to enable me to formulate an opinion: what I've read is true or false, right or wrong, pleasant or unpleasant. In ordinary life, on the other hand, there are always countless circumstances that escape my understanding, from the most general to the most banal: I often find myself facing situations in which I wouldn't know how to express an opinion, in which I prefer to suspend judgment.

While I wait for the unwritten world to become clear to my eyes, there is always within reach a written page that I can dive back into. I hasten to do that, with the greatest satisfaction: there at least, even if I understand only a small part of the whole, I can cultivate the illusion of keeping everything under control.

I think that in my youth, too, things went that way, but at the time I had the illusion that the written world and the unwritten world illuminated one another; that the experiences of life and the experiences of reading were in some way complementary, and every step forward in one field corresponded to a step forward in the other. Today I can say that I know much more about the written world than I once did: within books, experience is always possible, but its reach doesn't extend beyond the blank margin of the page. Instead, what happens in the world that surrounds me never stops surprising me, frightening me, disorienting me. I've witnessed many changes in my lifetime, in the vast world, in society, and many changes in myself, too, and yet I can't predict anything, not for myself or for the people I know, and even less regarding the future of the human race. I couldn't predict the future relations between the sexes, between the generations, future developments of society, of cities and nations, what type of peace there will be or what type of war, what significance money will have, which of the objects in daily use will disappear and which appear as new, what sort of vehicles and machines will be used, what the future of the sea will be, of rivers, animals, plants. I know very well that I share this ignorance with those who, on the contrary, claim to know: economists, sociologists, politicians. But the fact that I am not alone gives me no comfort.

I take some comfort in the thought that literature has always understood something more than other disciplines, but this reminds me that the ancients saw in letters a school of wisdom, and I realize how unattainable every idea of wisdom is today.

At this point you will ask: If you say that your true world is the written page, if only there do you feel at ease, why do you want to leave it, why do you want to venture into this vast world that you are unable to master? The answer is simple: To write. Because I'm a writer. What is expected of me is that I look around and capture some rapid images of what's happening, then return and, bent over my desk, resume work. In order to restart my factory of words I have to get new fuel from the wells of the unwritten.

But let's take a closer look at how things stand. Is that really how it happens? The principal philosophical currents of the moment say: No, none of this is true. The mind of the writer is obsessed by the contrasting positions of two philosophical currents. The first says: The world doesn't exist; only language exists. The second says: Common language has no meaning; the world is ineffable.

For the first, the materiality of language is raised above a world of shadows; for the second, it's the world that looms as a mute stone sphinx over a desert of words, like sand carried by the wind. The first current's main sources have come from Paris over the past twenty-five years; the second has been flowing from Vienna since the start of the century and has passed through various changes, regaining general acceptance in recent years in Italy as well. Both philosophies have strong arguments on their side. Both represent a challenge for the writer: the first requires the use of a language that responds only to itself, to its internal laws; the second, the use of a language that can face up to the silence of the world. Both exert on me their fascination and their influence. That means that I end up not following either, that I don't believe in either. What do I believe in, then?

Let's see for a moment if I can take advantage of this difficult situation. First of all, if we feel so intensely the incompatibility between the written and the not written, it's because we're much more aware of what the written world is: we can't forget even for a second that it's a world made of words, used according to the techniques and strategies proper to language, according to the special systems in which meanings and the relations between meanings are organized. We are aware that when a story is told to us (and almost all written texts tell a story, even a philosophical essay, even a corporation balance sheet, even a cooking recipe), this story is set in motion by a mechanism similar to the mechanisms of every other story.

This is a big step forward: we're now able to avoid a lot of confusion between what is linguistic and what isn't, and so we can see clearly the relationship between the two worlds.

All that's left is to cross-check, and verify that the external world is always there and doesn't depend on words, rather, is not reducible to words, and that no language, no writing can deplete it. I have only to turn my back on the words deposited in books, plunge into the world outside, hoping to reach the heart of silence, the true silence full of meaning . . . but how to get there?

Some, in order to have contact with the world outside, simply buy the newspaper every morning. I am not so naive. I know that from the papers I get a reading of the world made by others, or, rather, made by an anonymous machine, expert in choosing from the infinite dust of events those which can be sifted out as "news."

Others, to escape the grip of the written world, turn on

the television. But I know that all the images, even those most directly drawn from life, are part of a constructed story, like the ones in the newspapers. So I won't buy the newspaper, I won't turn on the television but will confine myself to going out for a walk.

But everything I see on the city streets already has its place in the context of homogenized information. This world I see, which is usually recognized as *the* world, appears to my eyes—mostly, anyway—already conquered, colonized by words, a world covered by a thick crust of discourses. The facts of our life are already classified, judged, commented on, even before they happen. We live in a world where everything is read even before it starts to exist.

Not only everything we see but our very eyes are saturated with written language. Over the centuries the habit of reading has transformed *Homo sapiens* into *Homo legens*, but this *Homo legens* isn't necessarily wiser than before. The man who didn't read knew how to see and hear many things that we no longer perceive: the tracks of the beasts he hunted, the signs of the approach of rain or wind. He knew the time of day from the shadow of a tree, the time of night by the distance of the stars above the horizon. And as for the heard, smelled, tasted, touched, his superiority to us can't be doubted.

Having said this, I had better clarify that I didn't come here to propose a return to illiteracy in order to recover the knowledge of Paleolithic tribes. I regret all we may have lost, but I never forget that the gains are greater than the losses. What I'm trying to understand is what we can do today.

I have to mention the particular difficulties I encounter as an Italian in both my relations with the world and my relations with language, that is, as a writer from a country that is continuously frustrating to those who try to understand it. Italy is a country where many mysterious things happen, which are every day widely discussed and commented on but never solved; where every event hides a secret plot, which is a secret and remains a secret; where no story comes to an end because the beginning is unknown, but between beginning and end we can enjoy an infinity of details. Italy is a country where society experiences very rapid changes, even in habits, in behavior: so rapid that we can't tell what direction we're moving in, and every new fact disappears, sunk by an avalanche of complaints and warnings of degradation and catastrophe, or by declarations of satisfaction with our traditional ability to get by and survive.

So the stories we can tell are marked on the one hand by a sense of the unknown and on the other by a need for structure, for carefully drawn lines, for harmony and geometry; this is our way of reacting to the shifting sands we feel under our feet.

As for language, it has been stricken by a kind of plague. Italian is becoming an increasingly abstract, artificial, ambiguous language; the simplest things are never said directly, concrete nouns are rarely used. This epidemic first infected politicians, bureaucrats, intellectuals, then became more general, as the larger masses increasingly acquired political and intellectual awareness. The writer's task is to fight this plague, ensure the survival of a direct, concrete language, but the problem is that everyday language, until yesterday the living source that writers could resort to, can no longer avoid infection.

In other words, I believe that we Italians are in the ideal situation to link our current difficulty in writing novels to general reflections on language and the world.

An important international tendency in our century's culture, what we call the phenomenological approach in philosophy and the alienation effect in literature, drives us to break the screen of words and concepts and see the world as if it were appearing to our gaze for the first time. Good, now I will try to make my mind blank, and look at the landscape with a gaze free of every cultural precedent. What happens? Our life is programmed for reading, and I realize that I am trying to *read* the landscape, the meadow, the waves of the sea. This programming doesn't mean that our eyes are obliged to follow an instinctive horizontal movement from left to right, then to the left a little lower down, and so on. (Obviously I'm speaking about eyes programmed to read Western pages; Japanese eyes are used to a vertical program.) More than an optical exercise, reading is a process that involves mind and eyes together, a process of abstraction or, rather, an extraction of concreteness by means of abstract operations, like recognizing distinctive marks, shattering everything we see into tiny pieces, rearranging them into meaningful segments, discovering around us regularities, differences, recurrences, singularities, substitutions, redundancies.

The comparison between the world and a book has had a long history starting in the Middle Ages and the Renaissance. What language is the book of the world written in? According to Galileo, it's the language of mathematics and geometry, a language of absolute exactitude. Can we read the world of today in this way? Maybe, if we're talking about the extremely distant: galaxies, quasars, supernovas. But as for our daily world, it seems to us written, rather, as in a mosaic of languages, like a wall covered with graffiti, writings traced one on top of the other, a palimpsest whose parchment has been scratched and rewritten many times, a collage by Schwitters, a layering of alphabets, of diverse citations, of slang terms, of flickering characters like those which appear on a computer screen.

Should we be trying to achieve an imitation of this language of the world? Some of the most important writers of our century have done that: we can find examples in the *Cantos* of Ezra Pound, or in Joyce, or in some dizzying passages of Gadda, who is always tempted by his obsession with connecting every detail to the entire universe.

But is imitation really the right way? I started from the irreconcilable difference between the written world and the unwritten world; if their two languages merge, my argument crumbles. The true challenge for a writer is to speak of the intricate tangle of our situation using a language so seemingly transparent that it creates a sense of hallucination, as Kafka did.

Perhaps the first step in renewing a relationship between language and world is the simplest: fix attention on an ordinary object, the most banal and familiar, and describe it minutely, as if it were the newest and most interesting thing in the universe.

One of the lessons we can take from modern poetry is to invest all our attention, all our love for detail, in something very far from any human image: an object or plant or animal in which we can identify our sense of reality, our morality, our I, as William Carlos Williams did with a cyclamen, Marianne Moore with a nautilus, Eugenio Montale with an eel.

In France, ever since Francis Ponge began to write prose poems on humble objects like a piece of soap or a piece of coal, the problem of the "thing in itself" has continued to mark literary projects, through Sartre and Camus, to reach its ultimate expression in the description of a quarter of a tomato by Robbe-Grillet. But I don't think the last word has been said yet. In Germany recently, Peter Handke wrote a novel based entirely on landscapes. And in Italy, too, what some of the new writers I've read lately have in common is a visual approach.

My interest in descriptions is also due to the fact that my most recent book, *Palomar*, includes a lot of descriptions. I try to work so that the description becomes a story, yet remains description. In each of these brief stories, a character thinks only on the basis of what he sees and is suspicious of any thoughts that come to him by other routes. My problem in writing this book was that I have never been what is called an observer; so the first operation I had to perform was to focus my attention on something and then describe it, or rather do the two things at the same time, because, not being an observer, if for example I observe an iguana at the zoo and I don't immediately write down everything I've seen, I forget it.

I have to say that most of the books I've written and those I have it in mind to write originate in the idea that writing such a book seemed impossible to me. When I'm convinced that a certain type of book is completely beyond the capacities of my temperament and my technical skills, I sit down at my desk and start writing it.

That's what happened with my novel *If on a winter's night a traveler*: I began by imagining all the types of novel that I will never write; then I tried to write them, to evoke in myself the creative energy of ten different imaginary novelists.

Another book I'm writing talks about the five senses, to demonstrate that modern man has lost the use of them. My problem in writing this book is that my sense of smell isn't very developed, I lack auditory attention, I'm not a gourmet, my tactile sensitivity is approximate, and I'm nearsighted. For each of the five senses I have to make an effort that allows me to master a range of sensations and nuances. I don't know if I'll succeed, but in this case as in the others my goal is not so much to make a book as to change myself, which I think should be the goal of every human undertaking.

You may object that you prefer books that convey a true experience, fully grasped. Well, so do I. But in my experience the motivation to write is always connected to the lack of something we would like to know and possess, something that escapes us. And since I am well acquainted with that type of motivation, it seems to me that I can also recognize it in the great writers whose voices seem to reach us from the peak of an absolute experience. What they convey is a sense of the approach to the experience, rather than a sense of the experience achieved; their secret is in knowing how to keep the force of desire intact.

In a certain sense, I believe that we always write about something we don't know: we write to make it possible for the unwritten world to express itself through us. At the moment my attention shifts from the regular order of the written lines and follows the mobile complexity that no sentence can contain or use up, I feel close to understanding that from the other side of the words, from the silent side, something is trying to emerge, to signify through language, like tapping on a prison wall.

[1983]

A Book, Books

Dear friends, I'm glad that I was able to take advantage of an invitation from the Feria del Libro to make my first visit to Buenos Aires. It's a city I've always wanted to know, and I'm especially glad to be with you at this moment, in a climate of freedom regained.

Excuse me if I speak in Italian; I hope that many of you will understand our language, just as I understand yours, although I don't feel confident enough to use it for an entire speech. I'm encouraged by the fact that many Argentineans are of Italian origin, which gives our language a special place in your culture, so I don't have to consider it completely foreign.

Speaking to you here at the Feria, I want to try to analyze the sensation I have whenever I visit a great book fair: a kind of vertigo as I get lost in this sea of printed paper, this boundless firmament of colored covers, this dust cloud of typographical characters; the opening up of spaces like an endless succession of mirrors that multiply the world; the expectation of a surprise encounter with a new title that piques my curiosity; the sudden desire to see reprinted an old book that can't be found; the dismay and at the same time the relief in thinking that my life has scarcely enough years to read or reread a limited number of the volumes spread out before me.

These sensations are different, by the way, from those which a great library offers: in libraries the past is deposited as if in geologic layers of silent words; at a book fair it's the new growth of the written vegetation as it propagates, it's the flow of freshly printed sentences trying to channel itself toward future readers, pressing to spill into their mental circuits.

I don't think it's coincidental that the big international book fairs take place in early fall: Frankfurt in October, Buenos Aires in April. For me as an Italian, early fall is the season of the grape harvest: as every year the harvest celebrates the abundance of grapes swelled with juice, so the book fair celebrates the renewal of a cycle, the multiplying of volumes. The same sense of abundance and profusion dominates both types of autumn festival; the fermentation of typographical ink emanates an atmosphere of intoxication no less contagious than that of the must that bubbles in the vats.

Books are made to be many, a single book has meaning only in that it's next to other books, in that it follows and precedes other books. So it has been ever since books were papyrus scrolls lined up on the shelves of libraries, vertical cylinders arrayed like organ pipes, each with its voice, serious or delicate, bold or melancholy. Our civilization is based on the multiplicity of books; truth is found only if we follow it from the pages of one volume to those of another, like a butterfly with multicolored wings that is nourished on different languages, on comparisons, on contradictions.

Certainly there have been civilizations and religions and peoples who are identified with a single book, "the Book," but it could contain a multiplicity of books, like what we justly call the Bible, that is *tà biblía*, "the books," plural, not "the book." And even when the sacred text is truly one book, in the singular, like the Koran, it requires an interminable production of commentaries and exegeses, so that one can say that the more definitive and indisputable a book is considered, the more it proliferates, filling entire libraries.

The idea of an absolute book also appears every so often in profane literature, like the Book with a capital B that Mallarmé longed for, but I would say it's a diabolical temptation. Better the bewildered and modest gesture of those who promote their own book as a gloss on books written before it, or consider their own work the chapter of a super-book made up of all the volumes already written or still to be written, by authors known or unknown, in all languages.

The popular imagination attributed supernatural powers to the written word and dreamed of a book that enabled whoever possessed it, and knew how to find the right word in its pages, to achieve world domination. The magic book turns up as a supernatural tool in fables, in legends, in chivalric adventures: usually its powers were used for evil, but the same evil magic could be transformed into divine aid if used by just hands.

In *Orlando Furioso* the wizard Atlantes with his magic book conjures a palace where everything is illusion, populated by the ghosts of the most valorous knights and the most beautiful ladies. The knight who got lost within those elusive walls, in pursuit of a shadow in which he recognized his mortal enemy or the beloved woman, couldn't find the way out, except when the book was closed and the palace disappeared into thin air. But when Astolfo, the knight who has a particular intimacy with everything that is marvelous, takes possession of the magic book, he will acquire the power to climb into the saddle of the hippogriff and fly to the moon.

In Ariosto's poem, which resounds with the iron clash of weapons—spears, swords, scimitars, but also the first gunshots, because in these pages gunpowder makes its first appearance in chivalric literature—the absolute weapon is the magic book. What is the power of the word that the magic book holds? Can the word change the world? Or, rather, does the word have the power to dissolve the world, to be a world itself, to replace the unwritten world with its own totality?

Orlando Furioso is a book that contains the whole world, and this world contains a book that wants to be the world. But what is written in this magic book, we don't know. Maybe the volume that Astolfo consults as he flies on the winged horse is precisely the poem that tells the story of

Astolfo and the winged horse and their journey to the moon.

The metaphors of the book as world and the world as book have a long history, from the Middle Ages up to today. Who is able to read the book of the world? God alone, or man, too? The metaphor of the book-world is at the center of theological discussions of divine wisdom and the limits of human knowledge.

At the beginning of the modern era, both Francis Bacon and Galileo Galilei set the book of Nature that God has written in his language, and that it is up to man to decipher, against the authority of books written in the languages of men. Tommaso Campanella condenses this idea into a sonnet: "The world is the book where the Eternal Mind / wrote its own thoughts." Galileo explains that the book of the world was written by God in a mathematical and geometric alphabet.

After all, Galileo's favorite poet was Ludovico Ariosto: as Astolfo on the hippogriff surveys the lands of the moon with the help of the magic book, so Galileo with the help of mathematical reasoning explores with his telescope the lunar landscape and describes its shadows and dazzling whiteness.

But there is also a passage where Galileo maintains that the whole world can be contained in a very small book: the alphabet. The alphabet, according to Galileo, is humankind's greatest invention, because with combinations of some twenty signs the entire multiform richness of the universe can be rendered. In the same way, he says, the painter's canvas is sufficient to represent all the visible through combinations of simple colors. The alphabet enables the swiftest transmission of thought between distant persons, between persons of different centuries, between the dead and the living . . .

Do the powers of the word reside then in the infinite potential that combinatorial art opens to us? From the Middle Ages of Ramón Lull to the seventeenth century of Leibniz, combinatorial art appears to the most ambitious minds as the key to all knowledge and kindles in them the dream of the universal book.

From China, Jesuit missionaries bring a book in which all human destinies are contained in the combinations of six broken or continuous lines: it's called the *I Ching*, the "Book of Changes." Leibniz studies the sixty-four hexagrams of this ancient Chinese book, not to interrogate the future but to get from it a system of binary calculation that two centuries later will become information technology.

And so wouldn't the magic book, the absolute book, whose mysteries go beyond the limits of every language, be a model of the electronic brain? But the computer is valuable for us only in that it can memorize and execute a great quantity of programs that we elaborate and insert in its microcircuits. Let's return to multiplicity as a precondition for every act of knowledge. As the computer has no meaning without programs, without its software, so, too, the book that claims to be considered "the Book" has no meaning without the surrounding context of many, many other books.

Another ancient temptation is to concentrate the knowledge of all books into a single discourse: the encyclopedia. We can say that this desire starts from the most reasonable motivations, from a need for order and method: to trace a map of the territories of human knowledge, to test the limits of our knowledge. Maybe no civilization, no era can help attempting the encyclopedia: but it's also true that this claim to unify many branches of knowledge will prove to be an illusion every time, because every type of knowledge has its method and its language that diverge from other methods and other languages and can't be inserted in a circular design such as the very word *encyclopedia* suggests.

But what I'd now like to point out is that the early modern age saw the birth of a literary genre, the novel, that from the start had an encyclopedic vocation. In the books of Pantagruel, Rabelais accumulates all the knowledge of the universities and of the taverns, all the languages of the educated and the common people. A half century later, Cervantes presents us with the encounter between the sublime of poetry and the prosaic of daily life, the ideal world of books and the imagination and the elementary common sense of proverbs, the hard knowledge of the dusty streets and stinking inns: an explosive mixture of elements that bursts into the madness of Don Quixote and inaugurates modern literature.

This encyclopedic vocation continued to be felt in the

history of the novel; in fact, in our century the most significant have been encyclopedia-novels, from *The Magic Mountain* to *The Man Without Qualities* and, especially, *Ulysses*, where Joyce assigns every chapter a different style and a different territory of human experience. In Italy the great encyclopedic novelist is Carlo Emilio Gadda, who in *That Awful Mess on Via Merulana* condenses into a crime-novel plot the dialects of Rome and half of Italy, baroque art and Virgil's epic, psychology and physiology, and most important a philosophy of knowledge.

Maybe novels are the only encyclopedias that truly compose a picture of the whole, starting from the singularity of human existences, of individual stories that are always partial, always contradictory, always ambiguous, never unequivocal. Totality is a concept of philosophers that will always remain abstract; what novelists seek is to weave a net that ties the experience preserved in books over the centuries to the dust of experience that we pass through every day in our lives and that seems increasingly elusive and indefinable.

A book, books. The thought that books are generated by books as if by a biological power of the written page can be distressing: if the written matter passes through the hand that writes, and the author is only a tool of something that *writes itself* independently of him, maybe it's not we who write books but books that write us.

Those who find this hypothesis distressing will prefer to believe that the page that writes is a mirror in which to project the image of the self: the book as the written equivalent of a person's most intimate self, the extension of individuality, manifestation of a unique and unrepeatable existence. Oneself as a book to decipher, the book as mirror or self-portrait: this, too, is a way of considering the writing that marks the beginning of modern culture, according to the lesson of Montaigne, and continues through Rousseau down to our days, to Proust and beyond. "This is no book, / Who touches this touches a man," said Walt Whitman.

But books in which a human being tells his story and describes himself with the evidence of a truth never before achieved are rare and extraordinary, and I don't think it would be useful if they were more numerous, unless we want to see a proliferation of the outbursts and narcissisms that literature already has in such abundance. A great book is valuable not because it teaches us to know a definite individual but because it presents to us a new way of understanding human life, applicable to others as well, and which we, too, can use to recognize ourselves. If every human person contained a book of himself and had only to deposit it on paper (or pop it out, like an egg), libraries would be crowded with endless populations of paper doubles of all the living and the dead, less perishable than the bodies of flesh and blood that will crowd the Valley of Jehoshaphat, a prospect that would certainly be most distressing of all. I prefer to think of an ideal library that welcomes exemplary models of experience, prototypes, the essential forms from which everything possible can be deduced.

To move on from general considerations to my own experience as a writer, I have to say that I am driven not by the desire to write *my* book, the book as equivalent of myself, but by the desire to have before me the book that I would like to read, and so I try to identify with the imaginary author of that book that is still to be written, an author who might even be very different from me.

For example, I recently published in Italy a book made up of descriptions. At the center of this book is a character called Palomar who thinks only through the minute observation of everything that happens before his eyes: an iguana at the zoo or cheeses on the counter in a shop. The problem is that I am not what is called an observer: I'm very distracted, absorbed in my thoughts, incapable of focusing my attention on what I see. Before writing each chapter of this book, I found that I needed to perform a preliminary operation: I set myself to observe things I'd had before my eyes hundreds of times and record every tiny detail in order to imprint it on my memory, which I had never done; it's an exercise that can be extremely difficult when, for example, it's a matter of the starry sky of a summer night or blades of grass in a lawn. I therefore had to try to change myself somehow, to make myself similar to the presumed author of the book I wanted to write. Thus writing a book becomes an experience of initiation, involves a continuing education of oneself, and this should be the goal of every human action.

When I was very young I thought my lack of life experience was a serious obstacle to writing; I thought I could allow myself to write only ironic and melancholy poems or poetic prose fed by dreams and childhood memories. But the novels I read at that time were about a brutal, vagabond life, about wars and adventures in distant lands; those novels excited me but seemed to belong to a world so alien to mine that they could have no relation to what I would ever be able to write. I didn't yet imagine that the collective experiences of my generation in the last period of the Second World War, with their tragedy and horror and the picaresque adventures in the stratagems for survival, would give legitimacy to my work as a debut writer narrating, precisely, an experience of life and death, which until a short time before I'd thought I could come to only as a reader.

Thus the first image that critics and the public had of me was the image of a realistic and popular writer, and I tried to write the books of this new self. But the miracle that had succeeded for me with the first novel and the first stories wasn't repeated, and everything I wrote seemed mannered.

The crisis lasted until I decided that I would write not the novel that I thought I had to write, and which others expected me to write, but the novel I would have liked to read, a book by an unknown author that seemed to have arrived from another time and another place, an old volume found in the attic, half eaten by mice, that I would surrender to with the absorption of childhood reading. It was at that point that I found the fantastic vein that the public and critics later judged best corresponded to my temperament.

But I've always tried not to remain a prisoner of any image of myself. I wish every book I write were the first, I wish I had a new name every time. I still get excited when I read books, especially if I feel that I would never write anything like them, and try to compare myself with their authors, to understand what makes me different from them, what they have that I don't. This thought works in me like a challenge. Exaggerating slightly, I could give this definition of my work: as soon as I'm convinced that a certain genre of literature is beyond my capabilities, I have no peace until I try my hand at it, to find out if it's really so unfeasible. And since I don't like to abandon a work halfway, I continue until my efforts take the form of a book.

I've always been attracted by the plant life of forests, and fiction of every type, every era, every country to me is like a forest of stories, where at first glance you confuse every plant with the others, but when you focus your attention you realize that no plant is the same as another.

Thirty years ago I rushed into the forest of the folktale, plunging into the folklore of the Italian regions, into the fables handed down by the voices of grandmothers in all the dialects, and I tried to classify and sort through a thick, tangled vegetation of marvels and enchantments.

That experience made me more attentive to certain elements, the way stories grow out of one another, the simplest and most effective structures that are recognizable as the skeleton of the most complicated stories, the oral beginnings of the art of storytelling, whose traces remain even when this art is turned into written works; it reinforced my interest in collections of Indian, Arabic, and Persian tales, whose influence can be seen in the development of Italian and other European stories.

In written literature, this infinite multiplicity of stories handed down from person to person is often rendered through a frame, a story in which the other stories are embedded. Boccaccio has a happy band of youths of both sexes meet in a Florentine villa to escape the plague that is devastating the city; there, for ten days, each youth in turn tells one story a day. Elaborations of this model characterize the evolution of the art of storytelling in the literature of the West.

In my most recent books, this traditional model has been transformed into the invention of devices generating stories that I felt the need to develop in increasingly complicated, ramified, faceted schemes, approaching the idea of a hyper-novel or novel raised to the nth power.

I attempted to write "apocryphal" novels—that is, novels that I imagine were written by an author who isn't me and doesn't exist—in my book *If on a winter's night a traveler*. It's a novel about the pleasure of reading novels; the protagonist is the Reader, who ten times starts to read a book that, owing to circumstances beyond his control, he can't finish. I therefore had to write the beginning of ten novels by imaginary authors, all in some way different from me and different from one another: one novel made up of suspicions and confused sensations; one of robust and full-blooded sensations; one introspective and symbolic; one revolutionary-existential; one cynical-brutal; one of obsessive manias; one logical and geometric; one erotic-perverse; one earthy-primordial; one apocalyptic-allegorical. Rather than identifying with the author of each of the ten novels, I tried to identify with the reader: to describe the pleasure of reading a given genre, rather than the actual text. At some moments I felt as if the creative energy of those ten nonexistent authors were passing through me. But mainly I was trying to provide evidence of the fact that every book originates in the presence of other books, in relation to and comparison with other books.

Now perhaps I should consider a question that is often heard today and is customary at a book fair: You speak of books as of something that there has always been and always will be, but are we really sure that the book has a future ahead of it? That it will survive the competition of audiovisual electronic devices? How will it be transformed or what will replace it? And what will become of the writer?

Well, my answer can only be one: loyalty to the book, come what may. Let's put it in the perspective of centuries. Books circulated for many centuries before Gutenberg's invention, and in future centuries they will certainly find new forms for survival.

The first publishing house whose activity we have detailed information about, through Cicero's letters, is the one founded in Rome around 50 BC by Titus Pomponius Atticus for the diffusion of Greek classics and new Latin works; it was organized not that differently from the publishers of our time, with the difference that in place of printers there was a large number of scribes.

Certainly the number of readers at the time wasn't equal to the print run of the bestsellers of today, but if we think that even today so many fundamental books continue to have a limited circulation, we see that even numeric comparisons are less discouraging than one might think. The important thing is for the ideal thread that runs through centuries of writing not to break. The thought that even during the Middle Ages of iron and fire, books found in convents a space where they could be preserved and multiply on the one hand reassures me, on the other worries me. The idea that we should all retreat to convents endowed with every comfort to publish books of quality, abandoning the cities to the barbarian invasion of videotapes, might even make me smile; but I wouldn't like the rest of the world to be deprived of books, of their silence full of whispers, of their reassuring calm or their subtle disquiet.

There is a continuity in the solitude that the writer carries with him like a fate inherent to his vocation, but from this solitude develops a desire and a capacity to communicate: the special communication that literature establishes between individuals, and that only in some eras and on some occasions can be amplified into mass communication. To know that Petrarch and Boccaccio exchanged parchment codices on which they had copied with refined graphic elegance in their own hand their own works or those of Dante convinces me that periods of splendor for literature can open up no matter what the external conditions are.

We know that the form of books has changed many times in history and certainly will continue to change. Not that this cheers me, because I am fond of books also as objects, in the form they have now, even if it's increasingly rare to see editions that express love for the book-as-object, which as a companion for our life should be beautifully made.

Of course many things will change, if it's true that with word processors our books will be composed directly by our own hands without going through the printer. Just as libraries will change, and perhaps will contain only microfilm. That saddens me a little, because we won't hear the rustling of pages.

Will our way of reading change? Maybe, but we can't predict how. We can say that we have direct testimony of an important revolution in the way of reading that occurred in the past because Saint Augustine described to us with amazement the moment he realized it. Visiting Saint Ambrose, Augustine noticed that the bishop of Milan was reading but in a way that he had never seen before: silently, using only his eyes and his mind, without emitting a sound, without even moving his lips. Augustine had passed through important schools and circles of scholars, yet he had never suspected that one could read as Ambrose was doing, without uttering the words.

But the future may hold other modes of reading that

we don't suspect. It seems to me wrong to deplore every technological novelty in the name of danger to humanistic values. I think that every new means of communication and diffusion of words, images, and sounds can contain new creative developments, new forms of expression. And I think that a more technologically advanced society will be richer in stimuli, in choices, in possibilities, in different tools, and will increasingly need to read, need things to read and people who read.

I don't think reading is comparable to any other means of learning and communication, because reading has a rhythm that is ruled by the will of the reader; reading opens spaces for interrogation and meditation and critical examination, in short, of freedom; reading is a relationship with ourselves and not only with the book, with our inner world through the world that the book opens up to us.

Maybe the time that could be meant for reading will increasingly be occupied by other things; this is already true today, but maybe it was still truer in the past for the majority of human beings. In any case, those who have a need to read, who take pleasure in reading (and reading is certainly a need-pleasure) will continue to have recourse to books, those of the past and those of the future.

[1984]

Why Do You Write?

The Paris daily *Libération* worked for months on a special issue that came out on March 22. Writers all over the world were asked: "Why do you write?" The survey recalled a historic precedent: a November 1919 issue of the journal *Littérature*, edited by André Breton, Louis Aragon, and Philippe Soupault. The same question was asked then, at a time when cataclysms and aftershocks were disrupting not only art and literature but all aspects of life and thought. The invitation from *Libération* to the writers included that reference, and I don't know if it intended to establish a parallel between that era and ours, after the sixties had signaled, especially in French culture, a push for fundamental innovations (in which the very notion of *écriture* was one of the battlefields), and after the most recent fading of radical thought. This comparison between the first and last decades of the century is enough to make us feel our era as quiet and dull in terms of both innovative urges and normalizing ones; but the big news is that we don't feel saddened by this calmer (at least apparently) pace, and no nostalgia for more active times surfaces even for an instant in our minds, since we're convinced that we can expect only nasty surprises.

Can this state of mind be reflected in the answer to a question like *Pourquoi écrivez-vous?* The fact is that many of the answers display an instinctive gesture of defense against a question that's too broad, against the insistence on posing problems that are too general. Samuel Beckett's answer is in this sense—there was no reason to doubt it—concisely exemplary: it consists of the three syllables of a colloquial expression: *Bon qu'à ça.* ("I'm no good for anything else.")

I will confine myself here to informing you how I handled it. Politely pressured by the written and telephonic insistence of the editors of *Libé* and by friends charged with convincing me, and assured that I could give a short answer, I had no recourse but to gather my strength and confront the feeling of annihilation that the question instills in me: Why do I write?

I had begun to rack my brain when Primo Levi's book *Other People's Trades* arrived (I've talked about it in these columns), and I see that one of the first chapters is entitled—by chance—"Why Do We Write?," an essay that probably originated as a response to a similar survey. The question, formulated in a more impersonal way ("we write" rather than "you write"), gave Levi an opportunity to set out a reasoned list (with his even-tempered and all-embracing spirit) of the motivations, good and less good, that impel people to write. First came the reasons that he was most sympathetic to, then those about which he had reservations or felt as less relevant.

The reasons considered by Primo Levi were nine. We write: (1) because we feel the urge or the need; (2) to entertain others or ourself; (3) to teach someone something; (4) to improve the world; (5) to spread our ideas (variant of the preceding); (6) to rid ourself of some source of anguish; (7) to become famous; (8) to become rich; (9) out of habit (the reason left for last because it's "the dreariest of all").

This list seemed to make my task much easier, because I had a base from which to start on a methodical reflection. But I soon realized that the difficulties were the same: What could I say, given that writing always costs me an effort, a violence against myself, and doesn't entertain me at all? (Even though I consider that entertaining readers, or at least not boring them, is my first and binding social duty.) Furthermore, I don't think I have a pedagogic vocation; I distrust those who claim to improve the world; I distrust particularly my own ideas, which are too often shown to be mistaken; et cetera. In short, answering this survey was like entering a crisis of depression.

I will spare you other ruminations in order not to violate the social imperative just uttered and move on immediately to the three reasons that I communicated to *Libération* as the conclusions of my examination of conscience.

Why do I write?

(1) Because I am dissatisfied with what I've already written and would like in some way to correct it, complete it,

offer an alternative. In this sense, there wasn't a "first time" when I started writing. Writing has always been an attempt to erase something I've already written and replace it with something that I still don't know if I'll succeed in writing.

(2) Because reading X (an old or a contemporary X), I have the thought: *Ah, how I'd like to write like X! Too bad it's completely beyond my capabilities!* Then I try to imagine this impossible undertaking, I think of the book I will never write but that I'd like to be able to read, to put beside other beloved books on an ideal shelf. And suddenly some words, some sentences appear in my mind . . . From then on I am no longer thinking of X, or of any other possible model. I'm thinking of that book, that book that hasn't yet been written and that could be *my* book! I try to write it . . .

(3) To learn something I don't know. I'm referring now not to the art of writing but to the rest: to some branch of knowledge or specific skill, or that more general knowledge called "life experience." It's not the desire to teach others what I know or think I know that makes me want to write but, on the contrary, the painful awareness of my incompetence. So would my first impulse be to write in order to pretend a competence I don't have? But in order to pretend, I have to somehow accumulate information, notions, observations, I have to succeed in imagining the slow accumulation of an experience. And this I can do only on the written page, where I hope to capture at least some trace of a knowledge or wisdom that I just touched in life and immediately lost.

[1985]

On Publishing

Notes for a Book Series
on Moral Inquiry

THE MORALITY OF DOING

The idea of the series should be to let moral guidelines emerge from practical activity, from technological and economic activity, from production—from work, in short (and work includes the organization of work). But do books of this type exist? I think we have only to reexamine from this point of view minor works of various literatures and some wonderful ones can be found, which can be grouped into two categories:

(a) *Memoirs* that range from the earliest memoirs of economic activity like the "Merchant of Prato" to those of the gentlemen farmers of the early nineteenth century, but including all the more entertaining writings by anyone who has practiced a trade with passion and skill and has written a book about it, such as the memoirs of Mark Twain as a pilot on the Mississippi riverboats or Conrad's wonderful *The Mirror of the Sea*, essays on the art of navigation. But you'd have to get up to modern industry, maybe to conclude that there's nothing, and already that would be a result, the indication of a gap.

(b) *Treatises*, naturally containing a poetic and moral argument, and here I don't think that the ancient treatises of classical and Renaissance authors (especially on farming) can hold any surprises; they're all a big bore. Rather, I think that here we should look at those Oriental (Japanese) books that hand down the rules of any elementary skill like the ritual of a higher wisdom (religious, but thus we stress their proper character as immanentistic ethics).

THE CONFRONTATION WITH NATURE

This is the basic situation where human activity originates; thus the poetic and moral wealth in the *testimony of explorers*, and all those who struggle with nature. A series of this type would have room for such books, classics and modern, which are naturally to be read right away, not kept among the classics. But the criterion has to be firmly tied to the current *morality of human limits*, I mean of their continuous expansion, today in the space age. In this category I'd like to have (if they exist) books that express the ethics and poetry of sports as a way of increasing man's powers, that is, a Hemingway or a Saint-Exupéry who had rid himself of his decadent traces.

THE MORALITY OF RESEARCH
(BOOKS BY SCIENTISTS)

Science, the exemplary mode of confronting nature, will be represented in the series by works in which science becomes the path of total knowledge, reintegration of a complete humanism. Two types:

(a) *Scientists' reflections:* books like the one of Einstein's ideas in Rostand's *Journal of a Biologist*;

(b) *The ethics of the method:* That is, when the scientific memoir becomes itself an exemplary text that transcends the importance of the theme being considered. And here I'm talking not just about Leonardo and Galileo, but I would insert some exemplary short works of Freud, and also the famous lessons of Charcot (in general I would tend to introduce psychology into the series as an example of scientific clarity, rather than as "soul").

THE MORALITY OF HISTORICAL ACTION

(a) *Testimony of revolutionaries:* The best books from a moral and spiritual point of view that our century has given us are the prison letters of political inmates. The man who is not passive toward history is the one most suited today to express an ethics tied to doing. It's easy to find precursors in the past. (Here a revival of Herzen would be successful.)

(b) *Testimony on the ethics of power* in which values emerge even if we don't approve of that power. And the same should be said for *the ethics of war*.

(c) *Testimony of ordinary spectators* in which history appears with its true flavor as it unfolds.

(d) *Exemplary short books by historians* that, as we said about books by scientists, have a value beyond what they narrate.

THE MORALITY OF EROS AND LOVE

Modern civilization aims (America) at an ethics of happiness that is mainly erotic happiness, and at the same time, after the crisis of the old sexual morality, it feels the need for a morality. The series will have works with various examples of the love relationship, the core of all relationships between the I and our neighbor, works that will be *testimony* both old and new of lovers, libertines, courtesans, good people, et cetera, and the *inventions of poets* essential for a survey of love today.

THE HUMAN PERSON

Is there something that can represent for us what "sanctity" is for those who believe in saints? That is, can an exemplary human value be expressed not in relation to particular things people do, or particular situations they find themselves in, but simply for a particular way of living their life, using existence itself as a means of expression? The works we choose will try to formul[ate] an inclusive response to this question.

(a) *Fulfillment by giving oneself to others:* Testimony regarding a particular type of modern man or woman of philanthropic action (Schweitzer Dolci Simone Weil);

(b) *Fulfillment by giving oneself to oneself:* Here we could bring in that part of the religious experience of one's own inner life that we recognize as true knowledge and at the same time the literature of modern secular inner life;

(c) *Education,* memoirs of teachers or of youth, or stories that are able to convey a modern idea of pedagogy in a broad sense;

(d) *Portraits:* Here I would bring in those special short works, biographies or profiles of people who are famous or not, written by great writers (for example the writings of Gorky on Tolstoy and Lenin) who have the power to convey the fascination of a unique personality, what is conveyed only through the living person.

PHILOSOPHY

(a) *Practical morality of the philosopher:* Here we'd publish minor writings of the great philosophers on problems of life and action, typical example Croce's writings on morality or practical life;

(b) *Philosophy of the practical:* This category is already represented case by case in the preceding categories.

POETRY AND ART

I put this last because naturally it's the driving force of the series and tends to loom over everything if it's not kept within strict limits; that is, if we want to create a series with a specific focus and not one of the usual universal ones, decided on criteria of pure taste.

(a) *Poetic knowledge of the self,* that is, diaristic, psychological, intimate, moralistic works by writers or poets, as well as correspondences;

(b) *The morality of poetic practice:* And here is the mine of writers' and artists' writings on their craft that we'd like to present here as a specific case of human "doing";

(c) *Poetry in itself is morality:* And so we can also include in the series minor creative works, valuable finds, et cetera; we just have to keep a sense of proportion;

(d) *Poetry as the first human voice:* And there we'd put all the testimony of the common people, popular fables, primitive poetry et cetera, et cetera, where poetry, religion, moral life are still a single thing.

[1960]

Plan for a Journal

This journal will publish works of creative literature (fiction, poetry, theater) and essays on particular aspects and problems and tendencies exemplified by the works published in the same issue. It will follow the discourse of Italian literature as it unfolds, through the work of writers who are young or not so young, new or with something new to say.

The journal will make it clear that it's a discourse—many discourses together, which can be articulated in a general conversation—that runs from book to book, from manuscript to manuscript, and will find the thread of this discourse even where it seems to be merely a messy tangle.

It's the right moment to try to "get our bearings on" many matters, and understand how we can move beyond. Many things have changed in the world in these years; Italy is also changing, and it is not very skilled at either renewing or preserving itself. (To hold on to the things you want to hold on to when all the rest is moving, all you can do is find the right way to move them.)

So the journal will review the new relationship today between language and dialect; and the new relationship between the south and what is no longer the south or even in the south, and what of the south has moved into the north; and the new relationship between things that are important to say and the need to start speaking in verse at a particular moment; and the problem of inserting into the structure of the story as it has been evolving so far the rhythm of life of those who work in the big factories six days a week; and how at a certain point it became difficult to talk about the war; and how at a certain point it became difficult to talk about love; and how at a certain point it becomes difficult to talk about people with potentially high vitality and morality rather than about people who are slightly dull and slightly sad and slightly mediocre.

These are all problems that can be profitably observed by the writer endowed with an independent poetic force, as well as by one endowed with merely an aptitude for bearing witness. And they are all very "Italian" problems, but precisely those which can compel us to break out of the shell of narrow local description in which Italian literature has a tendency to ossify.

Not that things are better outside of Italy, however. At first glance we might say that the lively discourse about literature in Europe and America even shortly after the Second World War, a discourse about man's relationship with the world, a philosophical and moral and historical and civic discourse, which literature opposed to theoretical discourse as a way of verification or antithesis, this discourse—entirely interrogative and voluntary—seems stuck there. On the one hand there are tendencies like the

French "new school" that are too technical and seem to want to make literature conform to the type of problems—more rigorous perhaps but much more limited—that have so far belonged to the figurative arts; on the other are the young self-important champions of unconditional revolution like the Americans of the Beat generation. This is how it seems at first glance; but in reality there hasn't been a total burning of bridges (and abandonment of all the most fertile fields, for a new shore where there's little left to chew on). We believe that deep down that discussion continues, and that all the new facts—French, English, American, Polish, Spanish, along with the Italians who are not so separate from this picture as they seem—need only to be seen in perspective, not all flattened.

We reject the image of a teeming, formless world of pure objectivity such as the overpopulated Earth might appear to the first Martian who arrives. We want the literature we'd like to discover or invent to mirror earthly humanity intent on a new relationship between the individual, others, space, time, what exists, what doesn't exist, for when we find ourselves on the spaceship, on the interplanetary station, landing on Mars.

Themes

major functions:
    laughter
    terror (false function: crying)
    journey—adventure—initiation—disorientation
    Eros

the obscene
aggression—violence—hatred
riddle
reintegration of justice—reparation for a wrong—
  redemption—metamorphosis that establishes a new
  order

narrative strategy:
  beginning
  end
  suspense
  time
  "rhymes" in fiction
  "stanzas" in fiction

symbolic places:
  the forest
  the house
    house from outside
    house from inside
    familiar house
    hostile house
    familiar house that becomes hostile
  the city
  Eden
  Hell
  journey of initiation (elsewhere—purgatory)
  the desert
  the crowd

real places (what they can mean as novelistic and
symbolic places): Chicago, Rome, Milan, Shanghai,
sewers, the concentration camps, school, the stock
exchange, et cetera

institutions:
description
landscape
how things are done (technical handbooks)
dialogue
conversation
the definition of a character (human types)
meditation
monologue
the dimension of memory

the I:
Saint Augustine
Stendhal

the character as:
object of identification
exciting
narcissistic
ironic
object of desire
object of loathing
dramatic
comic

protective figure
threatening figure

how to read:
  a spell
  a lullaby or nursery rhyme
  a myth
    primitive
    classical
  a fable
  a Buddhist legend
  a chanson de geste
  a historian
    of antiquity
    medieval
  a tragedy
    classical
    Elizabethan
    classicistic
  nineteenth-century serial novel
  romance novel
  nonsense rhyme
  news item
  police report
  car accident with compensation claim to the insurance
    agency
  memoirs of a general
  a "clinical case"
  how does the oral tradition survive today?

the obscene joke
the political joke

thus all types of stories not in a narrative form:
horoscopes
gravestones
bestiaries herbals lapidaries

stories condensed into images:
emblems
genealogical trees
rebus
fortune-telling
ex-votos
the plates illustrating arts and crafts in the Encyclopédie

major stylistic categories:
anthropomorphism
alienation
linguistic aggression
objectivity
transparency—depth

language:
common language—personal language
Italian
 as a convention
 as local moods
the old-fashioned—the modern

The various themes can be exemplified by:
(a) new Italian novel (serialized?) commissioned ad hoc
(b) recent foreign novel (serialized?) chosen ad hoc
(c) little-known classic or old popular novel et cetera
(anthologized and summarized?)
(d) classic retold by a contemporary writer (commissioned)
(e) anthologized examples with didactic framework
(f) bibliographical reviews

In every issue there could be:
(I) TEXTS
(1) an episode of a
(2) an episode of b
(3) an episode of c
(4) a d

(b and c can be disregarded and can fill possible gaps in a. Anyway something new should begin in every issue. After three or four episodes, if the novel isn't finished, we can break it off and send readers back to the book.)

(II) STORY AND NEWS STORY
(5) a news item (death of Pinelli; Casati-Stampa;
Gadolla): three or more writers are asked to tell it
(6) an area of Italian current affairs analyzed as
a "narrative field": characters, settings, roles,
actions, vocabulary, et cetera (e.g., the judiciary;
Reggio Calabria; immigrants), assigned to one or
more journalists

(7) an area of international current affairs analyzed in light of the meanings it has for us (e.g., Israelis-Arabs-Bedouins in mutual exchanges of oppressed-oppressor functions): assigned to a semiologist, a geographer, a sociologist, a historian, et cetera

(III) THEMES AND PROBLEMS

Presentations of themes or genres (see the list of themes and "how to read") with anthologies of examples and bibliographical surveys. These themes or genres should be sorted (in the same issue or alternating) according to the subject they are most relevant to:

(8) theme relevant to literature

(9) theme relevant to popular literature

(10) theme relevant to anthropology

(11) theme relevant to the current sociological-political context

(12) presentation of an author (with anthology and bibliography) (classic or popular or contemporary) relevant to one of the themes of the issue

(13) an author or a literary fact that has nothing to do with our themes in the rest of the issue (for example: Francis Ponge) to create a contrast, open a completely different horizon of reading, to demonstrate that we could also be wrong or that the important things are completely different

(IV) ILLUSTRATION

(14) the great illustrators (from the nineteenth century), foreign and Italian

(15) a contemporary graphic artist (invited to take up some pages with his offerings)

(16) contemporary painters and the story: interview with a painter or sculptor (neo-Dada or Pop or neo-Expressionist et cetera) to see the relationship of the artist's figurative world with writing, narrative, et cetera

(V) THE BIBLIOPHILE—THE COLLECTOR

The general orientation of taste is toward popular editions, not luxury editions; we turn toward the collector of old Sonzogno editions.

(17) how to collect books of . . . (editions on the market; foreign editions; antiquarian)

(18) presentation of a first edition of a classic that has a visual interest; or of a series; or of serialized novels et cetera

(19) presentation of a journal chosen from among the most important from the visual point of view (*Minothaure*) or thematically interesting (*La Ruota*, A. G. Bragaglia's pantheist journal)

[1970]

A New Series, Einaudi's
Centopagine Series

Centopagine ("A Hundred Pages") is a new Einaudi series featuring great writers of all times and all places, represented not by their monumental works, that is novels on a vast scale, but by works that belong to a no less illustrious and not at all minor genre: the short novel or long story. The name of the series shouldn't be taken literally: each volume will contain a complete novel and might have a hundred and fifty or two hundred pages, or maybe only ninety; the criterion for inclusion will be not so much the dimensions as the intensity and substance of a reading that can find its own space even on the less relaxed days of our daily life.

The Einaudi catalogue has an abundance of excellent translations of famous texts that can't be found on bookstore shelves and that in Centopagine will have their natural home; think merely of the great Russian novelists. But there will be many new translations, in some cases of works never before published in Italy, and forgotten or rare titles on which our current interests cast a new light. As with every series of classic novels, the nineteenth century remains an inexhaustible mine, a nineteenth (and early twentieth) century revisited with today's eyes on hallowed masterpieces as well as on perspectives opened up to our explorations. But there will also be voices from the preceding centuries, both rereadings of classics and suggestions for new discoveries. This modern outlook on reading will also be highlighted by introductions, written in large part for that purpose by Italian critics and writers.

The new offerings in the series will therefore be naturally in line with an approach that responds to a fundamental need for "primary materials" and doesn't become a precious collection of curious *trouvailles* or markers of taste.

The first batch of volumes is representative of this approach and its internal origins: beside works that were stalwarts of the old Universale Einaudi series, like Tolstoy's *The Kreutzer Sonata* and Dostoyevsky's *White Nights*, are new translations of classics of the short novel, like Maupassant's *Pierre and Jean* and Henry James's *Daisy Miller*; a jewel of German Romanticism that is one of the merriest and freshest books ever written, *Memoirs of a Good-for-Nothing*, by Joseph von Eichendorff; and a rediscovery from the Italian nineteenth century, *Fosca*, by Iginio Ugo Tarchetti.

It seems clear already that the Italian literature in Centopagine will hold the most unusual surprises. The Italian novel between Unification and the Great War is (apart from the few hallowed names) just waiting to be discovered. Of course, there is no comparison with the great foreign fictions: but there is so much to interest us in reading these minor writers of ours—as social picture, as language, as custom, as taste; the density of the information about ourselves, as if in a sort of national autobiography—that we are amply repaid for the disproportion.

The proof lies in the volume that inaugurates the series: *Fosca*, a novel by Iginio Ugo Tarchetti, a writer who died at thirty, in 1869, romantic and decadent and a little cursed. It's the story of a young officer's passion for an ugly, hypersensitive woman. But in what way is Fosca ugly? The author insists on her ugliness but barely describes it: the only—or almost—precise fact we can get is thinness, certainly a negative quality in an era that preferred Junoesque beauty but that other times and other fashions, before and after, have been quick to rehabilitate. Also, the features of her face, from the little Tarchetti says, and the snake-like contortions of her body foretell a stylization that figurative art will soon afterward carry to extremes. Among the various mysteries that the book doesn't explain (the psychosomatic illness that keeps Fosca's life tied to a thread; the role of the doctor who pulls the strings of the love story like a meticulous director, or, rather, like an absolute demiurge; the attitude of the colonel cousin who is a guardian of Fosca as distracted as he is susceptible) and the murky areas of the background (the garrison of officers whom we never see performing military duties but only discussing as if they were in a scientific salon; the locality that appears to be isolated at the ends of the earth yet is not far from Milan), the mystery of Fosca's fascinating ugliness assumes an almost symbolic meaning. Fosca is a character between art nouveau and D'Annunzio who appears at least twenty years in advance in a world that is (still) not hers, showing up like a visitor from another planet, or a mutant in the evolution of the species. Those who see her feel at once put off and attracted, as always happens before the facts—in art or in life—that warn us that something is changing.

CENTOPAGINE SERIES CATALOGUE

Iginio Ugo Tarchetti, *Fosca (Passion)*

Leo Tolstoy, *The Kreutzer Sonata*

Guy de Maupassant, *Pierre and Jean*

Fyodor Dostoyevsky, *White Nights*

Henry James, *Daisy Miller*

Edmondo De Amicis, *Amore e ginnastica (Love and Gymnastics)*

Joseph Conrad, *The Shadow Line*

Joseph von Eichendorff, *Memoirs of a Good-for-Nothing*

Denis Diderot, *Memoirs of a Nun*

Herman Melville, *Benito Cereno*

Aleksandr Pushkin, *The Captain's Daughter*

Mark Twain, *The Man That Corrupted Hadleyburg*

Anton Chekhov, *Ward No. 6*

Stendhal, *The Abbess of Castro*

Achim von Arnim, *Isabella of Egypt*

Achille Giovanni Cagna, *Alpinisti ciabattoni (Mountaineers in Slippers)*

Carlo Dossi, *L'Altrieri. Nero su bianco* (*The Day Before Yesterday: In Black and White*)

Thomas Nashe, *The Unfortunate Traveler*

Gaetano Carlo Chelli, *L'eredità Ferramonti* (*The Inheritance*)

Anonymous, *The Life of Lazarillo de Tormes*

Honoré de Balzac, *Ferragus*

E.T.A. Hoffmann, *Princess Brambilla*

Marchesa Colombi, *Un matrimonio in provincia* (*A Small-Town Marriage*)

Robert Louis Stevenson, *The Pavilion on the Links*

Thomas De Quincey, *Confessions of an English Opium Eater*

Angelo Costantini, *La vita di Scaramuccia* (*The Birth, Life, and Death of Scaramouche*)

William Beckford, *Vathek*

Leo Tolstoy, *Two Hussars*

La Fayette, *The Princess of Clèves*

Joseph Conrad, *Heart of Darkness*

Voltaire, *Zadig*

Charles Sealsfield, *The Hyacinth Prairie*

Robert Louis Stevenson, "Olalla"

Fyodor Dostoyevsky, *Uncle's Dream*

Edouard Dujardin, *The Laurels Are Cut Down*

Guido Nobili, *Memorie lontane* (*Distant Memories*)

Friedrich de la Motte-Fouqué, *Undine*

Nyta Jasmar, *Ricordi di una Telegrafista* (*Memoirs of a Telegraphist*)

Giovanni Boine, *Il peccato* (*The Sin*)

Henry James, *The Reverberator*

Ambrose Bierce, *Tales of Soldiers and Civilians*

Neera, *Teresa*

Giovanni Cena, *Gli Ammonitori* (*The Informers*)

Carlo Dossi, *Vita di Alberto Pisani* (*Life of Alberto Pisani*)

William Butler Yeats, *Rosa Alchemica*

Kate Chopin, *The Awakening*

Remigio Zena, *Confessione postuma. Quattro storie dall'altro mondo* (*Posthumous Confession and Four Stories from the Other World*)

Hans J. Ch. von Grimmelshausen, *Courage, the Adventuress and the False Messiah*

Emilio Praga and Roberto Sacchetti, *Memorie del presbiterio* (*Memories of the Presbytery*)

Honoré de Balzac, *The Girl with the Golden Eyes*

Prosper Mérimée, *Carmen and Other Stories*

Nikolai Leskov, *The Enchanted Wanderer*

Henry James, *The Aspern Papers*

Nikolai Gogol, *Evenings on a Farm Near Dikanka*

Luigi Pirandello, *Il turno* (*The Turn*)

E.T.A. Hoffmann, *The Devil's Elixirs*

Enrico Pea, *Moscardino. Il Volto Santo. Il servitore del diavolo* (*Moscardino: The Holy Face, the Devil's Servant*)

Denis Diderot, *Jacques the Fatalist and His Master*

Herculine Barbin, *Being the Recently Discovered Memoirs of a Nineteenth-Century French Hermaphrodite*

Anatole France, *The Queen Pedauque*

Charles Baudelaire, *La Fanfarlo*

Gustave Flaubert, *Three Stories*

Giuseppe Torelli, *Emiliano*

Fyodor Dostoyevsky, *Notes from Underground*

Laurence Sterne, *A Political Romance*

Carlo Dossi, *La Desinenza in A (The Ending in A)*

Honoré de Balzac, *The Lesser Bourgeoisie*

Fyodor Dostoyevsky, *The Eternal Husband*

———, *The Gambler*

William Butler Yeats, *John Sherman; and, Dhoya*

Théophile Gautier, *Spirite*

Antoine-François Prévost, *The Story of the Chevalier des Grieux and Manon Lescaut*

Henry James, *A London Life*

Federigo Tozzi, *Con gli occhi chiusi (With Eyes Closed)*

Henry James, *The Sacred Fount*

Theodore Fontane, *A Man of Honor*

Algernon Charles Swinburne, *A Year's Letters*

Einaudi Biblioteca Giovani
(Einaudi Young People's Library)

History and *stories*. For most of us, don't the great historical dates still evoke the mood of what we read when we were young? Isn't our first memory of the Ides of March the Shakespearean night when Brutus is watching in his garden, and don't we associate the Battle of Waterloo with Fabrizio del Dongo? The same is true for the atmosphere of an era or a civilization that we didn't experience: London of the Industrial Revolution is the city of Oliver Twist, tsarist Petersburg is the city of Dostoyevsky's Raskolnikov.

History, or what we gradually learn to recognize as a single thread that over time binds the multiform presence of human beings on the earth, presents itself from the start as an ebb and flow of *stories*, of tales that differ in rhythm and accent but are all charged with a force that imposes itself on the imagination, on reasoning, on choices. Later, when we've carefully woven this single, compact thread of history (in which the stories that had been our first point of reference are relegated almost to the rank of decorative element, of illustration outside the text), it starts to fall apart in our hands: we'll learn that continuity and synchrony are illusory, that even "universal history" isn't saved from being merely a particular point of view, yet another of our prejudices. But the *stories*, which have become part of our mental patrimony, with the force of emblems and symbols, and with their weight of meanings, will continue to work in us, to signify, to open new discourses.

This series of fifty books by novelists and by historians and memoirists as well—many of which are famous, others well known, all, however, with a proven "grip" on the reading of an audience of young people—aims at sketching a panorama that is at once the history of the world and an exemplification of attitudes toward the world, from the mythic mindset to the scientific, from the chivalric ethic to social protest. The fifty titles are representative: each was chosen after due consideration, none are superfluous; but that doesn't mean that they couldn't have been others. And although there are fifty they could become a hundred; and certainly they will, if not in this series, then as a first nucleus of readings that extends over the years, in the further choices of each reader. In other words, fifty books to read and to remember, books that *open up*: to other books and to the world.

We've said that historians are next to novelists, are read as novelists: Herodotus, Tacitus, Gibbon, Gregorovius are represented by a section of their monumental works that can be read independently, so that the reader isn't discouraged by the large volume. Alongside them are exceptional contemporary reporters like the John Reed of the Russian Revolution and the Edgar Snow of the Chinese Revolution. Then there is the broad range of relationships that writers have with the historical past, not excluding the polemical attitudes that lead a Bertolt Brecht to criticize the "greats."

On the other hand (we mustn't forget) every novelist is a *historian* of his time, whether Radiguet or Pasolini, if he bears direct witness to the behavior and language of a slice of society. But Poe or Kafka is no less a *historian* when he projects the hidden ghosts of his society, when he makes explicit the nightmares and prophecies of an era. The charge of truth that the story conveys is aimed between the two poles of the myth and the lived.

This reintroduction of *narrative* as history may seem against the general trend at a time when history—the subject that's taught in school, the subject of research by scholars, the subject of public discussion—sidelines "events" and "characters" in order to place in the foreground material supports, structures, institutions, the economy, statistics, figures, or ideological interpretation. However, precisely for that reason, today when we are more protected against the traps of *petite histoire*, against anecdotal mystifications, an invitation to rediscover that dimension of historical memory which is conveyed by the story seems to us especially important. This is a dimension that we can't lose without losing a crucial impulse of our conscious participation in changing the world.

CATALOGUE FOR EINAUDI
YOUNG PEOPLE'S LIBRARY *

Theodor H. Gaster, *The Oldest Stories in the World*

Herodotus, *The Histories*

Plutarch, *Lives of the Noble Greeks*

William Shakespeare, *From* Coriolanus *to* Cleopatra: *Three Roman Plays*

Bertolt Brecht, *The Business Affairs of Mr. Julius Caesar*

Suetonius and Tacitus, *Nero*

Edward Gibbon, *Decline and Fall of the Roman Empire*

Ferdinand Gregorovius, *History of the City of Rome in the Middle Ages*

Anonymous, *Erik the Red and Other Viking Sagas*

Marco Polo, *Il Milione (The Million)*

Anonymous, *The Thousand and One Nights*

Walter Scott, *Ivanhoe*

William H. Prescott, *History of the Conquest of Mexico*

Alexandre Dumas, *Queen Margot*

Bertolt Brecht, *Life of Galileo*

Saint-Simon, *La corte del Re Sole (Court of the Sun King)*

Daniel Defoe, *Robinson Crusoe*

Voltaire, *Candide*

Aleksandr Pushkin, *The Captain's Daughter*

Wolfgang Goethe, *The Sorrows of Young Werther*

Victor Hugo, *Ninety-Three*

---

* Edited by Mario Barenghi

Stendhal, *The Charterhouse of Parma*

James Fenimore Cooper, *The Last of the Mohicans*

Charles Dickens, *Oliver Twist*

Edgar Allan Poe, *The Narrative of Arthur Gordon Pym;*
    Murders in the Rue Morgue

Leo Tolstoy, *Sebastopol Sketches*

Herman Melville, *Benito Cereno; Billy Budd*

Ivan Turgenev, *Fathers and Sons*

Fyodor Dostoyevsky, *Crime and Punishment*

Guy de Maupassant, *Tales of the Franco-Prussian War*

Émile Zola, *Germinal*

Mark Twain, *The Adventures of Huckleberry Finn*

Robert Louis Stevenson, *Kidnapped*

Stephen Crane, *The Red Badge of Courage*

Frank Thiess, *Tsushima*

Jack London, *Martin Eden*

Joseph Conrad, *The Shadow Line; Heart of Darkness*

Thomas Mann, *Tonio Kröger; Death in Venice; Tristan*

Franz Kafka, *The Metamorphosis and Other Stories*

Mario Silvestri, *Isonzo 1917*

John Reed, *Ten Days That Shook the World*

Edgar Snow, *Red Star Over China*

Nuto Revelli, *La strada del davai (Mussolini's Death*
    March)

Robert Antelme, *The Human Race*

Beppe Fenoglio, *Racconti partigiani (Partisan Stories)*

Pier Paolo Pasolini, *Una vita violenta (A Violent Life)*

Leonardo Sciascia, *A ciascuno il suo (To Each His Own)*

José M. Arguedas, *Deep Rivers*

George Jackson, *Soledad Brothers*

Italo Calvino, *La memoria del mondo e altre storie cosmicomiche* (*World Memory and Other Cosmicomic Stories*)

The Mondadori Biblioteca Romantica

In May of 1930, along with the publication of the first six volumes of Mondadori's Biblioteca Romantica, a brochure appeared that served as a prospectus and as a *specimen*: it, too, had a green cloth binding and was printed on high-quality paper in the same typeface as the series. Besides the list of fifty volumes planned, with the names of the translators, it included an introduction by the editor of the series, G. A. Borgese.

The slogan (or, as was said at the time, "the motto and mission statement") that launched the Biblioteca Romantica was "The great foreign novelists become classic Italian writers." The principal literary innovation of this initiative lay in the fact that the translations were assigned largely to known writers, but there was an editorial innovation of equal importance: the launch into a vast market of a type of book that would appeal to collectors. The Biblioteca Romantica was made up of fifty volumes that were announced all at the same time: a corpus that was intended to be complete, and fully representative of world literature.

This was at the start of modern, high-quality publishing in Italy: for good reason guiding the Biblioteca Romantica was the type of critic who had a sense of literature as a global patrimony and not only as a national tradition (which said today may seem obvious, but wasn't at the time). And it should be remembered that Borgese planned the series and edited the initial volumes but couldn't follow through because the atmosphere of official Italy soon (in 1931) became so heavy that he emigrated to the United States, and did not return until after the war. Yet his name continued to appear on the frontispiece of the series until 1938, that is, with no. 46. Thus only the last four volumes appear without the name of the series editor.

The first title in the Biblioteca Romantica was *The Charterhouse of Parma*, in the translation by Ferdinando Martini. Borgese's introduction was included in the volume as an afterword. The other volumes were accompanied only by brief informational notes. The habit of overlong and over-academic introductions had not yet beaten down our publishers.

The Romantica program was completed in twelve years: it ended, as it had begun, with an epic, the two volumes of *War and Peace*, a title that in the meantime had become current: this was 1942. The twelve years of the Biblioteca Romantica go along with an era of changes on the cultural horizon of the Italian public and in the direction of publishing. We can consider Borgese's introduction of 1930 a document of a transitional phase.

The first thing that strikes us is the label *Romantic* placed on an entire series of books that, yes, belong mainly to the nineteenth century but that also include Swift's *Gulliver* and Voltaire's *Candide*, along with Zola and Maupassant, which no literary history would place under that banner. But Borgese explains in the introduction: "By romantic works we mean, historically, works of Christian and modern literatures; romantic, as the name itself says, is what originated in the legacy of Rome. In these literatures the happiest genre, the superior genre, is the epic in prose: the novel." *Romantic*, therefore, as opposed to classical antiquity, but above all *Romantic* as romance, or novel, without reference to the era or the school: the semantic zone of the term seems to overlap in part with that of *fiction*, a term then used little or not at all in the critical lexicon. The changes that the language has seen in the past fifty years could be the subject of an investigation that would hold many surprises. And I would also add a citation from Borgese that perhaps accounts for another connotation of the term *romantic*, that is, the one most closely tied to daily language: speaking of the format of the series, he notes that the publisher has provided it with all the special features that make it not only "prized by bibliophiles" but also pleasing "to women, the vast majority of the reading public."

Among the writers invited to make foreign classics Italian, besides Borgese himself, who translated *Werther*, were the best known of the time: Alfredo Panzini, for Henri Murger's *Vie de Bohème* (a translation from which Borgese, introducing the series, was quick to distance himself: it was the only exception to the standard of maximum fidelity tolerated), Marino Moretti for Maupassant, Lucio D'Ambra for De Musset. The pairs that stand out most in this first list, however, are three: Massimo Bontempelli for Chateaubriand's *Atala and René*, Aldo Palazzeschi for *Tartarin de Tarascon*, and Marinetti for Flaubert's *Tentations de St. Antoine*, the last a project that wasn't realized. Then a beautiful flower garden of women poets and writers, all chosen, coincidentally, to translate novels with a woman's name in the title: Grazia Deledda translates *Eugénie Grandet*, Ada Negri *Manon Lescaut*, Sibilla Aleramo *The Princess of Clèves*, the only book among these whose author is also a woman. In the initial prospectus Annie Vivanti was to do Hardy's *Tess of the d'Urbervilles*. How many of these translations can we consider to be truly the work of the person whose name is on them? Perhaps the archives of the publisher can answer this question, along with the biographies of the people in question and the critics of style. Those who have experience in editorial work know that translations very often pass through several hands. And Borgese himself in his introduction warned against the use of "ghostwriters" for the work of the translator.

Without getting into this thorny matter I will confine myself to some reflections suggested by these pairs. Palazzeschi-Daudet: here the matchup I would say sounds restrictive for the inventiveness of the Florentine poet and novelist, as if he were to be enclosed within (and this was, I think, the tendency of criticism of the time) the dimensions of a good-humored provincial caricature. And what to say of Bontempelli-Chateaubriand? The one with his love of the geometry of lucidity and the other all flamboyance and contrast of light and shadow? Another astonishing couple is Bacchelli-Voltaire, where sober corpulence and agile concision meet. But the pairing of Voltaire and Ugo Ojetti seems even stranger, and yet that was the name that first appeared in the prospectus, later replaced by Bacchelli. But certainly the most sensational coupling, although it remained in the planning stage, is Marinetti-Flaubert, with Bosch-like visions of the saint in the desert meeting the words-in-freedom of futurism . . .

Other encounters may have originated in a game of assonances and associations: to Francesco Pastonchi, a reciter of Dante who had great success in high society, is assigned not without irony *The Lady with the Camellias*; Angiolo Silvio Novaro, since he's from a city on the sea and is popular among young people for his poems on the seasons, is chosen to translate Stevenson.

Between the prospectus of 1930 and the catalogue of fifty titles that were in fact published in the space of twelve years, there are some differences and changes in both the texts and the editors, on account of which the number of writer-translators increases, with Corrado Alvaro unexpectedly translating Walter Scott, and the invaluable Bacchelli translating a chapter of *Astrée*, by Honoré d'Urfé (in addition to the great undertaking of the novels and stories of Voltaire).

But the main thing is the addition of many new names

that became famous precisely in those years. While Borgese's first list was characterized by figures typical of Italy around the turn of the century—Ferdinando Martini, Fausto Maria Martini, Guido Mazzoni, Guido Biagi, Fernando Palazzi, Giuseppe Lipparini—now alongside these old names are some who in the thirties and later became the principal ambassadors of foreign literature among us: Here is Diego Valeri, who finishes *Madame Bovary*, a text that Borgese in the introduction says that he had given up on because he couldn't find the right translator; here is Mario Praz, who presents one of the least-well-known texts of the series, *Esther Waters*, by George Moore; here is Carlo Linati, who will yoke his name to the introduction of Henry James in Italy and here presents him with *The American*; here is Lavinia Mazzucchetti, who enters with the phantasmagorical Hoffmann and the lucid Stifter. Giacomo Debenedetti, our first interpreter of Proust, appears in an unusual guise as a translator from English for George Eliot's *The Mill on the Floss*. And the first translator of Joyce, Alberto Rossi, presents Meredith's *The Tragic Comedians*, a text that in the prospectus was assigned to Lauro de Bosis, who had in the meantime left on his generous flight of no return.

And finally there is, as a novice translator, Elio Vittorini, who joins a Tuscan writer, Delfino Cinelli, in a great undertaking: the two volumes of stories by Edgar Allan Poe. Shortly afterward Vittorini became one of the mainstays of the Medusa, the other series from Mondadori that, also in the thirties, opens the windows onto the world of contemporary fiction.

Let's mention a volume that resurrected two classic translations: the inevitable *Sentimental Journey* of Sterne translated by Foscolo, and a more unusual work, which would be worth reprinting today, both for the work itself and for the translation, Schiller's *The Ghost-Seer*, translated by Giovanni Berchet.

We have paused to review the catalogue because it represents a sort of link at a moment of renewal of taste and cultural needs and critical horizons. But the essential fact is an awareness of the problem of translation. In presenting the series Borgese devotes to this subject a number of reflections, which culminate in the promulgation not of ten commandments for the translator but five:

"Translate directly from the text, using the best edition.

"Translate fully, without making cuts or taking liberties.

"In order for the translation to last, it needs to be written in plain current Italian, without archaic or vernacular flourishes, except in cases where particular accentuations serve to imitate certain characteristics of the text.

"For our contributors this other rule is superfluous (ordinary readers won't understand it, but publishers and literary people can):

"The translation has to be the genuine responsibility of the person whose name is on it, not entrusted to a young friend or family member and then validated by the authority of a famous name."

This last passage is worth a treatise in literary sociology, and proves to us that the worries we have to confront in editorial work haven't changed.

A step that takes us back, instead, to a sociocultural situation different from ours—note that I don't mean more backward, but certainly different—is a consideration of the place the French language holds in the culture of the average Italian, a place that is now largely occupied by English, though certainly not to the point where people read in the original language. Indicative of this is the fact that Borgese feels he has to explain why the series includes translations from French, given that "all Italians know French."

The reasons he identifies are two: first, that that statement isn't completely true, because even if many Italians understand French, they mutilate it when they pronounce it and in reading miss the musicality of the sentences; second, that he wanted to involve in the initiative some of the best Italian writers, and so he had no recourse but to have French books translated, because Italian literary people, Borgese says, "were and are rather mediocre students of other modern languages."

Given this familiarity of the language, one would expect a quirkier and more exciting choice of French titles; but all in all we wouldn't say that that is the case. Or, rather, the sixteenth and seventeenth centuries are worthily represented, and the inclusion of Choderlos de Laclos is certainly a gain for the series. But it seems to us that the choices from the second half of the nineteenth century leave something to be desired, despite a stroke of genius like Fromentin's *Dominique*. Sometimes there are extrinsic reasons to guide what is included: if in the case of Zola *The Ladies' Paradise* was chosen, it's owing to the fact—it is again Borgese who lets us know—that a translation by Ferdinando Martini existed.

Thus, moving on to German literature, Borgese anticipates the question "Why did we choose Goethe's *Wilhelm Meister's Theatrical Calling* instead of the classic and monumental *Meister* of which the *Theatrical Calling* is merely the first youthful draft?" And he explains that the greater *Meister* is "a book for poets and wise men" and that there was already an excellent translation on the market, by Spaini, a reason, it seems to me, already editorially and culturally sufficient. The German selection took advantage of the contribution of Borgese himself, who, besides *Werther*, was supposed to edit a miscellaneous volume including Eichendorff's *Good-for-Nothing* and Chamisso's *Schlemihl*, but because of his departure this volume, which would have been one of the jewels of the collection, wasn't produced. Nevertheless I would say that the German selection is the best of the series, that is, the least obvious and in its essentiality and liveliness the most rigorous, with the delightful Mörike of *Mozart's Journey to Prague* and the mini-collections of stories by Heine and Stifter.

As we continue to scan the choices in the various literatures one by one, we come to the English, which opens with Defoe's *Lady Roxana*: here, too, a less-well-known book by a great writer, and here, too, the reason can be traced to the available translation (by Guido Biagi). Altogether the English choices are anything but banal, with first-rank offerings by Jane Austen and Walter Pater, but I would say that it's not the most exciting dish on the menu: a pity, because it could be an opportunity to create a new audience for the English nineteenth century.

The Scandinavian literatures that around the same time found a warm welcome in a series parallel to this, UTET's Great Foreign Writers, are represented here by Jens Peter Jacobsen's *Maria Grubbe*. But the finite number of volumes in the Biblioteca Romantica didn't allow for much flexibility to provide a broader sample of the minor European literatures. The Spanish choices rely on the strength of Ferdinando Carlesi's translation of *Don Quixote* and a volume of picaresques translated by [Giuseppe] Ravegnani; my lack of expertise in the nineteenth century doesn't allow me to judge whether [Juan] Valera and [Jose Maria de] Pereda are worth the exclusion of [Benito] Pérez Galdós. Representing the Portuguese novel is [Jose Maria de] Eça de Queiroz, an author much read in Italy at the time and perhaps unjustly neglected today.

The touchstone of a series like this is Russian literature. A new demand for high-quality translations was displayed by the more discerning Italian public: we have only to recall an initiative like Alfredo Polledro's Genio Slavo series [published in Turin by Slavia], which brought back into circulation the great names of the Russian novel (until then mostly retranslated from German and French) in direct, complete, and faithful translations. This legacy was picked up in the late thirties by Giulio Einaudi, with the blue series of Foreign Novelists in Translation, whose backbone was the Russian classics, thanks mainly to Leone Ginzburg. The blue volumes of the Einaudi Foreign Novelists was in a way the successor to the Mondadori Romantica at the moment when the latter ended. Between these two, as far as the nineteenth-century Russian novels are concerned, the Biblioteca Romantica offers a selection that might best be called canonical, with the two greatest Tolstoys and the two greatest Dostoyevskys (or, if we prefer, two of the greatest Dostoyevskys, which are at least three), the Turgenev of *Fathers and Sons*, which we can consider in a way the series banner, in that it's an indispensable text that has no other editions, and a Gogol, unfortunately not the most representative (*Taras Bulba* and two novellas).

The name of Gogol reminds us of Tommaso Landolfi's extraordinary translation of *Petersburg Tales*, which is in the Rizzoli catalogue. Scanning the list of Romantica translators, we see that not only Landolfi but also others from the Florence of the hermetics, of *Solaria* and that whole milieu, are absent, as if the literary polemics of the time had dug an impassible abyss. The only name from that circle is Vittorini, the bold Sicilian who in those years made a stop at the Giubbe Rosse [café in Florence] but aimed ultimately at Milan; the Poe translations for the Romantica were his calling card for an operation that was accomplished first in the Medusa series and then in the Bompiani editions of the early forties, in which translation becomes a proposal for stylistic innovation in Italian prose.

We now come to the youngest of the literatures, American, to complete our review of the fifty Romantica titles.

American novelists are asserting themselves in Europe, and among the Mondadori editions the Medusa series, despite the obstacles of censorship, will be one of the first channels for this opening, especially with the Faulkner translated by Pavese. But even the more conservative Romantica feels the blast; the proof of it is that while the 1930 plan provided for only one Poe and one Hawthorne, in the end the Poe was doubled, to two volumes, and a James was added. The other great American novelist of the mid-nineteenth century, Melville, remains outside Borgese's plans, but it must be said that he had been discovered even in America only recently, and was, after all, a new name. It was a small Turinese publisher, Frassinelli, guided by the happy hand of Franco Antonicelli, who commissioned Pavese (this is still the thirties, which saw the genesis of many things) to translate *Moby Dick*. Later, from Einaudi and Bompiani respectively, came *Benito Cereno* and *Billy Budd*, the latter entrusted to another exceptional translator, Eugenio Montale.

I spoke about American literature last in order to end on a personal memory that's very important to me: Poe's *Narrative of Arthur Gordon Pym* in the Romantica was one of the first serious, complete readings of my youth. An uncle of mine had subscribed to the green volumes, had in fact signed up for one of the first subscriptions, which gave you the right to receive every volume with a personal ex libris. Among the gilded titles on the spines lined up on the shelf, I chose *Arthur Gordon Pym*, and it was one of the most emotional experiences of my life: physical emotion, because certain pages literally terrified me, and poetic emotion, like a call of destiny.

This is to mention one of the functions of the Biblioteca Romantica and certainly not the least of them: to provide a platform, to construct a foundation for literary culture, for the appeal of the great novel, for Italians who at the time were venturing into the world of books.

BIBLIOTECA ROMANTICA
MONDADORI CATALOGUE

Dostoyevsky, *Demons*
Daudet, *Tartarin de Tarascon*
Goldsmith, *The Vicar of Wakefield*
Goethe, *Wilhelm Meister's Theatrical Calling*
Stevenson, *Treasure Island*
Stifter, *The Bachelors*
Poe, *Tales of the Grotesque and Arabesque*
Voltaire, *Novels and Stories*
Dickens, *David Copperfield*
Eliot, *The Mill on the Floss*
Tolstoy, *War and Peace*
Murger, *Vie de Bohème*
Laclos, *Liaisons Dangereuses*
Flaubert, *Madame Bovary*
Prévost, *The Story of the Chevalier des Grieux and Manon Lescaut*
Zola, *The Ladies' Paradise*
Eça de Queiroz, *The Crime of Father Amaro*

James, *The American*

Jacobsen, *Maria Grubbe*

Bernardin de Saint-Pierre, *Paul and Virginia*

Scott, *Waverley*

Cervantes, *Don Quixote*

Balzac, *Eugénie Grandet*

Goethe, *The Sorrows of Young Werther*

Gautier, *Captain Fracasse*

Stendhal, *The Charterhouse of Parma*

Dumas, *The Lady with the Camellias*

Hawthorne, *The Scarlet Letter*

France, *Thaïs*

Maupassant, *A Life*

Fromentin, *Dominique*

Moore, *Esther Waters*

Swift, *Gulliver's Travels*

Balzac, *The Black Sheep*

Chekhov, *The Duel*

Heine, *The Rabbi of Bacharach*

Wilde, *The Portrait of Dorian Gray*

Musset, *The Confession of a Child of the Century*

La Fayette, *The Princess of Clèves*

Defoe, *Roxana: The Fortunate Mistress*

Mörike, *Mozart's Journey to Prague*

Austen, *Pride and Prejudice*

Turgenev, *Fathers and Sons*

Valera, *Peppina Jiménez*

Pereda, *Sotileza*

Gogol, *Taras Bulba*

Sterne, *Sentimental Journey;* Schiller, *The Ghost-Seer*
Tolstoy, *Anna Karenina*
Meredith, *The Tragic Comedians*
Poe, *The Narrative of Arthur Gordon Pym and Other Tales*

[1981]

On the Fantastic

The Knights of the Grail

When King Arthur is about to die, he orders his magic sword Excalibur to be thrown into the bottom of a lake, so that no unworthy hand can get possession of it. The faithful Girflet doesn't feel able to dispose of the royal sword: twice he pretends to throw it in the lake, but in reality he hides it and first throws his own sword into the water, then the sheath. Both times Arthur sees through the deception, because Girflet doesn't mention having noticed anything strange. Finally Girflet decides to obey, but before the sword touches the water a hand and arm rise out of the lake (but not the body they belong to), and the hand grabs the sword by the hilt, brandishes it in the air, and with it disappears into the depths.

This is the end of the *Lancelot-Grail*. Also in the final scene of the *Search for the Holy Grail* a hand appears without our seeing who it belongs to, but this one descends from heaven to seize the Grail and carry it up above the clouds. The two hands, the heavenly hand and the one that emerges from the depths—the one an element of the most well-known religious iconography and the other much more surprising and evocative—seem to represent the two aspects of the legends of the Breton cycle, Christian symbolism and druid paganism: the two keys in which we read the adventures of the Round Table today.

In Leo Spitzer's definition, "Adventure is a singular, extraordinary, and unexpected circumstance that comes from outside of man, it 'happens' to him and has to be overcome by him with courage and shrewdness, for a victory that represents a moral test of himself." In the medieval chivalric romance the term *adventure* appears constantly and sometimes with much wider meanings, which go beyond individual experience to become the exceptional situation of a place or an object or a series of phenomena, a departure from the norms of nature, a spell. The desolation that has struck the Terre Gaste, or Wasteland, the barren, wild land where Percival's exploits unfold, is "adventure."

"After the death of King Uther Pendragon, the father of the good King Arthur, the valiant men were impoverished, disinherited, unjustly ruined, their lands devastated." This sense of the ghostly, precarious life of a knight wandering through deserted and hostile lands, with the imperative to restore a past whose splendors have by now been canceled from every memory, permeates the entire cycle of Arthurian romances.

Epic poetry, if you look carefully, is sustained more by the emotions of defeat than by those of victory (even *The Iliad* is no exception, as it recounts a moment of impasse and crisis among the Achaeans), and this would confirm the hypotheses that the legends of King Arthur have distant historical origins. Whether one wants to connect the cycle to the struggles of the sixth-century Britons against the Saxons or the tenth-century Bretons against the Normans, it would be the celebration of a last glorious era for the Celts and the promise of revenge (with the return of Arthur from the Isle of the Blessed where he is received after death).

As for the origins of the Round Table as an object, Welsh, Irish, and Breton tradition says Arthur had it built so that none of his knights could boast a privileged place over the others. (Think of the discussions on the shape of the table before the start of the peace negotiations between the Americans and the Vietnamese in Paris.) A symbol of equality, therefore: In an English poem of the thirteenth century that certainly refers to much older traditions, a carpenter from Cornwall (in order to put an end to the disputes that raged among the knights) offers to make Arthur a table at which sixteen hundred men could sit without any arguments over places of honor. The biggest medieval round table that has been preserved is the one in Winchester, which can seat twenty-five people. Christian traditions, on the other hand, fix the number of places at twelve, plus one vacant: the Round Table as a replica of the table at the Last Supper and the first Communion table of Joseph of Arimathea.

But the circle is also the symbol of cosmic totality, linked to sun (and moon) worship: in primitive Celtic civilization, it's characteristic not only of magical objects but also of architecture. One contemporary commentator has identified the Round Table with the circular form of Stonehenge.

In any case, the important point is that the success of the chivalric cycles—whatever their origins—begins with a twelfth-century poet with a lightness of touch in every detail, a poet of psychological refinement, a maker of graceful rhyming couplets, whose evocation of a mysterious past is fascinating: Chrétien de Troyes. Finding good editions of the original text on the market is difficult, because in France today I'd say that medieval French, thorny but full of flavor, is read only by specialists: in the most widespread collections of *livres de poches,* Chrétien is found only in transcriptions into modern French prose. (It's rather as if we translated Dante and Boccaccio into modern Italian.)

A good prose translation into Italian, by Angela Bianchini, has just come out, including two of Chrétien's romances and many other texts from the Breton cycle, in the volume *Romanzi medievali d'amore e d'avventura* [*Medieval Romances of Love and Adventure*] (Milan: Garzanti, I Grandi Libri, 1981). The volume reproduces a Casini edition of some years ago, updating it in the wide-ranging introduction. The definition I cited above is from the preface that Spitzer wrote expressly for this work of Bianchini, his former student.

Chrétien's masterpiece is, although incomplete, *Perceval,* in which the childlike character is portrayed with surprising humor in speech and behavior, in the wild innocence that makes him invincible, and we follow him through a real journey of initiation. He discovers the chivalric life his mother vainly wished to keep him away from as a reality with the outlines of a dream. We can say that the chivalric adventure makes its entrance into literature with this aura of myth, and also with a hint of parody, as we see the knights' exploits imitated by the innocent spirit of this boy who has grown up in the woods. Thus we might say that chivalric literature is born and dies with two cases of sublime folly: Perceval and Don Quixote.

Perceval takes everything literally: First the advice of his mother, then that of the worthy man who confers knighthood on him. He is both a blunderer and a force of nature, but he is also pure, enlightened, almost a Zen monk.

His visit to the castle of the Fisher King is full of mysteries: What is the secret of the invalid king? What is the meaning of the three objects carried in procession: the bloody lance, the plate, and the cup called the grail? Why doesn't Perceval ask for explanations? And why is his silence a sin that will have grave consequences? The incomplete romance explains nothing, and from this uncertainty arose an entire library of "continuations" in various languages (the German was later happily taken up by Wagner in his *Parsifal*), in which the adventures of Perceval, Gawain, and Lancelot (whose adultery with Queen Guinevere, the wife of Arthur, is another sin with grim consequences) are woven together. It is Galahad, the virgin knight, who puts an end to the spell of the grail, and not Perceval, who is a happy fornicator, although in all innocence.

The most elaborate continuation is Robert de Boron's

mystical tale, in which the grail becomes the Holy Grail, the cup from which Jesus drank at the Last Supper and in which His blood was collected by Joseph of Arimathea. None of this was in Chrétien de Troyes, although he seems to start on the road of Christian symbology, saying (through the mouth of the Hermit King) that the grail contains a host that by itself is enough to nourish the Fisher King. Whatever Chrétien's intentions, it's likely that the symbology of the grail is also connected to Celtic rites regarding the cycle of vegetation and fertility, as many modern scholars are inclined to see. (The Fisher King's wound is literally "between his legs.")

But the mysteries of the incomplete romance don't stop there. Perceval's deceased father had suffered a wound like the Fisher King's (or Fisher Kings', because he, too, has an injured father). Then Perceval meets a girl cousin who reveals to him his kinship with that unlucky dynasty. But on the father's side or the mother's? All possible genealogies that can be derived from Chrétien's indications are tangled and contradictory.

Only in recent years, Jacques Roubaud, a poet who is also a mathematician, has succeeded in formulating a proposed genealogical tree that connects Perceval to the Fisher King, in fact to the various generations of Fisher Kings. Thus we get a new hypothesis to explain the secret around which the whole cycle revolves. In the middle is an incestuous act, in fact a series of incestuous acts, mother-son and father-daughter (while a brother-sister incest is at the origin of the troubles of King Arthur's family).

The incestuous interpretation doesn't contradict the mystical. Not at all. The genealogical chart of the family of the Fisher Kings would be the same as that of the family of Adam, and even that of the family of Jesus, just as (according to Roubaud) they were reconstructed by Joachim of Fiore!

This isn't the only thing in the book that I'm sorry I don't have space here to summarize in more detail (Jacques Roubaud, *Grail Fiction* [Paris: Gallimard, 1978]); it's overflowing with imagination and erudition, and with ideas that go from a Welsh fortune-teller's prophecy that fishermen (warriors of the people) will succeed hunters (defeated warrior nobility) to an interpretation of the grail as a book.

The central idea is this: Through Bleddri or Blaise, a Welsh bard of the eleventh century who moves to France, to the court of Poitiers, when Wales is invaded by the Normans, Celtic culture, now scattered through the forests and heaths, finds a way to survive by introducing the burning carnal passion of the stories of Tristan and Isolde and Lancelot and Guinevere into the cradle of Provençal poetry, courtly love, and chivalric idealism. Charged with this subversive ferment, the "material from Brittany" reaches Dante, for whom the story of adultery at the court of King Arthur is what urges the eyes of Paolo and Francesca to meet, makes their faces pale, and leads to the kiss of the mouth all trembling that decides the future fate of Western literature.

[1981]

Fantastic Tales of the
Nineteenth Century

The fantastic tale is one of the most typical creations of nineteenth-century fiction and one of the most meaningful for us, in the sense that it says many things about the inner life of the individual and about collective symbology. To our modern sensibility the supernatural element at the center of the plots always seems charged with meaning, like an uprising of the unconscious, the repressed, the forgotten, the removed from our rational attention. In that should be seen the modernity of the fantastic, the reason for the return of its success in our time. We feel that the fantastic says things that concern us directly, even if we are less willing than nineteenth-century readers to let ourselves be surprised by apparitions and phantasmagoria, or are willing to enjoy them in another way, as elements of the spirit of the time.

The fantastic tale originates in the terrain of eighteenth- and nineteenth-century philosophical speculation: its theme is the relationship between the reality of the world we inhabit and know through perception and the reality of the world of thought that lives in us and rules us. The problem of the reality of what is visible—extraordinary things that are perhaps hallucinations projected by our mind; ordinary things that under the most banal appearance may hide a disturbing, mysterious, terrifying second nature—is the essence of fantasy literature, whose best effects lie in the oscillation of irreconcilable levels of reality.

Tzvetan Todorov, in his *Introduction à la littérature fantastique* (*Introduction to Fantastic Literature*, 1970), maintains that what distinguishes "fantastic" fiction is precisely bewilderment in the face of an incredible fact, hesitation between a rational, realistic explanation and acceptance of the supernatural. The character of the incredulous positivist who often appears in this type of story, and is viewed with sympathy and sarcasm because he has to yield to what he can't explain, is not, however, completely rejected. The incredible fact that the fantastic tale recounts should, according to Todorov, always leave the possibility of rational explanation, even if it's a hallucination or a dream (a lid that fits all pots).

Whereas the "marvelous," says Todorov, can be distinguished from the "fantastic" in that it assumes acceptance of the unlikely and inexplicable, as in fables or the *Thousand and One Nights*. (The distinction is inherent in French literary terminology, where *fantastique* almost always refers to macabre elements, like apparitions from beyond the grave. Italian usage instead associates *fantastico* more freely with "fantasy"; in fact we speak of the "Ariostan fantastic," while according to the French terminology we should say the "Ariostan marvelous.")

The fantastic tale begins with German Romanticism at the start of the nineteenth century, but already in the second half of the eighteenth century the English "gothic" novel had explored a repertory of motives, settings, and effects (especially macabre, cruel, frightening) that the Romantic writers dipped into freely. And given that one of the earliest outstanding names among these (because of the perfect result of his *Peter Schlemihl*) belongs to a German, Adelbert von Chamisso, who was born French, and who brings a very French eighteenth-century lightness into his crystalline German prose, the French element also appears from the start as essential. The legacy left by the French eighteenth century to Romanticism's fantastic tale has two elements: the spectacular display of the "marvelous tale" (from the *féerique* of the court of Louis XIV to the Oriental phantasmagoria of the *Thousand and One Nights*, discovered and translated by Galland) and the swift, sharp linearity of the Voltairean "philosophical tale," where nothing is superfluous, everything is aiming toward an end.

As the eighteenth-century "philosophical tale" had been the paradoxical expression of enlightenment Reason, so the "fantastic tale" arises in Germany as the waking dream of philosophical idealism, with the declared intention of representing the reality of the inner, subjective world, the mind of the imagination, giving it a dignity equal to or greater than that of the objective world of the senses. So it's also a philosophical story, and here one name stands out over all: Hoffmann.

Every anthology has to impose rules and limits; ours imposed the rule of including a single work for each author, which seemed particularly cruel when it came to choosing a single story to represent all of Hoffmann. I chose the most typical and well known (because it's what we could call an "obligatory" text), *The Sandman*, in which characters and images of a quiet bourgeois life are transformed into grotesque, diabolical, terrifying apparitions, as in a bad dream. But I could also have relied on a Hoffmann in which the grotesque is almost absent, like *The Mines of Falun*, where the romantic poetry of nature touches the sublime through the fascination of the mineral world.

The mines in which the young Ellis buries himself to the point where he prefers them to the light of the sun and the embrace of his bride are one of the great symbols of the ideal inner life. And here is another essential point that every discourse on the fantastic has to reckon with: any attempt to define the meaning of a symbol (the shadow lost by Chamisso's Peter Schlemihl, the mines where Hoffmann's Ellis gets lost, the Jews' alley in Arnim's *The Majoratsherren*) only impoverishes the wealth of possibilities.

Apart from Hoffmann, the masterpieces of the German Romantic fantastic are too long to include in an anthology whose aim is to provide as broad a panorama as possible. A length of under fifty pages is another limit I imposed on myself, and it forced me to give up some of my favorite works, which all have the dimensions of the long story or short novel: the Chamisso I already mentioned, Arnim's *Isabella of Egypt* and other wonderful writings, and Eichendorff's *Memoirs of a Good-for-Nothing.* Including only a few of the best sections would have meant breaking the third rule I set for myself: including only complete stories. (I made a single exception, for Potocki, but his novel *The Manuscript Found in Saragossa* contains stories that have a certain autonomy, although they're closely interwoven.)

If we consider how widespread Hoffmann's explicit influence is on the various European literatures, we can say that, at least for the first half of the nineteenth century, "fantastic tale" is synonymous with "Hoffmann-like tale." In Russian literature Hoffmann's influence bears wonderful fruit like Gogol's *Petersburg Tales*; but it has to be said that before any European inspiration Gogol had written extraordinary macabre stories in the two books of Ukrainian tales. The critical tradition has always looked at nineteenth-century Russian fiction from the perspective of realism, but a parallel current of the fantastic—from Pushkin to Dostoyevsky—is equally evident; and it's in this area that a great writer like Leskov achieves his full proportions.

In France, Hoffmann has a strong influence on Charles Nodier, on Balzac (on the explicitly fantastic Balzac and on the realist Balzac with his grotesque nocturnal evocations), and on Théophile Gautier, who is at the start of a branch growing out of the Romantic trunk that became important in the fantastic tale's development: aestheticism.

As for the philosophical background, in France the fantastic is colored by early esotericism, from Nodier to Nerval, and by Swedenborgian theosophy, in Balzac and Gautier. And Gérard de Nerval creates a new genre of the fantastic: the dream story (*Sylvie, Aurélia*), sustained by lyrical density rather than by plot. As for [Prosper] Mérimée, with his Mediterranean stories (but also northern: the evocative Lithuania of *Lokis*), with his skill at capturing the light and soul of a place in an image that immediately becomes emblematic, he opens a new dimension to the fantastic: exoticism.

England puts a special intellectual pleasure into playing with the macabre and terrifying: the most famous example is Mary Shelley's *Frankenstein*. The sentimentality and humor of the Victorian novel leave a margin for a revival of the "black," "gothic" imagination, with a new spirit: the ghost story is born, whose authors perhaps give an ironic wink but meanwhile stake something of themselves, an inner truth that doesn't fall within the mannerisms of the genre. Dickens's propensity for the grotesque and the macabre is expressed not only in the great novels but also in the minor production of Christmas fables and ghost stories. I say *production* because Dickens (like Balzac) planned and disseminated his own work with the determination of someone operating in an industrial and commercial world (his indisputable masterpieces also originated in that way), and edited journals of fiction written mainly by him but for which he also organized contributions from friends. Among those writers of his circle (including the first author of detective novels, Wilkie Collins), there is one who has an important place in the history of the fantastic: Le Fanu, from an Irish Protestant family, the first exemplar of the "professional" author of ghost stories, in that he wrote almost nothing else besides ghost and horror stories. He thus establishes a "specialization" of the fantastic story that developed widely in our century (at the level of both popular and high-quality literature, but often straddling the two). That doesn't imply that Le Fanu should be considered a mere hack (as Bram Stoker, the creator of Dracula, was later), on the contrary: animating his stories is the drama of the religious controversies, the popular Irish imagination, and a grotesque nocturnal poetic vein (see *Judge Harbottle*) in which we recognize Hoffmann's influence yet again.

Common to all these diverse authors I've named so far is the emphasis on a visual evocativeness. And it's not a coincidence; as I said at the start, the true theme of the nineteenth-century fantastic tale is the reality of what is seen: to believe or not to believe in phantasmagoric apparitions, to see behind the everyday appearance another world, enchanted or infernal. It's as if more than any other narrative genre, the fantastic tale were obliged to "show us," to take shape in a series of images, to entrust its communicative force to the power of creating "figures." Mastery in manipulating words or in pursuing the flashes of an abstract thought counts far less than the vividness of a complex and unusual scene. The element of "spectacle" is essential to the fantastic narrative: it's natural that the cinema has found so much sustenance in it.

But we can't generalize. If in the majority of cases the Romantic imagination creates around itself a space populated by visionary apparitions, there is also the fantastic tale in which the supernatural remains invisible, is "felt" rather than "seen," becomes part of an inner dimension, like state of mind or conjecture. Even Hoffmann, who so liked to evoke distressing and diabolical images, has stories that, unfolding with a strict economy of the spectacular element, are created entirely from images of daily life. In *The Deserted House*, for example, the closed windows of a run-down cottage amid the wealthy edifices of Unter den Linden, a woman's arm and then a girl's face looking out are enough to create a mysterious expectation, and all the more when these movements are observed not directly but reflected in an ordinary mirror that acquires the function of a magic mirror.

We find the clearest example of these two directions in Poe. His most typical stories are those in which a dead woman, dressed in white, emerges bleeding from a coffin in a dark house whose opulent furnishings emanate an air of decay; "The Fall of the House of Usher" constitutes the richest elaboration of this model. But let's look instead at "The Telltale Heart": the visual suggestiveness is reduced to the minimum, focused on an eye wide open in the darkness, and all the tension is concentrated in the murderer's monologue.

To deal with the "visionary" aspects of the fantastic and those I would call "mental" or "abstract" or "psychological" or "daily," I had first thought of choosing two stories, representative of the two directions, by every author. But I soon realized that in the early nineteenth century the "visionary" fantastic clearly predominated, just as the "daily" fantastic predominated toward the end of the century, to reach its intangible peak of elusiveness with Henry James. I understood, that is, that by leaving out only a minimum of works from the original project, I could unify the chronological order and the stylistic classification, organizing the first volume under the banner of the "visionary fantastic," and including works of the first three decades of the century, and under the banner of the "daily fantastic" the second, which goes up to the start of the twentieth century. A little strain is inevitable in operations like this, based on contrasting definitions: in some cases the labels are interchangeable and stories in one series could also be assigned to the other; but what's important is that the general direction be clear, that is, toward the internalization of the supernatural.

Poe was, after Hoffmann, the author who had the greatest influence on the European fantastic: Baudelaire's translation was supposed to function as the manifesto of a new approach to literary taste; and the macabre and "horror" effects were more readily acknowledged in its success than the rational lucidity that is Poe's most vital distinguishing quality. I mention his European success first because at home the figure of Poe did not seem as emblematic, such that he was identified with a separate literary genre. Beside him, or slightly preceding him, was another great American who had achieved an extraordinary intensity in the fantastic tale: Nathaniel Hawthorne.

Among the authors represented in this anthology, Hawthorne is certainly the one who goes farthest into the moral and religious depths, both in the drama of the individual conscience and in presenting unadorned a world forged by extreme religiosity, like that of Puritan society. Many of his stories are masterpieces (of the visionary fantastic, like the sabbath of "Young Goodman Brown," or the introspective fantastic, like "Egotism; or, The Bosom-Serpent") but not all: when he abandons American settings (as in the too famous "Rappaccini's Daughter") his inventiveness can indulge in more predictable effects. But at his most successful, the moral allegories, always based on the indelible presence of sin in the heart of man, have a power of visualizing the inner drama that in our century was achieved only by Franz Kafka. (There is even an anticipation of Kafka's *Castle* in one of Hawthorne's best and most disturbing stories: "My Kinsman, Major Molineux.")

It has to be said that in the literature of the United States even before Hawthorne and Poe the fantastic had a tradition and a classic of its own: Washington Irving. Nor should we forget an emblematic story like "Peter Rugg, the Missing Man," by William Austin (1824). A mysterious divine curse condemns a man to drive his carriage ceaselessly, along with his daughter, pursued by a storm across the immense geography of the continent. The story expresses with primitive force the elements of the nascent American myth: the power of nature, individual predestination, adventurous tension.

Thus Poe (unlike the Romantics of the early nineteenth century) inherits a tradition of the fantastic that is already mature, and this he hands down to his followers, who often are merely epigones and mannerists (although rich in the color of the era, like Ambrose Bierce). Not until Henry James will we come to a new turning point.

In France, Poe, having become French through Baudelaire, wasn't long in gaining followers. And the most interesting of them in the specific area of the short story is Villiers de l'Isle-Adam, who in "Véra" creates an effective setting for the theme of love that continues beyond the grave, and in "A Torture by Hope" one of the greatest examples of the purely psychological fantastic. (Roger Callois and Borges, in their anthologies of the fantastic, choose, respectively, "Véra" and "A Torture by Hope"; both, especially the second, are excellent choices, and if I offer a third story it is mainly in order not to repeat the selections of others.)

The pathways that the fantastic will take in the twentieth century open up mainly in England. And in England we can distinguish a refined type of writer who likes to disguise himself as a popular writer, and succeeds because he does it with enjoyment and professional commitment, and no trace of condescension, which is possible only when one knows that without the techniques of the trade no artistic knowledge is of value. Robert Louis Stevenson is the happiest example of this state of mind; but alongside him we have to consider two extraordinary cases of inventive genius and, at the same time, craftsmanlike precision: Kipling and Wells.

The fantastic of Kipling's Indian stories is exotic not in the aestheticizing and decadent sense but in that it arises from the conflict between the religious, moral, and social world of India and the English world. The supernatural is very often an invisible if terrifying presence, as in "The Mark of the Beast"; sometimes, as in "The Bridge Builders," the scene of daily work is torn apart and the ancient divinities of Hindu mythology appear in a vision. Kipling also wrote many fantastic stories with English settings where the supernatural is almost always invisible (as in "They") and the anguish of death is paramount.

With Wells, science fiction begins, offering a new horizon of the imagination that develops swiftly in the second half of our century. But Wells's genius lies not only in hypothesizing the wonders and terrors of the future, in unfurling apocalyptic visions; his extraordinary stories are always based on an intellectual trick that can be very simple. "The Story of the Late Mr. Elvesham" is about a young man who is chosen by an old man, a stranger, as his sole heir on condition that he agrees to take the old man's name. And here he is waking in the old man's house; he looks at his hands, and they're all wrinkled; he looks in the mirror, and he is the old man. He realizes that at the same moment, he who was the old man has taken his identity and person and is living his youth. Outwardly everything has the same, normal appearance of before; but the reality is a boundless fear.

The author who most subtly combines the refinement of an accomplished writer and the impetus of the popular narrator (among his favorite authors, he always cited Dumas) is Robert Louis Stevenson. In his short life as an invalid he managed to create so many perfect things, from adventure novels to *Dr. Jekyll* and many shorter fantastic stories: "Olalla," the story of a vampire in Napoleonic Spain (the same setting as Potocki; I don't know if he had ever read him); "Thrown Janet," a story about Scottish witches' obsessions; "Island Nights' Entertainments," in which with a light hand he catches the magic of exoticism (but also exports Scottish themes, adapting them to Polynesian settings); "Markheim," which follows the path of the internalized fantastic, as in Poe's "Telltale Heart," but in which the Puritan conscience has a more conspicuous presence.

One of Stevenson's most enthusiastic admirers and friends is Henry James, a writer who has nothing at all popular about him; and it's with this writer, whom we don't know whether to call American or English or European, that the nineteenth-century fantastic has its final incarnation—or rather disincarnation, in that it becomes more than ever invisible and impalpable, a psychological emanation or vibration. Here we have to put in the background the intellectual world in which the work of Henry James has its origin, and in particular the theories of his brother, the philosopher William James, regarding the psychic reality of experience: and so we might say that at the end of the century the fantastic tale again becomes the philosophical tale, as it was at the start of the century.

The ghosts of Henry James's ghost stories are as elusive as ever: they can be faceless and formless incarnations of evil like the diabolical servants of *The Turn of the Screw* or visible apparitions that give sensible form to a dominant thought, as in "Sir Edmund Orme," or mystifications that unleash the true presence of the supernatural, as in "The Ghostly Rental." In one of the most evocative and emotional stories, "The Jolly Corner," the ghost barely glimpsed by the protagonist is the self he would have been if his life had taken another course; in "Private Life" there is a man who exists only when others look at him, otherwise he dissolves, and one who, instead, exists twice, because he has a double who writes the books that he would never be able to write.

With James, an author who belongs to the nineteenth century chronologically but to our century as a literary taste, this review concludes. I've left out the Italian authors because I didn't want them to appear only out of obligation: the fantastic remains in nineteenth-century Italian literature a truly "minor" field. Special collections (*Poesie e racconti* by Arrigo Boito, and *Racconti neri della scapigliatura*),* like certain works by writers better known for other

---

* A. Boito, *Poesie e racconti* (Milan: Oscar Mondadori, 1981); G. Finzi, ed., *Racconti neri della scapigliatura* (Milan: Oscar Mondadori, 1980)

aspects of their oeuvre, from De Marchi to Capuana, can offer valuable discoveries and interesting documentation on the level of taste. Among the other literatures that I've left out, Spanish has a well-known author of fantastic tales, G. A. Bécquer. But this anthology doesn't aspire to completeness. It's a panorama centered on some examples that I wanted to offer, and above all it's a book just to read.

[1983]

Seven Flasks of Tears

"'Seven flasks of tears have I filled, / seven long years of bitter tears: / you sleep despite my desperate cries, / the cock crows, and you won't wake.'" Thus Carducci [in "Before San Guido"] recalling the stories his grandmother told. The lines sound like a genuine example of Tuscan folklore, and the first conclusion we can draw is this: the weeping of popular narrative can be assessed in quantitative terms, in units of measure: "seven flasks of tears."

Unlike other psychological manifestations, crying consists of a material production: it is made concrete in tears. In the special logic of fables, every object has its practical efficacy: a given quantity of tears should obtain compensation for the sorrow that was the cause of the tears, for example to revive the beloved person (given that the fable always tries to reestablish a lost harmony or repair an injustice of fate).

The first literary testimony of popular fabulist motifs, G. B. Basile's *Pentamerone*, in the seventeenth-century Neapolitan baroque, opens with the story of Princess Zosa, condemned (in retaliation for an untimely laugh) to fill a pitcher with tears in three days; if she does this she will be able to revive the prince. (But she falls asleep before the pitcher is full and her rights are usurped by a lying slave.)

The Cinderella of the Brothers Grimm (Aschenputtel) is different from the better known one of Perrault in that she waters her mother's grave with tears: out of it grows a magic tree that fulfills all the desires of the forsaken girl. The famous Russian folklorist Vladimir Propp (*Oedipus in the Light of Folklore*) studied the motif of the tree that grows out of the grave, linking it to traditions of ritual weeping.

From the material aspect of shedding tears we move on to the social: crying as a ritual institution, the codification of mourning, that is, an attempt to limit the crisis of the loss that destroys the structure of the world (see the famous book by Ernesto De Marino [*Magic: A Theory from the South*, 1959]). It's as if the relief brought by weeping extended to the universe, in order to reestablish an image of harmony. Already in the classical myths the abundance of tears had that function: Ovid tells stories of nymphs who weep so much they are transformed into fountains.

Fables also represent other social aspects of crying: its relevance to behavior in front of others. Abandoned in the woods, Hop-o'-My-Thumb (Pollicino; Perrault's Petit Poucet) doesn't cry, while his brothers burst into tears; thus in the Grimms, in the same situation, Hansel doesn't cry, while his sister Gretel does. In these cases crying is devalued as a weakness: in fact it's the one who doesn't cry (Hop-o'-My-Thumb, Hansel) who gets busy finding a solution. But in these same fairy tales crying is also valued as a sign of moral sensitivity, piety, goodness: in Perrault, the mother weeps at the thought of having to abandon her children in the woods, and the wife of the ogre weeps thinking of the fate that awaits the unfortunates who have knocked at her door. (These tears are absent, however, in the Brothers Grimm, who must have had a fairly negative view of women: it's the mother of Hansel and Gretel who decides and cruelly insists on abandoning them in the woods, where in the end they'll find a devouring witch rather than a male ogre.)

We can say, in short, that when we try to define more carefully a phenomenon like crying, which might be thought to belong more than any other to the sphere of psychology, of feelings, of the soul, we accentuate either its physiological materiality (like Descartes, who to specify what distinguishes the passions of the soul had first to recognize everything that pertains to the body) or its cultural, that is, linguistic, aspect.

The two aspects are not completely separate, since language begins with the wail of the newborn who wants to be fed or at least get his mother's attention: and he does it by crying. Darwin sees this clearly, in his entirely biological conception (see the wonderful volume *The Expression of the Emotions in Man and Animals*, 1872). The origin of crying is explained by Darwin on two levels: phylogenetically, as a mechanism of secretion to protect the cornea, which develops when our ancestors descend from trees and, adapting to life on earth, encounter the annoying problem of dust in their eyes; and ontogenetically, as the tendency of infants to wail when they're uncomfortable (an effort that leads them to contract the orbicular muscle, provoking the lachrymal secretion). That tendency is perpetuated in adulthood as a conditioned reflex that causes only crying, not wailing.

For the other aspect, the cultural, this statement of the great ethnologist Marcel Mauss (*Il linguaggio dei sentimenti* ["The Obligatory Expression of Feelings"] [Milan: Adelphi, 1975]) is sufficient: "Tears, and every sort of oral expression of feelings, are not exclusively psychological or physiological phenomena but are social phenomena, distinguished above all by lack of spontaneity and the most perfect obligation." Using as an example mourning rituals among the Australian aborigines, Mauss demonstrates that crying is an elaborate and codified language, but "this convention and this regularity do not at all exclude sincerity. No more than in our own funeral customs. It is all, at the same time, social and obligatory, and yet violent and natural; search and expression of sorrow go together."

I think this should be kept in mind today when, it seems to me, crying is being rehabilitated as emotional spontaneity in contrast to the ethics of "stoic and manly" self-repression. All right, but don't forget that the military and "Spartan" era in which some European generations, up to and including mine, were raised had two ever-present faces: one teary-eyed and the other dry-eyed, with a good measure of smugness and deception in both.

Mauss's essay drew inspiration from a study by Georges

Dumas in *Traité de psychologie* (*Treatise on Psychology*), 1923, that had first described "the language of tears." Dumas's essay has a richness and intelligence that we're no longer used to (the descriptive psychology of the nineteenth century provided a type of empirical knowledge whose loss is not made up for by the gains of psychoanalysis). In it he says that the child cries to attract the compassion of others, the adult to demonstrate to others his own compassion: "It's also true that we sometimes weep alone, in the presence only of our own memories, but most of the time because we are mentally addressing someone and imagine ourselves in a scene of social life."

Dumas makes the interesting observation that the eyes fill with tears when a strong emotion can't be translated into movements, gestures, action. This explains tears of rage and impotence. (According to Darwin, crying is not specific to human beings; there is at least one animal that weeps hot tears—the elephant in captivity, when it can't unleash the energy of its enormous muscular mass.) And this would also explain how we can shed tears in the theater or reading a book; that is, contemplating from the immobility of our chairs facts that would provoke an active reaction if they were taking place in real life.

This leads me to mention the value and negative value of emotional and sentimental literature. Ulysses at the court of the Phaeacians listens to a bard who sings of his adversities (as if *The Odyssey* were already circulating); and that unshakable pillar bursts into sobs. The episode defines the emotive mechanism well: we are moved because we identify with the story that's being told; and on the other hand what in life can be confronted dry-eyed becomes a torture when we are present as a spectator at a play.

We could review the history of the epic, tragedy, and the novel to identify the various strategies in the management of emotion. I think the triumph of the weepy sentimental begins in the eighteenth century, with the novels of Richardson, but also at that time the tears of unfortunate girls become a stimulus of perverse pleasure in Sade's teeming phantasmagoria. From then on, a suspicion of sadism attaches to novelists who enjoy striking the chords of pitiful sentimentality and spare no effects to make readers male and female cry. We have the example of De Amicis's *Cuore*, written with the intention of giving a population of cynics a sentimental education, and forgetting that the worse risk is to end up with weepy cynics.

The most complete example of the phenomenology of crying in literature is in Jules Verne's *Michel Strogoff*. The tsar's courier is captured by the Tartars, along with other prisoners, but his identity has not yet been securely established. To force him to reveal himself, the Tartars make the prisoners parade in front of Strogoff's old mother, certain that emotion will betray them. But mother and son, restraining their tears, remain impassive. The Tartars then start whipping the old woman, and Strogoff leaps up, tears the knout out of the torturer's hand, and slashes his face. There's no longer any doubt that it's he: Will he be killed? No, he will be blinded, as a spy who wished to see too much. The burning blade of a scimitar is run over his eyes, while his mother faints. The tsar's courier is blinded. After various other events the final coup de théâtre is based on the fact that the supposed blind man saw very clearly. How in the world? When Strogoff saw that his mother was compelled to be present at the torture, his eyes filled with tears that made a screen protecting them from the flash of the blade, saving his sight.

Tears as sentiment and as signal, tears restrained as proof of strength of mind, tears as physiological protection for the eyes and as magic tool of salvation: it seems to me that nothing is missing.

[1984]

The Fantastic in Italian Literature

I will begin with a quotation:

RUYSCH (*outside his laboratory, looking through the keyhole*):* Good Lord! Who taught these dead people music, singing like cocks at midnight? The truth is, I'm in a cold sweat, and nearly deader than they are. I didn't think that because I saved them from decay they would be revived. So it is: with all my philosophy, I'm shaking from head to toe. That devil that tempted me to have those people in my house was evil. I don't know what to do. If I leave them shut in here, how do I know they won't break down the door, or go out through the keyhole, and come and find me in bed? Calling for help because I'm afraid of the dead doesn't appeal to me. Come on, let's be brave, and try to make them afraid.

(*Entering*) Children, what's the game we're play-

---

* The stage direction was added from Leopardi and is not in Calvino. (*Translator's note*)

ing? Don't you remember you're dead? What's all this uproar? Maybe you're proud of that visit from the tsar, and you think you're not subject to the laws anymore? I imagine you intended this as a joke, not for real. If you are revived, I rejoice with you; but I don't have so much that I can support the living, as well as the dead; and so take yourselves out of my house. If it's true what is said about vampires, and you are those, look for other blood to drink; I am not willing to let mine be sucked, as I have been liberal with the fake blood, which I put in your veins. In short, if you will continue to be peaceful and silent, as you were up to now, we will remain in pleasant harmony, and you will lack nothing in my house; if not, be warned that I will grab the bar of the door and kill you all.

DEAD PERSON: Don't get angry; I promise you we'll all stay dead as we are, without your killing us.

RUYSCH: So what's this idea of singing that's got into you?

DEAD PERSON: A short time ago, at midnight exactly, the great mathematical year was completed for the first time, about which the ancients write so many things; and this likewise is the first time that the dead have spoken. And all the dead in every cemetery and sepulcher, in the depths of the sea, beneath the snow and the sand, under the open sky, and wherever they are to be found, have like us sung the song you have just heard.

We might call this a perfect setup for a fantastic story. But it's the start of one of Leopardi's dialogues: the *Dialogue Between Frederik Ruysch and His Mummies*. Frederik Ruysch was a Dutch scientist who lived from 1638 to 1731 and was famous throughout Europe as the inventor of a system of mummification of corpses that gave them a lifelike appearance. Leopardi, who had read a eulogy of Ruysch written by Fontenelle, imagines that one night the Dutch scientist surprises the dead singing and talking. (And here Leopardi also leans on a classic tradition: the marvels that accompany the completion of the *annus magnus*, or cosmic cycle, that Cicero talks about in *De natura deorum*.) Given that the dead have the faculty of speech for a quarter of an hour, Ruysch interrogates them on the sensations they felt at the moment of passing: Pain? Fear? In keeping with Leopardi's philosophy, the mummies explain that death is the cessation of every faculty of feeling, therefore of all pain, therefore it is what might be defined as a pleasure. And yet all the dead say that up to the last they continued to hope to be able to go on living, even for an hour or two. Ruysch asks:

> But how did you know at the end, that the spirit had left the body? Tell me: How did you know you were dead? They don't answer. Children, don't you understand me? A quarter of an hour must have passed. Let's try them a little. They're good and dead again: there's no danger that they'll frighten me again: let's go back to bed.

So the dialogue concludes. The date when Leopardi wrote it takes us back to the years when German Romanticism was disseminating throughout Europe a taste for stories in which fear of the macabre and the supernatural was tinged with irony. It's unlikely that this vogue had reached Leopardi, who didn't love the Romantics and didn't read novels or stories. Still, the dialogue of Ruysch and the mummies introduces some of the themes that more often return in the fantastic fiction of the nineteenth century: the scientist who challenges the laws of nature until one night his audacity is put to a hard test; the ancient myth that turns out to be true; the supernatural world that opens up for a fleeting moment and immediately closes shut again. All the rest is typically Leopardian, and oriented in a very different direction: the rejection of every terrestrial or extraterrestrial illusion, the reality of life seen as suffering without redemption. But Leopardi wouldn't be Leopardi without the lightness of an ever-present irony, without the affirmation that hope, even if vain, is the only positive moment of human life, and that our sole comfort is in the treasures of imagination and the beauty of poetic language. These are characteristics that Leopardi shares with the spirit of his contemporaries who founded fantastic literature: Chamisso, Hoffmann, Arnim, Eichendorff. And if we recall that the fantastic narrators of Romanticism drew on the nascent German idealist philosophy, and that this had as its background the crisis of Rousseau's faith in the benevolence of nature and the crisis of Voltaire's faith in the progress of civilization, we can see that Leopardi emerges from the same situation, even if his response is different. So there is a historical and philosophical bond, common to the Romantics and the anti-Romantic Leopardi, which is at the origin of the modern fantastic, and it's the bond that ties the fantastic tale as it originates in Germany in the early nineteenth century to its direct predecessor and simultaneously opposes it: that is, the *conte philosophique* of the Century of Enlightenment. As the philosophical tale was the paradoxical expression of enlightenment Reason, so the fantastic tale originates as a waking dream of philosophical idealism, with the stated intention of representing the reality of the inner subjective world, giving it a dignity equal to or greater than the world of objectivity and the senses. So it, too, is a philosophical tale, and such it remains until today, even through all the changes in the intellectual landscape.

I lingered on this point to try to understand how the fantastic element in Italian literature fails just when it triumphs in other European literatures. The "horror" fantastic asserts itself in German, French, English, and Russian literature but in Italy remains a marginal element, not represented by important works; for example, Italy did not have a romantic revival of the popular world of legends, such as Spain had with Gustavo Adolfo Bécquer.

And I lingered on Leopardi in particular because in this great lyric poet and prose writer, profoundly immersed in classical culture and perhaps for that reason the most modern then and now, the Leopardi who despised all novels except *Don Quixote*, there exists a nucleus of the fantastic that we glimpse in some of his dialogues, or in the fragment of a poem that describes a dream in which the moon separates from the sky and comes to rest on a meadow.

ALCETA
Listen, Melisso: I want to tell you a dream
I had last night, which comes to mind,
seeing the moon again. I was standing
at the window that looks out on the meadow
staring up, when suddenly the moon
unhooked herself. And it seemed to me
that as she fell,
the nearer she got the bigger she looked, until
she hit the ground in the middle of the meadow,
big as a bucket, and vomited
a cloud of sparks that shrieked as loud
as when you dunk a live coal in the water
and drown it. So, as I said,
the moon died in the middle of the meadow,
little by little slowly darkening,
and the grass was smoking all around.
Then, looking up into the sky, I saw
something still there, a glimmer or a shadow,
or the niche that she'd been torn away from,
which made me cold with fear. And I'm still anxious.

MELISSO
You were right to be afraid, when the moon
fell so easily into your field.

ALCETA
Who knows? Don't we often see
stars fall in summer?

MELISSO
     There are so many stars
that if one or another of them falls
it's no great loss, since there are thousands left.
But there's just this one moon up in the sky,
*which no one saw fall ever—except in dreams.**

This is the true seed from which the Italian fantastic was able to emerge because the fantastic, contrary to what may be believed, requires a clear mind, control of reason over instinctive or unconscious inspiration, stylistic discipline; it requires knowing at the same time how to separate and how to mix fiction and truth, play and fear, attraction and repulsion, that is, to read the world on multiple levels and in multiple languages at the same time.

Maybe we have to go farther back into the history of literature and see how, during the eighteenth century, all the continents of the imagination were explored, from the *féeries* of the Sun King's court to Galland's translation of the *Thousand and One Nights* to the English gothic novel. In Italy the theatrical fables of Carlo Gozzi mark not a beginning but an end: the end of the tradition of the marvelous that had been the most generous lifeblood of Italian liter-

---

* Giacomo Leopardi, *Canti*, trans. Jonathan Galassi (New York: Farrar, Straus and Giroux, 2010)

ature for centuries. I here adopt the distinction made by French criticism between the "marvelous," of the *contes des fées,* or fairy tales, and the *Thousand and One Nights,* and the "fantastic," which implies an interior dimension, a doubt about seeing and believing. But the distinction isn't always possible, and in Italy the term *fantastic* has a much broader meaning, which includes the marvelous, the fabulous, the mythological. Thus the chivalric poems revisited by the poets of the Renaissance: Pulci, Boiardo, Ariosto, Tasso, and the baroque mythological poem of Cavalier Marino. Thus the storytellers who gave literary form to the folktale, Masuccio Salernitano, Straparola, and the baroque Neapolitan Giambattista Basile; thus Bandello, in whose infinite repertory of dramatic stories Shakespeare found the seed of many of his plays.

We can say that the marvelous has always been present in the Italian tradition: the book from Latin antiquity that has been continuously read, even during the Middle Ages, is Ovid's *Metamorphosis.* Perhaps that trend stops in the eighteenth century, and both Italian classicism and Italian Romanticism were originally too preoccupied with proving themselves serious and responsible to give in to the fantastic.

What could have been the obstacle? An exaggerated devotion to reason? On the contrary: perhaps too little. Fantastic literature is always—or almost always—sustained by a rational plan, a structure of ideas, a thought following an internal logic to its ultimate consequences.

Or might the obstacle have been a too lively moral preoccupation? No, for those who explore their own conscience, the sole means of expression is symbols; and it's in the symbolic dimension that fantastic literature lives. The symbol as image of an interior reality not otherwise definable: the lost shadow of Chamisso's Peter Schlemihl in what is perhaps the best fantastic tale ever written, or the mines of Falun in Hoffmann's stupendous story, which was later reworked for the theater by Hofmannsthal. Italy, instead, acquired a new fantastic life in the works of foreign writers. It could be said that Italy and Spain had a parallel fortune in international literary themes. One of the first and most evocative examples of the Romantic fantastic is *Manuscript Found at Saragozza*, written in French by the Polish count Jan Potocki in 1805, and rediscovered only twenty-five years ago by Roger Callois, a great connoisseur of the fantastic in every time and place. Potocki's book offers a complete repertory of the literary conventions, portraying Spain as the country of mysterious, adventure-filled exoticism. These apparitions and atmospheres continue to sustain the works of foreign writers up to Robert Louis Stevenson, whose "Olalla" starts with the same situation as Potocki's novel: an officer of the Napoleonic wars who gets lost among Iberian mysteries, grappling with insidious vampire women.

(Could Stevenson have read Potocki? I don't know if any research has been done to determine that. If he hadn't read it, that is an even more convincing proof that this repertory of themes had entered the collective imagination.)

The same can be said for Italy. In the tradition of the

"gothic novel," ghost stories, the shadowy supernatural, Italy has always been a favorite setting. Old cities in which the medieval and Renaissance past, dense with crimes and mysteries, is indissolubly interwoven with everyday life seem built purposely to suggest that doubling of reality which sets off the narrative mechanism of this literary genre. At least that's the case for the writers of fantastic tales who have felt most strongly attracted by Italy, from Hoffmann to Hawthorne, from Théophile Gautier to Henry James. Even earlier, the English "horror novels" situated their cursed castles in an improbable Otranto (Walpole) or in the Apennine Mountains (Radcliffe). Eichendorff's *The Marble Statue* takes place in Lucca; more recently Vernon Lee, a knowledgeable English Italianist, wrote fantastic stories set in Urbino and Foligno.

Why only foreign writers? Evidently, this effect of disorientation and doubling acts on those who look at our cities from a distance that makes them exotic, while for Italian writers of the nineteenth century what prevailed was either the cult of local history (and so they went directly into the past, via historical novels) or the daily reality of provincial traditions (and this portrait of an ambience dominates even in the twentieth century, in the few examples of first-rate ghost stories that Italian literature can boast, such as those of Tommaso Landolfi and Mario Soldati).

Only in our century, when fantastic literature, having lost any romantic vagueness, established itself as a lucid mental construction, could an Italian fantastic come into being, and that happened just when Italian literature was identified above all with the legacy of Leopardi, that is, with a disenchanted, bitter, ironic clarity of gaze.

When I began writing, the contemporary Italian authors in whom I recognized an inflection of the fantastic were two masters of the older generation, Aldo Palazzeschi, a poet and storyteller whose grotesque imagination had an extraordinary lightness, and Massimo Bontempelli, with his geometric, crystalline imagination, and, especially, two writers of the generation in between, Dino Buzzati and Tommaso Landolfi. Buzzati and Landolfi were two absolutely opposite types of writers. Buzzati, who had a northern fantastic streak and an instinctive narrative mastery, was a journalist and wrote his stories tirelessly for newspapers, far from literary and intellectual circles, with extraordinary results when he didn't give in to the facility of his inspiration; Landolfi, on the other hand, was an ultrasophisticated, polyglot intellectual, the wonderful translator of Leskov and Hofmannsthal, a last aristocratic gambler and dandy, and his stories are refined pastiches of Romanticism, horror, surrealism, and southern laziness.

But I have to say that, after the Italian classics, my true masters were a great number of foreign writers, and I think that their example led me to try out new forms of fantastic literature. Most of them are from the nineteenth century, but I later added the great authors of our century who were most important for me: Kafka, whom I will never finish exploring and reflecting on; Borges, who opened up a fantastic world of perfect clarity where I seem to have lived forever but that doesn't cease to surprise me; Samuel

Beckett, who presents an extreme experience of the world after the end of the world.

Only in the past ten years has a passion for fantastic literature asserted itself in Italy and indeed become a fashion, and translations of the classics of the genre have multiplied; for a long time I had considered it a personal passion of mine, shared by few. Last year I published an anthology of nineteenth-century fantastic tales in two volumes: the first dedicated mainly to Hoffmann's influence on European literatures, the second to the influence of Edgar Allan Poe. At the same time my anthology choices tried to exemplify what in my view are the two great tendencies of the imagination: the "visionary" fantastic, which evokes spectacular powers, and the "mental" or "abstract" or "psychological" or "everyday" fantastic (each of these qualifiers illuminates an aspect of that tendency, which becomes dominant in the second half of the century, reaching its intangible peak of elusiveness with Henry James).

I will allude here to the main passages of my commentary.*

In my anthology I didn't include Italian authors because, as I said, the fantastic tale was only a minor genre among us in the last century and I didn't want to present my compatriots out of obligation. But there is one author I could certainly have put on the level of the greatest international successes of fantastic literature with passages like this:

---

* A passage taken from the introduction to *Fantastic Tales of the Nineteenth Century*, here on pp. 208–22, has been omitted.

Then a beautiful Girl with blue hair and a white face like a wax image appeared at the window, eyes closed and hands crossed on the chest, who, without moving her lips, said in a little voice that seemed to come from the other world:

"There's no one in this house. They're all dead."

"At least you could open the door!"

"I'm dead, too."

"Dead? Then what are you doing like that at the window?"

"I'm waiting for the coffin that's coming to take me away."

It's one of the most famous books in Italian literature, and famous throughout the world, and it may be the book that has most influenced my imaginary world and my style, because—and I think the majority of my compatriots could say the same thing—it was the first book I read (in fact I already knew the book chapter by chapter before learning to read): *Pinocchio*.

The centenary of *Pinocchio* (1882) was celebrated two years ago. The author of *Pinocchio*, Carlo Collodi, was certainly not Hoffmann or Poe; but the house that turns white in the night, with a girl like a wax statue who looks out a window, would certainly have appealed to Poe. And similarly Hoffmann would have liked the Little Butter Man who drives a silent cart at night, its wheels bound with straw and rags, drawn by twelve pairs of donkeys shod in boots . . . In *Pinocchio* every presence acquires a visual force that is unforgettable: black rabbits that carry a coffin; assassins cloaked in coal sacks who run leaping . . .

Adding the name of *Pinocchio* to this review of favorites that I started with the name of Leopardi, I feel I have paid a debt of gratitude and can conclude my contribution to your conference.

[1985]

Notturno Italiano

The mistake was thinking that to write fantastic tales you had first of all "to believe in it": in the supernatural, in spirits, in magic. The contrary (or almost) is true: the German Romantics, and before them the English "gothics," and after them the American classics of horror and the French symbolists and *maudits* first of all enjoyed telling stories in that genre. They wanted to apply to those constructs and those effects their imagination, their irony, their logic and rationality, paradoxical as they might be. Of course, they had a pronounced taste for the disturbing and the distressing and the macabre, that is, the "nocturnal" aspects of the popular and literary and individual imagination: and thus the willingness to accept the mysterious without immediately having to make it fit with causes and effects, and that sense of "anything is possible" (real or pretended) that allows us to suspend disbelief and realistic judgment and ask ourselves what would emerge "if it were true that . . ."

In short, yes, "they believed in it": "they believed" utterly, but as the writer and the poet believe in their own poetic world, as Ariosto believed in the hippogriff and

Shakespeare in Ariel and Caliban. While those who "believed in it" in another way, as a practice, as science, as lived
"experience"—occultists, illuminati, spiritualists—neither
could nor would ever play with those things; fantastic
literature knows them as characters, not as authors. (I'm
simplifying: I'm well aware that there have been authors
who "believed in it" in both ways; but that doesn't affect
the general sense of what I'm saying.)

The fact is that at the start of the last century, the Italian
Romantics, in the grip of their ethical and patriotic imper-
atives, were eager to insist that they had nothing in common with the "nocturnal" and phantasmagorical arsenal
of northern Romanticism, that the evocation of witches'
sabbaths and other obscurantist superstitions was repug-
nant to the sane popular Italian mind. Of programmatic
declarations like this there were many: of Romantics like
Carlo Porta and Manzoni, of anti-Romantics like Leopardi and Giordani, up to Benedetto Croce. They explain
clearly why the category "fantastic literature" is so empty
in our literary history, precisely in the era when it was
most flourishing elsewhere; they also explain one of the
reasons (certainly not the only one) that our nineteenth
century is so different from that of other great literatures,
less preoccupied than ours with pedagogic respectability
but much more stimulating to the palate, the imagination,
and the intellect.

Enrico Ghidetti, who opens the introduction to his collection of Italian "horror" stories with those citations, finds
no works worthy of being anthologized until around 1870,

fifty years later than the European vogue, and no (what's more important) true originality with respect to foreign examples until this century.

I'm referring to two volumes entitled *Notturno italiano*, the first devoted to fantastic tales of the nineteenth century and the second to those of the twentieth, published by Editori Riuniti, both edited by Enrico Ghidetti (the second in collaboration with Leonardo Lattarulo), who for years has been exploring areas of Italian literature of the past that have remained in the shadows (to him we owe editions of Paolo Valera, Iginio Ugo Tarchetti, the minor Capuana). The overall story of a literary period is revealed not so much by its most celebrated monuments as by the galaxy of the minor and minimal. Scholars like Ghidetti, motivated by this mission (another was the late Glauco Viazzi), have the virtue of rescuing from rapid oblivion voices that perhaps haven't yet said to us all they have to say. (If for nothing else as testimony of trends and fashions of the time; thus we also meet in these pages names that sound unknown—at least to me—like Molineri, Giordano-Zocchi, Bazzero in the nineteenth century, and Enrico Boni and Persio Falchi in the early twentieth.)

The nineteenth-century volume offers more confirmations than surprises. Confirmations: The most gifted (in two opposite directions) are the Boito brothers, Arrigo, always overloaded and congested, and the crude, cold Camillo; the most promising invention (but not always sustained) is Tarchetti's (as here the idea of opposing the deadly power of a jinx by resorting to another, even more powerful jinx). The better constructed and more intense fantastic tales come later, on the threshold of our century, with Remigio Zena (*Confessione postuma* [*Posthumous Confession*], but I will also remember *La cavalcata* [*The Cavalcade*]). And the rare quality of inventive, imaginative, entertaining writing can be found in Faldella (but his stories are uninteresting) and in Imbriani (here represented by what is defined as a "porno-fable," that is, with a different meaning of fantasy, though still "transgressive": the popular marvelous reinvented by the literary game).

When more celebrated authors like Verga or Serao venture into the fantastic they don't do too well; Capuana's bourgeois vampirism is a little better, because it has few pretenses; as for Fogazzaro, he is unrecognizable in the fake-Renaissance flavor of the Venetian tale "Màlgari," but it has its moments of grace, as when the reflections in the sea become the heads and hands of Nereids.

Surprises: Sacchetti and De Roberto. "Da uno spiraglio" ("Through a Crack"), by Roberto Sacchetti, takes place in the valley of Gressoney, where a German dialect is spoken; perhaps that's what triggers the northern fascination of the story, in which a sensitive blind girl moves among the cliffs like a sleepwalker. Federico De Roberto's story is not so much a story as a refined meditation on the impossibility of words to express the silent language of thought, on the ineffability of the interior monologue; the only possible expression of feelings is found in music, in the voice of the organ.

The second volume demonstrates how much richer and

more confident and original the Italian literature of the twentieth century is than that of the nineteenth. Statistically, compared with the twenty-one "nocturnal" authors whom Ghidetti records for the nineteenth century (and I would say none are missing, except perhaps Emilio De Marchi), the twentieth-century volume has thirty-six and could have added many others. An image emerges of an *other* Italian fiction that can coexist with the more substantiated image, that is, the one in which reality of setting, memory, feelings of existence dominate (not a few writers straddle the two).

In the contemporary fantastic the gamble on the imagination, on formal and conceptual invention, is explicit; now you couldn't even pose the problem of "believing or not believing in it." Rather, there is a type of story that we could call the "everyday fantastic," widespread especially in the Anglo-Saxon sphere but almost absent among us, in which everything that happens is part of the usual reality and the supernatural lies only in a mysterious connection or disconnection that emerges amid the facts of every day: "believing or not believing" is a dizzying glimmer that appears for a moment. One could say that this type of story has in Italy a single enthusiast: the Mario Soldati of *Storie di spettri* (*Ghost Stories*), 1962, who with exemplary elegance and restraint reconnects the *notturno* of the late nineteenth century and that of the late twentieth.

If we start reading the works from the beginning, in chronological order, and want to indicate the moment when the Italian fantastic tale separates from nineteenth-century models and becomes something else (or a hundred something elses), we could say 1907, the date of "Il Pilota cieco" ("The Blind Pilot"), by Giovanni Papini, the youthful Papini dear to Borges, who took off from there, all precision and negativity, so different from the Papini we knew later.

For some of the principal exponents of the fantastic in the twentieth century (on the global scale, not just Italian), like Savinio, Buzzati, Landolfi, the selection in *Notturno italiano* sticks to the most famous and now canonical stories: "Casa 'La Vita'" ("The House of Life"), "Sette piani" ("Seven Floors"), "La moglie di Gogol" ("Gogol's Wife"). I was really glad about the Palazzeschi choice, "Ritratto della regina" ("Portrait of the Queen"), a very imaginative fantasy on Palazzeschi in love with a voluptuously female fish. Then there are two names that instill a desire to search again in memory and in the library: Arturo Loria, who should be reevaluated as an Italian master of the short story, for psychological intensity and atmosphere; and Nicola Lisi, whose delicate spells I remember with gratitude.

And there is no lack of surprises. In 1937 Beniamino Joppolo wrote a short story in which a respectable modern-day family secretly has at home an uncle who is a monkey (biological evolution in that family functioned late but at high velocity); the nephew tries to hide this from his bride, who instead finds the fact scientifically interesting and promising. The funny thing is that twenty-seven years later, knowing nothing about it, I wrote a story that, although very different, has exactly the same setup: In the Carboniferous period, a family of land animals has an uncle who has remained a fish; the nephew would like to hide it from his fiancée, who instead is excited about it. Which proves that narrative structures exist on their own, like geometric figures or Platonic ideas or abstract archetypes, and assert themselves in the individual imagination of single authors. It should be noted that no critic (that I recall) has ever discovered this analogy: and that proves that there is no literature less well known than Italian.

The volume contains two jewels. As a perfect modern elaboration of the themes of "gothic" romanticism there is a story by Giorgio Vigolo in which an unknown city, metaphysical and dreamlike, appears in a breach in space and time beyond a Roman palazzo in the neighborhood of Campo de' Fiori. As an absolute innovation of completely mental, geometric "white magic" there is a story by Bontempelli, "Quasi d'amore" ("Almost Love"). It takes place in a hotel like Marienbad and, more precisely, in the window where the shadows of the garden in the dark mingle with the reflections of the illuminated dining room: the hypothesis of an *other* space where the contact between reflections on the inside and shadows on the outside becomes tangible is stunningly verified with a kiss stolen at a distance. An extraordinary piece: a few pages of impeccable art deco stylization and subtle skill in exploiting this labile encounter of inside and outside, transparency and opacity in the surface of the glass. (A metaphor, if you think about it, of literature, and perhaps of the very essence of . . . of what? Well!)

Can we find among the stories chosen by Ghidetti and Lattarulo an element that characterizes the Italian fantastic, or at least a noticeable tendency, a recurring theme? Two authors as different, in fact opposite, as F. T. Marinetti and Tomasi di Lampedusa have told, each in his way, a modern man's love for a mermaid: a classical mermaid, half woman and half fish. Lampedusa has her appear to a professor of Greek in the sea in Sicily, Marinetti creates her himself out of Mediterranean male desire, swimming at Capri.

Recalling that an "atypical" story of Soldati's, "Il caso Motta" ("The Motta Case"), has the same theme, and reading here "Alcina," by Guido Gozzano, in which amid the temples of Agrigento a hunchbacked English archaeologist is transformed into a nymph, I should designate this mythical nucleus, with all its possible variants, as having the most genetic force. And maybe it's true: many modern European writers have attempted the difficult operation of evoking classical myths, whether with irony or fascination, playing on the distance between the northern imagination and the Greco-Latin—whereas Italian writers have taken it on with the familiarity and ease of those who find themselves at home. I think especially of Savinio, whose extreme confidence with mythology—justified by a childhood in Greece—is never parodic irreverence but identification with its continuous polymorphic transformations.

And I also think that perfectly in keeping with this trend is the wonderful story about centaurs that closes *Notturno italiano*, by Primo Levi, a writer whose background is completely different from Savinio's.

The Metamorphoses, in other words, continue their metamorphic life in the literature of today. I mean Ovid's work, the principal source of Italian literature for many centuries; and I mean the book of Apuleius, the origin novel, which not surprisingly inspired Savinio and not surprisingly was translated by Bontempelli.

[1984]

Science, History, Anthropology

The Genealogical Forest

In the preceding "Taccuino,"* Mr. Palomar, who in Mexico had seen a gigantic tree with a very irregular shape, and then in a church a baroque plaster relief depicting a tree with people hanging from the branches, had started digressing on the shape of trees in nature and in culture, and on the symbolism of genealogical trees.

Following the thread of these reflections, he happened to remember the most regular genealogical tree possible, devised by two Italians, a graphic artist and a writer, based on a diagram that starts with one individual of today and goes back to the two parents, the four parents of the parents, the sixteen parents of those four, and so on, taking no account of brothers and sisters but only of direct ancestors. Given that each person has a father and a mother (even "unknown" parents have to appear in a genealogy of this type), the result will be a roughly triangular figure, which has little to do with a tree, because from a point-like apex it spreads into a fan.

---

* "Taccuino di signor Palomar" was a series that ran in the *Corriere della Sera* in the 1970s.

With a diagram like that, you have only to fill in each box with name, last name, dates, place-names, and you have a novel, a novel not written (except for those facts that we could call auxiliary materials of the traditional narrative, but which are already quite difficult to assemble, and, indeed, hardly anyone tries it anymore) but entirely implied in the situations it suggests: a "conceptual" novel.

It's what Carla Vasio has done in *Romanzo storico* (*Historical Novel*), which was published last year by Milano Libri and is one of the most extraordinary Italian books of recent times. We say *book*, but in reality it's a single page, folded and bound, that, based on a drawing devised by the graphic artist Enzo Mari (the result of a series of attempts at a possible universal genealogical tree), contains the name, last name, profession, and place and date of birth and death of five hundred and eleven characters, representing nine generations, that is, going back to the end of the eighteenth century: the closest forebears of a child born in Milan in 1974.

The "novel" consists only in these essential facts, but there is more than enough novelistic material, further enriched by a painstaking accumulation of historical facts. Those bare facts are enough to go back from parents to parents and imagine how they lived, how they met, how they died. (In the case of violent deaths the how is indicated: snake bite for a Tyrolese farmer, stabbing in Marseilles for a smuggler.)

The genealogy of ordinary families is much more lively and picturesque than that of royalty, especially a genealogy

like this in which the author's imagination (always historically plausible) can track the numerous illegitimate descen-
dants. As in every family history, in this genealogical map
there are static, repetitious areas (a family of wood carvers in Ortisei who for five generations are wood carvers;
a branch of Sardinian families who for generations don't
leave the island, although they have very eventful lives and
deaths), sudden leaps from a closed world of peasant mar-
riages to a diversity of ancestors (through the encounter of
a peasant woman with a passing stranger, a Napoleonic soldier, a gypsy), vertical cross-sections of a society linked by
illegitimate origins (Neapolitan sailors, Bourbon officials,
a dynasty of notaries), and more eventful areas, in which
from one generation to the next we here can see a range of
social situations out of a nineteenth-century French novel,
there a summary of Spanish history, and these reconnect
in a distant ramification in the Islamic world, consolidating
the elements of the Mediterranean crucible.

Passing through another crucible of civilization, which
started to boil almost five hundred years ago with the
Spanish soldiers of the conquest landing on the shores of
Mexico, Mr. Palomar recalls the outline of that concise
Historical Novel (in which two fundamental attitudes of
the Italian mind—the sense of dense, stratified history and
the essential nature and functionality of design—merge
in the lasting intention to conceptualize and actualize experience).

It's evening. He's sitting under the porticos of the *zocalo*
in Oaxaca, the square that is the heart of every old colonial

city, green with well-watered low trees that are called al-
mendros but have nothing to do with almonds. The band,
wearing black, plays in the art nouveau–style kiosk. Flags
and slogans greet the visit of the official electoral candidate. The local families walk up and down. The American
hippies wait for the old woman who provides mescal. The
ragged peddlers set out colored fabrics.

When it seems to him that a moment, a place contains
all the elements of the matter, Mr. Palomar feels a sensation like relief, as if starting out from a picture that is
somehow simplified or more absolute he would be able to
rethink everything in an orderly way. But it's a sensation
that doesn't last; the skein immediately gets tangled up
again.

[1976]

Cosmological Models

The irreversibility of time has two aspects. One is manifested in all those processes that, whether they are biological, geological, or astronomical, involve the passage from a simpler and more uniform state to one that is more complex and differentiated: here the "arrow of time" indicates an increase in order, in information. The other aspect is the sugar cube dissolving in the coffee, the perfume evaporating out of the open flask, energy degrading into heat: here the arrow of time marks the opposite direction: an increase in disorder, entropy, dissolution of the universe into a formless dust.

But neither arrow, not "historical" time or "thermodynamic" time, is observable at the microscopic level: the path of a single molecule includes neither information nor entropy, and could very well unfold backward, like film shot in reverse, without any law of physics being disturbed. The time of molecules and atoms is symmetrical and reversible.

To resolve the contradiction between the two arrows of macroscopic time and the absence of arrows of microscopic time, an astronomer at Harvard, David Layzer, in an article in the December issue of *Scientific American*, proposes a new cosmogonic model. It's a, so to speak, "cold" variant of the classic Big Bang theory, the initial explosion.

The difference is that here we no longer have to imagine as a precondition that all the matter of the universe is maximally concentrated in one point; instead it's assumed that in the beginning the universe was devoid of any structure (or information), just as it was without disorder (or entropy)—a frozen universe crystallized into an alloy of metallic hydrogen and helium.

It is in this initial phase of the universe that the properties of time are determined; or, rather, in the first quarter of an hour (a very special quarter of an hour, before any clock or solar system), through the effect of expansion (not explained here, but accepted as a fact). The frozen universe, expanding, shatters into fragments of planetary dimensions that move randomly like molecules of a gas and so end up aggregating in groups, from which the stars will form, along with the galaxies and the clusters of galaxies that we can observe today. Irreversible time begins the moment a first beginning of order and a first beginning of disorder are generated together in the universe, and from that moment they will simply grow together. The universe begins creating itself and destroying itself at the same moment, and so it continues and will continue: without ever unmaking itself completely. And this is certainly an advantage over other models of the universe that can't avert the inevitability of cosmic death.

But how is it possible, if a fundamental law says that the increase of entropy implies a decrease in information, and vice versa?

No, Layzer explains, the velocity of expansion, greatest at the start, is related to changes in density and temperature, and the facts of the system change continually. "Cosmological" time (time of the spatial expansion), "historical" time (time of the construction of macroscopic forms), and "thermodynamic" time (time of the degradation of the universe into randomly wandering particles) are three arrows that proceed in parallel but follow different rhythms, and influence one another by turns. (Thus Layzer, a partisan of the Big Bang, reaches the balanced and harmonic stability of the main rival theory, that of the "steady state.")

And microscopic time? Much of the article is devoted to attempts to move from macroscopic information (and what it implies about predictability, determination, the direction of time) to microscopic information, that is, the movements of molecules, atoms, particles.

If in theory we can conceive the possibility of establishing all the microscopic information of a closed system, in practice we know that closed systems don't exist, that the rest of the universe doesn't stop interfering even in the most heavily armored container. We would then have to consider the entire universe a finite, closed system, of which we can conceive, at least in principle, a complete microscopic description.

Would the arrow of time then become an arbitrary convention? Would past and future become interchangeable? No: The universe can be infinite or finite, it doesn't much matter; what is certain is that it is unlimited, that is, not closed, that is, open at every point and in every direction to all the rest of itself. Information can be only macroscopic, never microscopic. And the foundations of this order, which is in broad terms structured, and which heavenly bodies, biological life, and consciousness work incessantly to produce, rest on an impalpable, unpredictable landslide of microscopic events. If the future of the universe appears less precarious than what we might have feared, that doesn't make it more knowable. Layzer concludes: "Not even the ultimate computer—the universe itself—ever contains enough information to completely specify its own future states."

Mr. Palomar collects cosmological models. He reads and rereads the new article, makes a written summary to be sure of having grasped the essential points, then archives it in his collection, where many other universes are lined up next to one another like butterflies pierced by a pin.

He doesn't claim to offer an opinion on the greater or lesser reliability of one or the other hypothesis, nor does he venture to show any preference. However things are, he expects nothing good from the universe. That's why he feels the need to keep an eye on it.

In general he's more sensitive to suggestions of plastic images than to philosophical implications. Of this whole demonstration what most impressed him is a drawing that illustrates an incidental digression: it depicts a series of representations of probability in various phases of the evolution of a system in time.

In the first drawing, probability is represented as a small sphere in the middle of a large cube; in the second, the sphere has extruded snail horns or little branches of a coral-like plant; in the third, the sphere occupies a large part of the cube but in reality has not increased in volume: it has extended like a bush with increasingly complicated and slender branches.

Mr. Palomar decides to start another collection: of images whose attraction he can't explain and that he feels could signify many things.

[1976]

Montezuma and Cortés

In the gardens of the ancient imperial palace of Mexico
two sumptuously dressed characters are intently playing
totoloque. One of the players is the emperor of the Aztecs
Motecuhzoma (the name will be simplified by the Euro-
peans to Moctezuma or Montezuma), the other is Hernán
Cortés, the Spanish captain who has conquered Mexico.
They calculate the toss of the small gold balls carefully; the
stakes are a handful of jewels, trifling in that city overflowing with gold and precious stones. But if the players are passionate about the match it's because the game represents
the true relationship between them, the great match unde-
cided since the day the Spanish landed on the beaches of
what will be Veracruz. A match whose stakes are immense:
for the Mexicans the end of the world (they don't know it
yet, but they have a presentiment); for the Spanish the start
of a new era. (They don't know it, either, but they know
that in play is their personal fate: as triumphant conquistadores or as failed adventurers; or, even worse, as victims
with their throats cut by obsidian knives on the altar of the
god Huitzilopochtli.)

In the great match, the Spanish have the advantage (the Emperor Montezuma is the prisoner of his foreign guest) and certainly the final outcome is also taken for granted (but one can't yet know: the Spanish have sunk the ships behind them, they're alone, four hundred men isolated on an unknown and hostile continent), but the rules of the game are gradually being set.

An escort of dignitaries from both camps watches the two players toss: grave and impassive the Mexicans, the Spanish always ready to cause a ruckus. Keeping score for Montezuma is a captain, his nephew, for Cortés his right-hand man, Pedro de Alvarado. Alvarado is a hidalgo, like many of those who followed Cortés on the great adventure, but he is also a tough soldier, as they all are, whether of high or low birth; his charm and noble bearing have made him immediately famous at the court of Montezuma, earning him the privilege of being called by the name of the sun god, Tonatiuh. The emperor keeps a sharp watch and notices that Alvarado gives Cortés points even when he loses. Montezuma complains to Cortés: "Tell Tonatiuh not to cheat!" And the chorus of soldiers wails and sneers, before the dismayed Mexican princes.

One question has been torturing Montezuma ever since the Spanish entered his territories: Are they the gods of the prophecy, these foreigners? Aztec mythology tells of a dethroned god, Quetzalcoatl, exiled beyond the ocean; the exiled god's return will mean the end of the Mexican empire and its gods, the start of a new era. If the whites are the sons of Quetzalcoatl who have returned from the west, then it's pointless to oppose them. Now, the whites have miraculous and terrible powers, they command thunder and lightning (firearms), but at the same time they display an eager, disorderly rudeness: the first qualities are recognizable as divine, the second would expose them as human beings. All Montezuma's uncertainties are concentrated on this doubt.

A gigantic Spanish sailor, who guards the august prisoner at night, emits disgusting sounds. Montezuma summons him and asks him not to do it anymore, out of respect for his person; he sends him away with the gift of a gold object. The next night the sailor repeats the sounds, hoping for another gift. That's what the Spanish are like: hardly gods! And yet these unpredictable contrasts make the foreigners even more mysterious: the negative qualities could be signs of the arbitrariness that governs divine behavior. The more vile acts the Spanish commit, the higher might be their origin. For Montezuma the great match at stake is linked to a bet on the divine nature of the invaders of his kingdom.

Whether the whites are gods or men, Montezuma has certainly made the wrong moves from the start: he wanted to keep them distant and ingratiate himself at the same time: through his ambassadors he warned them against coming to see him, thus revealing his fear, and he sent them precious gifts that opened their eyes to the treasures of the New World, exciting their greed; then he tried to annihilate them by laying an ambush in the city of Cholula, with the result that the Cholulani, his allies, were massacred and fear of the whites grew among the populations in the interior. Having failed to keep them away or overpower them, he finally decided to welcome the Spanish as guests—strange hospitality, dominated by a sense of insecurity on both sides, until the guests, to clarify the situation, sequestered the master of the house as a hostage.

Cortés instead managed to play two cards at the same time with absolute evenhandedness and confidence: defender of the populations oppressed by Montezuma and supporter of Montezuma's sovereignty. In one of his first stops on the continent, at Cempoala, to ally himself with the tribes of the Totonachi, burdened by taxes from the Mexicans, he captures and ill-treats Montezuma's tax collectors; then in the middle of the night he frees two of them, heaps kindnesses on them, and sends them back to their sovereign with offers of peace. After defeating the Tlaxcalani, traditional enemies of the Mexicans, in a bloody battle, he forces them to surrender and to form an alliance, but the negotiations take place in the presence of the ambassadors whom Montezuma has decided to send to bring Cortés under control and make him abandon his march on Mexico. Cortés seems to do everything he can to draw the suspicions of all. How can he propose an alliance with the ones while he's negotiating with the others? That is what both the Tlaxcalani and the Mexicans will say to him; and yet this double game conducted in the light of the sun becomes a sign of power: the Tlaxcalani will follow him as his faithful allies to the last, and Montezuma will open the doors of his city even if he appears with the armies of the enemy Tlaxcalani. And when Cortés imprisons him by surprise, Montezuma adapts to being his hostage, because he sees in his imprisonment a confirmation of his own dangerous power: he knows that for Cortés he is useful as an emperor, in the fullness of his dignity and authority.

A strange relationship is established between the Spaniard and Montezuma. Cortés overwhelms the monarch with attentions, tries to dissipate the melancholy of his prison, consoles him, amuses him. For his part Montezuma displays a magnanimous and generous attitude even toward his jailers. The jewels he wins from Cortés in the *tocoloque* games he distributes among the Spanish soldiers who are guarding him, and who immediately brawl, grabbing the precious objects out of his hands. Cortés gives his winnings to Montezuma's grandchildren, but he cheats counting the points. The Spaniards are partly grand lords, partly mean; they always want something more than what is given to them. All the gold and rubies that circulate there are Montezuma's, in the end, even the gifts that Cortés gives: they are gifts of the Aztec emperor or plunder from the cities of his empire. But Montezuma doesn't seem to have any objections: it's in giving that he confirms his own majesty. Maybe he'd prefer the Spanish, starting with Cortés, to be a little less pressing in asking for gifts, in extorting treasures, and a little less quarrelsome in dividing up the booty, but even here the Mexican feels a reason for his superiority, the greatness of the sacrifice that the foreigners don't know and that he tastes every day. But where do you get if you continue along that path? Is the emperor about to admit that the true superiority is in defeat?

The other path would be that of resistance. But the Mexicans would have to revolt to free the imprisoned sovereign. Now, whoever freed Montezuma from the hands of the Spaniards would establish an advantage over him. His nephew Cacama is plotting to free him; Montezuma understands that if his nephew is successful he will become the emperor of Mexico in his place. Power has this logic, that as soon as it discovers it is weak it needs a stronger power to sustain it. So Montezuma as a prisoner suppresses the revolt of the free Cacama, or, rather, lends his imperial authority to Cortés so that he can put down with his iron hand the anti-Spanish revolt. Is he deluded that he is still exercising his sovereignty or does he already know he is only a tool of Cortés? Cortés, not satisfied with the service done for him, immediately asks to be paid: a tribute for the Emperor Charles V. Montezuma can only hope to be freed by the gods. But the gods have turned their backs on him.

No, the games are not over yet: news reaches Mexico City, a dramatic turn not only for Cortés, who expected it, but for Montezuma, who never ceases to be astonished by these white men. A powerful Spanish army has landed under the command of Panfilo de Narvaez, sent to capture and disarm Cortés by order of the Emperor Charles V. Suddenly the imprisoned king understands that Cortés is only one element in a much more complex reality, in which he may be revealed not as one invested with a transcendent authority but as an adventurer outside the law. The whites' machine of power is as complicated and unstable as the Aztec Empire, and can be turned upside down at any moment. While Cortés prepares his army for the clash with Narvaez, Montezuma pulls the strings of a wary double game with the new arrivals, who he hopes will free him. But Cortés knows how to maneuver on the battlefield just as well as in the conflicts of skill in the Spanish colonial bureaucracy: he manages to defeat Narvaez and get back at Montezuma, reproaching him for his disloyalty. The fiction of an alliance between them has vanished.

Just as the illusion of the Aztecs' peaceful acceptance of Spanish dominion vanishes: the insurrection that had long been brewing under the ashes breaks out. Cortés suppresses it by slaughtering the population and destroying the magnificent capital. When the outcome is still uncertain, Cortés tries to take advantage one last time of Montezuma's little remaining authority: he sends him to preach peace to the ferocious crowd. The crowd responds by throwing stones, Montezuma falls down dead.

If Montezuma, unlike many other of the conquered whose traces history has erased, appears to us a rounded character, with his Hamlet-like anguish, it is thanks to the meticulous chronicle of the conquest of Mexico left to us by one of Cortés's soldiers: Bernal Díaz del Castillo. In a case rare in history, one of the most extraordinary human adventures found an eyewitness capable of telling the story, day by day, with a great wealth of detail and—as far as possible for a soldier on one side—with objectivity. Bernal Díaz reports the facts as he saw them, nothing but the facts; but these reported facts evoke states of mind and inner tensions, and the *Historia de la Conquista de Nueva España* is a great book, especially in restoring to us the atmosphere of mistrust surrounding everything. That universal mistrust dominates Montezuma in the presence of the mysterious superiority of the foreigners who command "lightning and thunder" as well as the Spaniards themselves, who can't get rid of the suspicion that they are the true besieged, and sleep in their clothes, with all their weapons, not even taking off gorgets and thigh armor. "I got so used to it, that even now, after the conquest," writes Díaz, "I go to bed dressed, and after a brief sleep I have to get up in the middle of the night, to look at the sky and the stars, and walk a bit outside."

In the first encounter with Cortés described by Bernal Díaz, Montezuma, sparkling with jewels, climbs down from the litter, four dignitaries supporting him by the arms, and advances under a canopy of green feathers toward the armor-clad Spaniards. For the conquistadores authority lies completely in images of strength, while the Aztec sovereign reveals his majesty through signs of extreme weakness. From the first conversations with Cortés, Montezuma displays no solemnity: he laughs, indulges in a bland self-irony, plays down his wealth, mocks those who think he is a god. He seems to be trying in this way to extend a limited influence even over the Spanish.

When Cortés, who has already been a guest of Mexico for four days, visits the pyramid of Huitzilopochtli, Montezuma is waiting for him at the top; he has certainly been carried up there, and sends eight dignitaries to help Cortés on the stairway. Cortés avoids them, climbs the steps rapidly, without taking a breath. "You must be tired," Montezuma says, welcoming him amid the sacrificial altars. "The Spanish are never tired," replies that champion of an efficiency that will remain the supreme value of the West. Meekly the emperor takes the soldier by the hand, leads him to the edge of the terrace to contemplate the grand city on the lake. The harmony is brief: Cortés is quick to declare his indignation at the bloody rites in homage to the idols. Montezuma, offended, responds in the dismayed and depressed tone of his darker moments.

Montezuma's mood is unstable, oscillating between extremes. Even as a prisoner he is often heard laughing and joking with his concubines and officials, eating his favorite dishes, which have a base of red pepper. Of the novelties introduced by the Spaniards what amuses him most is the sailboats that Cortés has built to sail on the lake. Bernal Díaz recounts a happy day that Cortés gives the prisoner: crossing the lake in a sailboat with a good wind, a hunting party in the woods on the opposite shore, an artillery salvo during the return that fills the monarch with joy. For a moment, in this grim story, oppression appears as the chink in a world at peace, and immediately hilarity grips Montezuma. He's a mature man, certainly older than the thirty-five-year-old Cortés, and if he seems to us a child compared with his adversary it's perhaps only because of our old criterion of contrast between "primitive" cultures and Europe; in reality, every one of his gestures contains a gravity, a deliberation that contrasts with this childlike image.

Through Díaz del Castillo and later historians, down to successful popularizers like [W. H.] Prescott, Montezuma enters our history as seen by European eyes; but already a good number of sources from the sixteenth century, pictographic and then written, provide a chronicle of the conquest as seen by the conquered. Curiosity about this absolute difference that each of the two peoples represented for the other dominates the accounts. And the stronger the difference the harder each tries to force the unknown into known schemes, or at least into the categories of its own culture, such as for the Spanish chivalric poems, and for the Mexicans the prophecies of their mythology.

This biography of Montezuma is the work of C. A. Burland, an authoritative English scholar of Aztec antiquities, and is based mainly on Indian sources and on what archaeology and anthropology have revealed to us about the ancient Mexicans. So it's a biography that takes the point of view of the person whose biography it is. Two-thirds of the book is in fact devoted to the life of Montezuma before the arrival of the "floating houses" that disembarked mysterious strangers clothed in "gray stone" (iron), astride "deer without horns" (horses), capable of commanding lightning and thunder. This part reconstructs his education as a great priest-astrologer and warrior, the role he played in the creation of the rapacious and oppressive Aztec Empire and in the growth of the capital (Tehochtitlán, or Cactus Rock, as Burland translates it), and the ecclesiastical-political-military career that led him to be elected to the highest (if not absolute) power as Spokesman of the Council of Four. (Thus the literal translation of the office that the Spaniards identified with that of emperor.)

Only two dense chapters are devoted by Burland to the tragic rush of events on which historians of the conquest lingered, but the contradictions of Montezuma's behavior can be largely explained by the code (mythological and ethical) under which the Aztec sovereign lived that terrible crisis. The unexpected invasion of beings incomprehensible in language and behavior is for Montezuma the external manifestation of a battle between gods: Huitzilopochtli, the Blue Snake, patron of the Aztecs, and Quetzalcoatl, the Plumed Serpent, the god exiled from Mexico, whom the prophecy said would return from the west to resume his place, casting the other gods off the throne.

All this is known: it was known also to Cortés, who tried to play as much as he could on his identification with a god or one sent by the god. (His lover and interpreter and very skilled Mexican counselor, Doña Marina, had—according to Burland—a considerable role in setting this scene.) But Burland emphasizes that the battle between the gods took place first of all within the mind of Montezuma, whose individual patron was Quetzalcoatl, and so, if Cortés was the god in person or, more likely, sent by him, he couldn't go against his wishes; while, at the same time, as lord of the Aztecs, he had to sustain the cult of the Hummingbird of the South, of whom the foreigners—inspired or not by

the Plumed Serpent—were certainly mortal enemies. The
result is a psychologically less mysterious Montezuma, already pledged to an openly inauspicious fate, and straining
to the end to make the events in which he is involved coincide with the prophecies of the sacred books.

Is this the *true* Montezuma? We have to say that the
Montezuma of Bernal Díaz is not in any way denied or
eclipsed by this. Rather: with all its shadows, the portrait
drawn from life by the Spanish soldier remains the richest, the most emotional, and every new historical investigation only illuminates particular aspects of it. Burland
convincingly reconstructs the religious code by which the
Aztec chief tried to interpret the invasion and to live his
bewildering experience. This mythic reading of the present assumes in Burland's book a concreteness, a logic that
up to now escaped us: but perhaps it was for Montezuma
only a means of stifling the anguish of the unknown, the
persistent uncertainty regarding the practical and moral
choices, the distress at feeling the edifice of power that until then had sustained him crumble under his feet.

Builders of stepped pyramidal temples, the Aztecs had
founded on the plateaus of Mexico a pyramidal empire, in
which the hierarchy of powers made a stairway between
the heaven of the gods and the earth swarming with men.
Less than a century before, one of the barbaric nomadic
tribes had asserted itself over the others, had combined
their religions into a complex pantheon and the arts of
individual villages (the jewels of Xochimilco, the colored
feather mats of Amantitlán) into a multiform civilization.

From a palace whose gardens contained all the known species of plants, whose cages held all the birds, whose menageries all the beasts (and with a pavilion that housed Lilliputian or other deformed examples of the human race, a collection of living phenomena), Montezuma exercised his authority over the dignitaries of the court, and these ruled the officials who controlled the zones of the capital and the villages of farmers and artisans. A corps of collectors brought to the capital the corn and cacao harvests, bales of cotton, jade and emeralds. The emperor withdrew the share that was due to the public offices and redistributed the products to the families of the poor. Through the increasingly complicated collection of taxes, Montezuma perpetuated (or so he believed) the frugal equality of the ancient tribes.

At this point the foreigners arrived, offspring of a civilization that for millennia had known and used the mechanisms of power in good and evil, and which had seen many empires rise, become invincible, and fall. Their gaze had only to rest on the shining marble pyramid to expose fissures, breaches, nests of serpents, termites. Cortés's eyes can distinguish from afar every tiny crack in the edifice and choose the point in which to prize it open. The true great disparity between them lies not in the blades of Toledo against the splinters of obsidian, in the horses and firearms unknown to the Mexicans, but in the fact that Montezuma, head of an empire modeled on the order of the firmament and on the equilibrium of forces of the gods, feels insecure, at the mercy of a precarious universe; while Cortés, who proceeds through a world in which everything is unknown to him, keeps a solid grip on causes and effects, means and ends.

While Cortés advances in the exploration of Mexico, a Florentine official has recently explored the history of antiquity and of his own time to explain how the power of those who govern depends not on divine wills but on a prudent use of power relations. Without having read Machiavelli, both Montezuma and Cortés move on his horizon: if the Spaniard wins it's because he always knows, without hesitation, what he wants. Today we understand how ephemeral Cortés's victories are, and how irreparable the destruction he brings with him; while the figure of Montezuma appears to us not only in the sad light of the weak and conquered but fixed in a suspended tension, as if the match between him and his enemy were still open. If his victory can be ruled out from the start, it's not that his defeat is certain. There is in Montezuma a bewildered and receptive attitude that we feel is close and present, like that of the man who with his warning systems in crisis tries desperately to keep his eyes open, to understand.

[1976]

Cannibals and Kings
by Marvin Harris

No matter how little reading we've done in ethnology, we've learned that one can speak about cannibalism only with the respect due to the religious rites of other cultures, which shouldn't be judged by our limited Eurocentric standard. Connecting the consumption of human flesh in any way with culinary gluttony or, worse still, with economic-nutritional usefulness should be avoided by cultivated persons as the grossest vulgarity.

Even for Marvin Harris (*Cannibals and Kings: The Origins of Cultures*), the number of documented cases of anthropophagy (the most recent some ten years ago) in a hundred societies scattered throughout the two Americas, black Africa, southwest Asia, Malaysia, Indonesia, and Oceania is quantitatively too small to have any value that is not symbolic-ritual. The same should be said for human sacrifices (which can be found in the past of every human civilization, including European), whose connections to cannibalism are only occasional. But what Harris pauses to consider is the most famous example of a civilization in which human sacrifice was practiced habitually on a large scale: the Aztecs, in Mexico, among whom, for at least a century before the Spanish conquest, the ritual killing of large numbers of prisoners of war was a central fact of the entire religious, government, and military system of their complex and refined civilization, with daily sacrifices of individual victims in various sanctuaries and mass sacrifices of thousands of victims (up to fifteen thousand at a time, it seems) on the occasion of celebrations and victories.

It can be said that we know everything about the Aztecs' religion and the cosmological rationales that ordered them to nourish the solar divinities with beating hearts and rivers of human blood. Similarly, we know everything about the way prisoners crowned with flowers were made to climb up onto the altars where the priests extracted the heart with stone knives and rolled the body down the steps of the pyramid. But what happened to the body when it reached the bottom of the steps? Much less is said about this detail, but contemporary witnesses of the conquest (Bernardino de Sahagún, Diego Durán) leave no doubts: the bodies were eaten at great banquets. (I find scant information on the way in which they were cooked: sauces based on hot peppers seem to be the most important ingredient.)

One finds the custom of ritually eating individual sacrificed prisoners of war among other peoples of America, from the Tupinambá of Brazil to the Huron of Canada, according to the testimony of shipwrecked sailors and missionaries of the seventeenth and eighteenth centuries; but only in the Aztec Empire does cannibalism assume these giant destructive dimensions. Why? Marvin Harris, after studying the reasons for the rise and fall of the preceding Mexican state cultures (Olmec and Maya), describes the characteristics of the Aztecs' success on the semi-arid plateaus. He notes that although the intensification of agriculture didn't have the same catastrophic results as in the forest and marshy areas, it led to a precarious equilibrium between population growth and food resources.

Human sacrifice as a method of population control? But population control has been practiced since prehistoric times through the infanticide of female children, while the slaughter of males for that purpose is essentially unproductive. Better to consider the problems of food. Between the end of the last ice age and the European conquest, the large meat mammals disappeared from America. Edible animals known to the Aztecs were turkey, duck, rabbit, dogs, and, at most, deer (besides fish). Was cannibalism, then, intended to compensate for a lack of fats and proteins? Harris rules out the notion that for a population of two million inhabitants even a generous availability of cannibalistic banquets would have resolved anything from the alimentary point of view. (The most reliable calculations would presume an average of one man eaten a year for a hundred eaters.)

Harris's thesis is more complex: he takes account of the nutritional value of human flesh but also of the system of power, whose development he has followed from the most primitive agricultural communities to the formation of the great empires of antiquity, and the role of the "great providers" or redistributors of meat, edible plants, and goods of various kinds among the population.

In the function of these "great providers" Harris sees the original nucleus of the dominant classes of the first states. The Mexican empire would have been a particular case of this system from the point of view of agricultural resources and religious-military organization.

> If an occasional finger or toe was all anyone could expect, the system would probably not have worked. But if the meat was supplied in concentrated packages to the nobility, soldiers, and their retainers, and if the supply was synchronized to compensate for deficits in the agricultural cycle, the payoff for Moctezuma and the ruling class might have been sufficient to stave off political collapse.

I have to say that I welcomed Marvin Harris's conclusions with a certain relief. Even with all my willingness to understand the religious motivation of the Aztecs' human sacrifices in the context of a given system of relationships with natural and supernatural forces, there remained an impression of waste that no spiritual implication and no cultural functionality could balance. Now, knowing, first, that the body of the victim, once the heart had been given to the gods, was not a leftover to throw away but was used and appreciated and, second, that meals of human flesh were an important contribution to the need for calories, allows me to better evaluate the advantages of an operation of which I saw mainly the costs. (Even if the balance remains at a loss, as in the majority of the economic practices of our time.)

What I've reported is only one example of the satisfactions that reading *Cannibals and Kings* offers. Starting with the communities of hunter-gatherers of the Paleolithic (who had a more prosperous and restful life than we think), the American anthropologist Marvin Harris explains the history of human societies according to a method that he calls *cultural determinism* and that is based on the relation between availability of nutritional resources, population growth, and processes for increasing the first and reducing the second. Many will view the claim to explain the origin of the various forms of family, religious, state, and military life on the basis of the consumption of proteins as deserving the label "vulgar materialism," understood as pejorative. But the power—and the moral necessity—of every type of "materialism" lies in its "vulgarity," that is, in the determination to bring everything back to the basic problems of survival. Also, many phenomena put up a resistance to Harris's "cultural materialism" that seemingly can't be overcome by tools that are too simple; for example, alimentary interdictions (pork is unclean for Jews and Arabs, the cow sacred for Indians). And yet it's clear that in studying them we can't disregard the relationships between the availability of beasts for meat and the evolution of religions from sacrificial rites to spiritual symbolism or vegetarianism.

The horizon that contemporary ethnology has opened to us seems intended purposely to deny any economic determinism. In primitive economic activity the "gift" counts much more than interest, symbolic value more than usefulness, and in human relations codifications count more than any utilitarian motive. These are the initial facts that Marvin Harris is obliged to take account of; therefore, the course of his reasoning is never mechanical or predictable. In explaining the origins of wars (with wonderful ethnographic examples: battles of Australian tribes based on obscene insults shouted by old women), he notes that it's the "culture of war" and not war in itself that can be seen as a system to decrease demographic pressure. It's the "culture of war" that authorizes male supremacy (and not vice versa) and encourages infanticide of girls (otherwise no less valued than males).

Infanticide (especially of girls but often extended to both sexes) was the great safety valve for the survival of the species, whenever a population reached its limits of expansion. (The "contraceptive revolution" is a modern achievement; and as for primitive abortion techniques, they were butchery and continued to be until today, with the legalization of abortion.)

If in prehistory the practice of infanticide can only be hypothesized, based on probable rates of demographic growth, in historical times we have impressive documentation, such as in England in the Middle Ages and during the Industrial Revolution. In the thirteenth and fourteenth centuries the "accidental" suffocation of newborns because the mother fell asleep on them ("overlaying") was so frequent that priests punished it only with a light penance. In London in the eighteenth century the government, to make up for the enormous number of infanticides, established foundling hospitals that were soon transformed into elimination camps. But around the end of the century, infant mortality decreased: What happened? There was an increased need for young workers in manufacturing, because they were paid less and were more docile. Children, Harris says, "were now given the dubious privilege of living to the age at which they could begin to work in a factory for a few years before they succumbed to tuberculosis."

Since 1979 was the "Year of the Child," I thought I couldn't bring it to a better conclusion than by reading and reflecting on these last chapters of *Cannibals and Kings*.

[1980]

Carlo Ginzburg, "Clues: Roots of an Evidential Paradigm"

If the image that comes to mind when we think of logical-mathematical rationality is a sphere, or the five Platonic solids that can be inscribed in it, evidential and individualizing knowledge has for us today the image of an ear, or, rather, a collection of different ears: as in the tables in which Giovanni Morelli catalogued the details useful for recognizing the style of the great painters, or those in which the criminal anthropologist Alphonse Bertillon offered a method of classification for people wanted by the police; or even just two ears, cut off and sent in a package by mail, whose mystery only Sherlock Holmes was able to solve at first glance.

In Carlo Ginzburg's essay "Clues: Roots of an Evidential Paradigm," the ear indicates individual uniqueness in two ways: in nature, for the variety of forms of pavilions and lobes; and in painters' pictures, because every artist has his way of making ears that emerges unconsciously, given that ears are details we don't think about. Corresponding to the galaxy of ears that opens the essay—with the young Freud excited about Morelli's discovery—is a vortex of finger-prints at the conclusion, with the history of the discovery of this true writing of individuality and its use as a method of generalized social control: from a Bengalese custom (perhaps for a divinatory purpose) to its adoption by an English colonial official.

Carlo Ginzburg's essay has already been talked about and will continue to be talked about, both for the large number of ideas that are woven into it, like threads in a carpet (in a weave that is still provisional—the author warns us—and that will likely become denser), and for its stated intention of representing an epistemological para-digm opposed to that of the science called Galilean, based on the generalization, quantification, and repeatability of phenomena. For good reason it appears in the collection of essays *Crisi della ragione* (*Crisis of Reason*) (Turin: Einaudi, 1980), edited by Aldo Gargani, who has prefaced it with a stimulating essay on the crisis of the logical-mathematical model of traditional rationality.

But is this opposition completely relevant? The mere name of Galileo warns us that things are not so simple. The observer of sunspots and moon spots, of irregular-ities in the movements of the planets, the reasoner who had no scruples about accumulating evidence to reduce the Earth to the rank of planet among others: What goal did he set for science if not the realization of singularity against a presumed norm, in the macroscopic case of the solar system seen for the first time in its individuality as a collection of degradable and asymmetrical objects, rather than as a rational, harmonious paradigm perfectly stable on multiple levels, like the Aristotelian-Ptolemaic model? Of course, that meant that Galileo had to "understand the language" in which "the book of the universe" was written, that is, mathematics (and Ginzburg rightly emphasizes in this metaphor the reference to philology, with the idea that the book is not immediately legible, in order to establish the study of a language that is neither anthropocentric nor anthropomorphic). But isn't this the direction of every type of knowledge? Recognition of the singularity that escapes the norm; construction of a more sophisticated model, which applies to a rougher, more rugged reality; a new rupture in the mesh of the system; and so on.

Things aren't too different in another methodology that Ginzburg refers to repeatedly: that of the narrator. "Man has been a hunter for thousands of years. In the course of countless chases he learned to reconstruct the shapes and movements of invisible prey from tracks in the mud, broken branches, excrement, tufts of fur, snagged feathers, stagnating odors . . . He learned how to execute complex mental operations with lightning speed, in the depths of a forest or in a clearing with its hidden dangers."

With the speed of association worthy of an old hunter, Ginzburg connects the origins of the art of storytelling to hunting. He recognizes the tracks of the tracker's methodological principles in an old Oriental fable about a lost camel (or horse), which a wise man (or three brothers) can describe without having seen; accused of theft, he demonstrates that he got all those details from tracks on the ground. Voltaire makes this story an episode in *Zadig*; and out of it comes all of Sherlock Holmes, not to mention much theorizing about the inductive method.

Ginzburg is also right in a more general sense. The arc along which he fixes certain points—from the fable to the novel (which "provided the bourgeoisie with a replacement for and, at the same time, a reformulation of initiation rites—or access to experience in general") and to Proust, who constructs his novel "on a rigorous evidential paradigm"—is based on a mental form that is in essence "hunting." Storytelling is the operation by means of which a series of facts that is assumed to have a meaning and a design is chosen from among the innumerable facts that form the continuous fabric of human lives: the clues and tracks of a story with a beginning and an end, of a specific existential journey, of a destiny.

This holds for more primitive and linear narratives as much as for the novel, which is overflowing with inessential details and nuances of atmosphere; these, too, are tracks, and extremely indispensable, of a narrative strategy whose effect of truth coincides with the peculiar singularity of lived experience. In the fable (which is the story of something lost and found), the tracks that the narrative records are usually not those of the lost object (the "Zadig case" is an exception) but those of the reason for the loss (prohibitions that were not respected) and of the pathways to being found (magical reparatory actions). And here the art of narration intersects with the art of divination, in turn intersecting with medical semiotics and in general the scientific induction of causes and effects (as Ginzburg points out on the basis of Jean Bottéro's Mesopotamian studies).

What I'd like to say is that the story (unlike the hunter's pursuit—for the hunter, only the singularity of the episode and the experience exist) offers singularity and geometry at the same time: it becomes a story when the singularity of the facts is composed into a schema, whether it's rigid or fluid.

Every new story is a victory of singularity over the already ossified schema, as long as a set of exceptions to the schema are not configured as schemata themselves. In other words, I find in the practice of telling stories the same phases of movement that I tried to outline above, talking about Galilean science. Thus the literary critic aims at going back and forth between two basic operations: emphasizing the singularity in the text that is most obedient to the rules of a genre; and revealing the schema, the archaic structure, the traditional *topos*, the collective archetype hidden in a text that is apparently animated only by individual inspiration, by extemporaneous innovation.

In the object of evidential knowledge Ginzburg distinguishes between nature and culture. In fact the examples mainly track "involuntary signs" of spontaneity (the way an artist paints ears, or the pen strokes interpreted by the graphologist, or the slips investigated by the psychoanalyst); we are therefore more on the side of nature, or, rather, of layers closer to nature, hidden under cultural layers. In my view, the dividing line is between activity whose value lies in the track of the individual and activity whose value lies in impersonality. The idea of "style" as a personal brand rather than as a rule of uniformity is relatively recent. In many artisanal productions, just as in the "masterpiece" that until a short time ago was required for apprentices in the engineering industries, what counted was knowing how to make an object indistinguishable from the others. To subdivide the vast field covered by the "evidential paradigm" we have to start with a classification of the values that are the object of study. Or of the negative values, the crimes.

Here we are, then, at the worry that runs through Ginzburg's entire essay, first implicit, then stated, up to the final distressing evocation of the criminal archive that no one escapes. Evidential knowledge, individual and concrete, or rather this "body of local types of knowledge," transmissible only through practical experience, outside the abstraction of the written rules, inspires certainly in Ginzburg an allegiance made up of instinctive sympathy, professional passion (the career of the historian), ideological affinity (because he comes "from the low," and "it is very different from any form of 'superior' knowledge, which is always restricted to an elite"). (But is that really true: as for epistemological democracy, the universality of the Cartesian and Kantian I, the impersonality of experimental science—aren't they grand premises of equality and commonality of language?) At the same time he can't hide the fact that not only in the novels of Conan Doyle does the "evidential" quickly become "police" but spying for traces of hidden truth quickly becomes spying as general control.

Certainly the evaluation of "hunting" knowledge changes depending on whether we take the hunter's view or that of the hunted: but the basic point is the impetus of vital interest that pushes the hunter (we always think of the Paleolithic) toward the capture—but also toward the perpetuation—of the prey. An example closer to hunting, as the pursuit of a singularity that is manifested in clues to decipher, is love. "Someone has said that falling in love is the overestimation of the marginal differences that exist between one woman and the next (or between one man and the other)," Ginzburg writes.

Is the power that wants to establish close control over individuals—a power that is increasingly threatening today in the era of electronic records—animated by an excess of love for the citizens? But both the hunter and the lover seek traces of the *existence* of something that might also not exist. Police knowledge seeks the traces of a crime. The curse of our century is that every cognitive interest is transformed into an accusation. And this is not only on the part of the state toward the individual; it's the intellectual gaze that is always in search of a crime to try, a disgrace to report, a secret to violate. If we think about it for a moment, it's not a vocation to be proud of.

I recall the outburst of a writer against contemporary criticism in general because, drawing on both Marxism and psychoanalysis, all it can do is investigate, look for hidden, guilty motivations. He was a Polish writer, and if that can explain the allergy to feeling that he was under surveillance, his rejection makes sense even where the observing gaze is less institutionalized.

In a book that I talked about here recently (Marvin Harris's *Cannibals and Kings*) there is a passage that intersects with Ginzburg's essay, illustrating the move from the nomadic life of hunters to settlement in the village.

From a study of the Mehinacu Indians of Brazil we learn that the hunter's aptitude for picking up the tiniest clues brings to the lives around him more disadvantages than advantages, because it destroys all privacy: "[The Mehinacu] can tell from the print of a heel or a buttock where a couple stopped and had sexual relations off the path. Lost arrows give away the owner's prize fishing spot; an ax resting against a tree tells a story of interrupted work. No one leaves or enters the village without being noticed. One must whisper to secure privacy—with walls of thatch there are no closed doors. The village is filled with irritating gossip about men who are impotent or who ejaculate too quickly, and about women's behavior during coitus."

We notice immediately that in the village acuteness of observation has a component that it doesn't have in the forest: making one's neighbor feel guilty, in the form of gossiping malice, general ill will. And we can say that the metropolitan civilization of large numbers and widespread inquisitive individual conscience presents many analogies with the village of the Mehinacu Indians.

[1980]

Ilya Prigogine and Isabelle Stengers, La Nouvelle Alliance

Jacques Monod's book *Chance and Necessity* (1970) was intended as a bold and unillusioned statement of man's solitude, of man a stranger to the universe. No law of nature could have predicted the origin of life or the chain of extremely "unlikely" evolutionary events that led to man; but the pathways opened by chance—indifferent to every purpose—proceed between the iron walls of physical and biological necessity, which is likewise indifferent to who profits from it and who is damaged by it. From that derives the attitude of tragic dignity needed to confront the fall from the illusion of anthropocentrism to the absolute marginality that is our place among things. Monod wrote: "The ancient covenant is in pieces; man knows at last that he is alone in the universe's unfeeling immensity, out of which he emerged only by chance."

Exactly ten years later, another book of philosophy and history of science comes out in France and is announced as an event with the reach of Monod's, to which it is a response: the authors are a Nobel Prize winner in chemistry (Russian by birth, Belgian by adoption) and a collaborator. They say that Monod treated with perfect clarity and rigor the philosophical consequences of classical science, which was understood to establish universal laws of a nature seen as a simple and reversible mechanism; but the perspective of science has changed, and today attention is focused on irreversible processes that, while also generated by chance and necessity, put in play notions of structure, function, history.

Monod's vision is corrected not in its assumptions but in its perspectives: "Irreversibility is a source of order at all levels. Irreversibility is the mechanism that brings order out of chaos." Therefore the macroscopic and human world shouldn't be seen as a marginal exception in the universe of the immensely large and the immensely small. In that sense what the authors, starting with the title of the book, call "the new alliance" can be established (Ilya Prigogine and Isabelle Stengers: *La Nouvelle Alliance. Métamorphose de la science* [Paris: Gallimard, 1980]).

Thermodynamics (which up until yesterday was announcing the inevitable death of the universe, the triumph of entropy, the irreversible degradation of all energy into heat) today, through "the discovery of processes of spontaneous organization and dissipative structures" (Prigogine's specialty), claims that it can explain to us how more complex organizations, that is, the forms of the living world, are not an accident of nature but are situated on its main street, on the course of its most logical development.

La Nouvelle Alliance is a book of the history of science and at the same time of science being made (especially the chapters on thermodynamics and "order through fluctuations," which deal with ongoing studies as well), but it's also a passionate meditation on man and the universe that refuses to separate the "two cultures," and tightly weaves into a single discourse the pathways opened by scientists and the questions of philosophers; nor does it consider the ways of poetry extraneous or distant.

Now, I have to say that my first reaction when I see the statements of a scientist incline toward the "poetic" is distrust; one of the first fundamental principles of our (or at least of my) intellectual education insists that science should appear with a rugged and unadorned face. If what I consider a poetic suggestion jumps out from the results of science's impassive proceedings, I welcome it, but I have to be the one who discovers it; if it's science itself that says to me, "Did you see how poetic I am!" that's not for me, in fact my impulse is to reject it. Here with Prigogine, who on the margins of the most complex proofs lets flow an emotional evocation of dizzying horizons, I should be on my guard, mobilize all my suspicions and allergies: but no, I seem to recognize the sound of something solid that supports the argument, whatever its rhetorical wrapping. Without claiming to enter into the merits of material too far outside my competence, as an unbiased and willing reader I have to say that *La Nouvelle Alliance* is a fascinating book on the history of science that explains clearly connections and distinctions and turning points that we tend to underestimate, and read as a philosophy book it can't fail to leave its mark.

Prigogine's point of departure is the separation between the human world and physical nature that takes place with Newton: on the one hand "the world we live, love, and die in," our habitat, made up of qualities and perceptions and intentions, and on the other the world of quantity and geometry, simple laws that can be reduced to mathematical forms, nature seen as a machine, nature regular and harmonious but irremediably "stupid." Among the book's finest chapters are the ones on the Newtonian revolution and the birth of modern science, an encounter between technology and theory that would have been unthinkable in the time of the Greeks; for them the very terms *machine* and *mechanical* implied deceptions aimed at nature, and science excluded manipulation, that is, experiment.

An experiment is "art," a specious interrogation of nature, a mise-en-scène (up to the experiment that happens only in thought, like the trains and elevators of Einstein's arguments). Galileo, who excludes from his interests Aristotle's *why*s to concentrate his research on the *how*, wants to reach the *global* truth of nature, written in the language of mathematics, unique for all phenomena, and proof of the homogeneity of everything. In the origins of Western science theological resonances can't be ruled out: the idea of a legislator god whose word (mathematical) is incarnated in nature and is rationally intelligible to man. An accord quickly becomes possible between scientists, in the name of the universality of mathematical language, and theologians, in the name of the omnipotence of divine law. Leibniz alone remains to insist on the multiplicity of worlds and listen intently to the countless different "mathematical voices."

Lucretian atomism, the science of chance and collisions, gradually yields the field to the idea of *attraction* that Newton had taken from his unrepudiated alchemical interests. Despite the objections of Diderot, who demanded knowledge centered on living matter ("Look at this egg: with it you can overthrow all the schools of theology . . ."), the triumphant edifice of eighteenth-century science is supported by Newton's dynamics, which were later extended by Laplace to a universal system. In Laplace's world, which is "simple and clear, without shadow or depth . . . man, as an inhabitant taking part in a natural becoming, is inconceivable. . . . He is the residue of a total opacity." Such a world, whose future and past the demon Laplace hypothesizes could, starting from the observation of an instantaneous state, calculate, "is nothing but an immense tautology, eternal and arbitrary, necessary and absurd, in every single detail as much as in its totality."

Kant only apparently overturns the situation: man as transcendental subject imposes laws on nature through science, while at the start of science philosophy continues its ancient meditation on human destiny; in fact it's precisely with Kant that, with the distinction confirmed between science and wisdom, science and truth, the separation between the "two cultures" is sanctioned.

At this point a big coup de théâtre. 1811: a science mathematically rigorous but completely alien to Newtonianism is born, the science of heat, contemporaneous with and part of the Industrial Revolution. In physics from then on, two universals will coexist, gravitation and heat. Philosophers and scientists, from Auguste Comte to Helmholtz, will try to overcome their opposition. The principle of conservation of energy will be assumed as a unifier of science that restores a balanced and peaceful image of the universe. But "others, like Nietzsche, detected the dim echo of a nature creator and destroyer, whose power science had had to recognize in order to muffle its dark noise."

The spectacle of thermal engines, of the red-hot boilers of locomotives which burn fuel irreversibly in order to produce movement, was eloquent enough in itself: "Fuel used by the steam engine disappears forever." The science of heat introduces into the harmonious Newtonian world the arrow of time, irreversibility, loss. "The obsession with the exhaustion of resources and engines stopping, and the idea of an irreversible decline, certainly translates this anguish particular to the modern world."

Between technology and cosmology there's only one step, which will be taken by Clausius in 1865, with the concept of entropy. Just as the biological sciences and the social and cultural sciences defined an evolution toward greater complexity and an increase in innovation, thermodynamics promised dissipation of energy, non-recoverability of initial conditions, evolution toward disorder.

I have summarized and paraphrased half of Prigogine and Stengers's book, up to its most dramatic point of suspense. In the second half it steps back from the formless abyss of the dissipation of heat and proceeds, if not toward a happy ending, toward a logic in which the organization of living beings, man and his history are not at all extraneous accidents. I would be less successful in summarizing those chapters, given the technical complexity of the arguments. But Prigogine's discourse moves continually— sometimes in the same sentence—from the formula to the philosopher's reflection, maybe what we least expect to meet in that context; so that even the reader more acquainted with one of the two cultures exclusively can find the thread again every time it escapes him.

Among these citations of philosophers, it seems to me that what "makes headlines" is the fact that Henri Bergson, an author who for years was not named except with condescension or rejection, is here considered with great attention, as having established the most complete divorce between science and "spirit" but also as having addressed to science a criticism that science is now making its own.

Every so often, more or less unexpectedly, contemporary French philosophical-literary names surface. Among these, an important place is given to Michel Serres—evidence of an ongoing and frequent dialogue. Not surprisingly it was Serres, the author of *Hermes ou la communication* and interpreter of Leibniz and Lucretius, who greeted the publication of *La Nouvelle Alliance* in an article in *Le Monde* charged with lyrical enthusiasm and a density of knowledge that we might call Lucretian, and, above all, an optimism such as we have not heard for a long time.

"The universalists of the past noticed the moral law only on nights of good weather: a rather rare circumstance on the shores of the Baltic," Michel Serres writes. "Finally day breaks over things that I can't predict, as I cannot predict myself. Only a stone, a celestial body, a fool can, sometimes, be predictable. Finally day breaks over a circumstantial, differentiated, risky, improbable world, as concrete, multicolored, unexpected, and, yes, beautiful as the one I see, feel, touch, admire."

[1980]

Arnold van Gennep,
The Rites of Passage

The Rites of Passage, by Arnold van Gennep, a classic of anthropology (1909), which is now being reintroduced in the Universale scientifica Boringhieri series (or perhaps introduced for the first time in Italian, edited by Francesco Remotti), is a small book but contains a global conception of society and human existence, based on separations, of places, sexes, ages, families, groups, functions, not to mention the fundamental passages that separate the life of the individual from pre-life and post-life: birth and death.

Van Gennep, whose virtues as a researcher are known from monumental works on French folklore, in ethnology limited himself to organizing facts gathered by others, but he can easily be considered among the inventors of great theoretical systems based on a simple unifying concept that can explain any phenomenon. Such for him was the *rite de passage,* the rite of passage, which in every culture, primitive or not, is accompanied by special ceremonies.

Culture is, precisely, an awareness of passages, or transitions, and of the need to mark them with corresponding ceremonies: the material passage that links the inside with the outside, that is, the gates of the house and the city, the frontiers of the territory; the rites of departure and return; the rites of incorporating the stranger into the group or the tribe and the rites of separation that include vendetta and war; the rites that accompany pregnancy; birth, the entrance of the baby into the community, circumcision or baptism; rites of puberty and initiation, priestly ordinations, coronations, initiations into secret societies or professional corporations, and corresponding expulsions or excommunications; rites of engagement or marriage, not to mention repudiation and divorce; and the complex ritual of funeral ceremonies.

Every, or almost every, passage has a corresponding marginal area, or border zone, outside of space and time, considered sacred or impure, taboo: the threshold, the goodbye, pregnancy, engagement, mourning.

If we add the agricultural rites of seasonal transitions and the rites that go along with the phases of the moon, the revolutions of the planets, and the zodiac cycles, we can see that the system of ritual passages connects human affairs to the cosmos, in a universal diagram characterized by sharp strokes, by gaps and dividing lines.

The most evocative image of this conception of the world is presented by the monumental gates in the Far East that stand isolated, apparently not communicating with anything. These isolated portals "not only became independent monuments of architectural value (for example, porticoes of deities, of emperors, of widows) but also, at least in Shintoism and Taoism, are used as ceremonial instruments (see description of childhood ceremonies). This evolution from the magic portal to the monument seems also to have occurred in the case of the Roman arch of triumph. The victor was first required to separate himself from the enemy world through a series of rites, in order to be able to return to the Roman world by passing through the arch. The rite of incorporation in this case was a sacrifice to Jupiter Capitoline and to the deities protecting the city."

Of this universe of differences that surrounded the men of antiquity and societies that he calls "semi-civilized," van Gennep, writing at the start of the twentieth century, already speaks as of a lost world, in an era that is heading toward uniformity and lack of differentiation. In modern society (from the Renaissance on) he sees the separation between the sacred and the profane increasing, while in the earlier phases they mingled in every area of existence (special rites continue to be necessary, for example, to move from the lay state to the priesthood); the separation between classes, categories, professions is maintained but only on the basis of economics and education (incorporations and changes in social status are no longer marked by particular rituals) and is no longer locally circumscribed with regard to the uniformity of groups; he finds the separation between the sexes diminished and even the solidarity among those belonging to the same sex, sanctioned (in primitive societies) by periods of exclusion of men or women.

Writing in the last years of the Belle Époque, he also includes in the separations that are being eliminated the borders between nations, which are "visible—in an exaggerated fashion—only on maps." But even if for us this remains a system of dividing lines that is still concretely in force, we have to agree that it is increasingly artificial, in that adjacent nations tend increasingly to resemble one another.

In the world of mass societies we inhabit, the perspective has changed a little from the present in which van Gennep was writing, but the corrections don't change the basic discourse. The growing push to uniformity between the sexes doesn't exclude sexist solidarity; there is no hierarchical separation between ages, and no system of initiations and incorporations into adulthood, but a youth culture has been established as a separate and stable zone (even in terms of the market); increasingly homogeneous cultural horizons correspond to the vast economic distance between classes; the split between the geographic locations of the "less evolved" (to use the old vocabulary) and the metropolis is, on the other hand, constantly growing (while in the preindustrial world the awareness of one's own innate difference was possessive and proud on both sides and contempt for the other was mutual).

However, we're talking not about larger or smaller differences and separations but, rather, about the fact that today no separations are consecrated by rituals, in fact one might say they can't even be justified by ideology. It's a sign that these separations are felt as nonfunctional stumbling blocks, consciously pushed aside already as negative and expendable.

Perhaps it's precisely because this world of passages seems increasingly distant from us that we seem to understand it perfectly: every critical situation was classified within clear lines, institutionalized and in some way exorcised, but for that very reason its effective value as a crisis was recognized; while our world, in which passages are faded, diluted, or minimized, is configured as a condition of diffuse and continuous crisis.

Reading van Gennep we can't help wondering, with regard to every event in our daily life or in our fundamental experiences, what unconscious or implicit "rites of passage" we are led to perform: certainly they exist, and we practice them continuously even if we can't recognize them as such. If you think about it, our entire era is habitually defined as "a transitional period" or period "of passage": passage toward what we don't know, or we have less and less of an idea. We still have a tendency to consider the situation of transition and crisis sacred. But since we lack an inside and an outside from which or into which to pass, the sacralized passage becomes permanent and without alternatives, and usurps the homage that is due to it as a passage.

Let's take doors: we live in the era of keys, and each of us goes around with a bunch of keys hanging from our belt like a jailer; with the doors of today only the locks count, the system that ensures the material maintenance of possession. Gone is the symbolic meaning of the threshold, guarded by griffins or sphinxes or winged dragons or other sacred beasts, as at the entrance to the houses of the Egyptians, the Assyrian-Babylonians, and even today the Chinese. The monster guardians of doors could be considered an enduring feature of them; our absurd life as carriers of keys appears to us a makeshift remedy to a condition of emergency, though we know there are no possible alternatives.

To demonstrate that the main door of a house, consecrated by special rites and oriented in a favorable direction, had the spiritual prerogatives of a margin between the external world and the familiar one, while for impure functions such as removing corpses (and for women the periods considered impure), windows or secondary or back doors were used, van Gennep adds, with admirable candor: "Therefore thieves . . . prefer to enter otherwise than through the door."

[1981]

Long Journey to the Center of the Brain *by Renato and Rosellina Balbi*

It's hot. I'm aware of it, I'm intelligent, I have a well-developed brain, a brain that has twenty-one levels. I generally use only the twenty-first, the most evolved, and keep the others in reserve, underneath. But to know that it's hot I'd likely need only level number four, which was formed during the Silurian period, when I was a fish, in a salty estuary. That is, I as I passed through the Silurian period in that phase of fetal life between the eleventh week after conception and the thirteenth.

Now I'm walking down the street, moving my limbs, an operation I could already perform pretty well using level number five, which comes to me from my time as an amphibian during the Carboniferous, or from the fourth month of my intrauterine life. But I have to say that if I had stopped at that level I would be moving without knowing where to go, like a poor skinned dog ("generic" motility, not "specific"); whereas I do know where I'm heading—I'm looking for a bar to have a beer—which means that my brain has at least three more levels, up to number eight, common to marsupials, swimmers, and climbers. That level sends me back to the good times of the Jurassic, or to when I was a newborn, in the first month of life, intent entirely on the satisfaction of my needs.

Naturally I didn't skip levels six and seven; the thirst that is driving me toward the bar has its origin in level six, when the sucking reflex formed, while with level seven I was able to regulate my body temperature, just like a good old platypus.

At this moment it's the pleasure principle that guides my steps: I am, therefore, at level nine, like the insectivores of the Cretaceous; it's an exceedingly hedonistic phase, corresponding to the third and fourth month of my infant life. And in this search I use sight, like the squirrels of the Paleocene, when learning began for those remote arboreal ancestors of ours, just as it did for me between four and six months.

The crowded bar reawakens the aggressive instinct belonging to carnivores, which has been buried in the eleventh level of my brain since the Eocene: I would walk over the bodies of all the other customers just to get hold of that beer, as the recollection of its taste now stands out in my memory. I am in fact capable of desiring an object I can't see, like the lemuroids, early ancestors of monkeys, and children from eight to ten (level twelve). With the capacity for representation (level fourteen, anthropoid apes) comes envy of all those who are ahead of me in the line to get their receipt from the cashier. Paying before consuming means making plans for the future: level fifteen, Australopithecus, who has succeeded in achieving the erect position (or the child of a year and a half).

"A beer," someone ahead of me says to the cashier; and I have only to say (given that I've acquired the word by reaching the stage of imitation, level sixteen), "Me, too."

"Domestic or imported?" I'm asked, and suddenly I leap to level seventeen, which assumes a social conscience and capacity for individual choices: in a few words I'm forced to reveal myself as *Homo sapiens*. Here the problems begin, because level nineteen induces me to let myself be influenced by the authority of the tribe's shamans: the first beer that occurs to me is the most widely advertised. Will I manage to reach level twenty, which implies a critical spirit and rational will? I know that it is accompanied by worries about responsibility, apprehension . . . The bartender gets impatient, I stammer . . . level twenty-one seems very far away . . .

This page of my intimate diary was written under the influence of a really stimulating book, *Lungo viaggio al centro del cervello* (*Long Journey to the Center of the Brain*) (Rome: Laterza, 1981), the work of a neuropsychiatrist, Renato Balbi (professor at the University of Naples), and an essayist and journalist, Rosellina Balbi (his sister, who is responsible for the culture pages of the daily *Repubblica*). I took from the book all the notions I used, I hope not too arbitrarily. In fact this clear, evocative, and concise exposition of the evolution of the brain in the animal and then the human world is addressed to the nonspecialist reader. The stages of this process (given that ontogeny recapitulates phylogeny) repeat also in the individual, from the formation of the embryo to fetal life and infancy. The development of each successive level inhibits the functioning of the lower level by assuming its tasks, but the lower levels don't disappear and can resume their functions when the upper level isn't activated: which happens normally during sleep, or in special cases like hypnosis or injury and illnesses. In this way we get an original and convincing explanation of the processes of the dream (also in reference to psychoanalysis: Will we get to the point of situating the unconscious in a layer of the brain?), sleepwalking, hypnosis, the effects of neuroleptics and antianxiety drugs. An interesting and surprising chapter is the one on the tragedy of thalidomide. But these theories connect to the most diverse fields: even the techniques of advertising and the "hidden persuaders."

[1981]

Disturbing the Universe
by *Freeman Dyson*

Among the books that came out in Italy in 1981 there is at least one that has to be read, and that is *Disturbing the Universe*, by Freeman Dyson (Turin: Boringhieri). It came out a couple of months ago, and I expected that right away it would be constantly cited in the newspapers, especially in front-page articles, because on many subjects that front pages discuss continually—from atomic rearmament to nuclear power plants—or sporadically, from genetic engineering to solar energy, the experiences and reflections of this man who has been engaged with these problems, always in crucial moments and places and roles, have to leave an impression on the reader.

And yet nothing: it seems to me that this book isn't being talked about at all, as if no one were aware of it. I will try to talk about it, even though I'm not the most suitable reviewer, and even though it deals with so many issues it's a difficult book to summarize. I will try to give a general outline and convey how Dyson never tries to persuade the reader to think in one way rather than another but, precisely for this reason, in my view, manages to communicate something invaluable. Dyson goes to the heart of a problem just as it is experienced by those who have a direct and concrete responsibility for it; his approach is never what one expects, and at no stage of his journey do his conclusions coincide with the opinion he started with.

Published two years ago in the United States, as part of a series of volumes in which, at the invitation of the Sloan Foundation, famous scientists present their worldview on the basis of their experiences, both human and scientific, *Disturbing the Universe* is the autobiography of a first-rate physicist. Born in England in 1923, he becomes a professor at Princeton at the age of thirty and takes American citizenship at a time when the generation of physicists before him is racked by polemics (and by processes) on the responsibility of the scientist in the atomic age. From the portrait that [Luigi A.] Radicati presents in the introduction to the Italian edition, a versatile, restless type of scientist emerges, who isn't content with one field of investigation or an established opinion, but considers every point of arrival a new point of departure.

Radicati writes: "When everyone expects from him (the great scientist) the solution to the fundamental problems of quantum field theory, here he is designing reactors or planning futuristic nuclear rockets (the concrete, dynamic scientist). When elite science lines up behind Oppenheimer he forms a friendship with his archenemy Teller and frequents the Livermore military laboratory. A militarist, then? No, because shortly afterward we find him in Washington, involved, with a seriousness that not many liberals have displayed, in problems of disarmament and nuclear safety."

The first chapters show us a man whose fundamental motivations are of a moral order, sustained at the same time by reason (along with the wish to act in accord with what reason indicates to him as just) and imagination (literature has in this memoir no less a place than science, and the title is a line from Eliot: "Do I dare / Disturb the universe?").

For those who want their reading to be condensed (reserving the right to extend it later) I advise them to begin with chapter 3, which serves as an introduction to one of the book's main themes, that is, the science-war connection. It recounts Dyson's experience, during the Second World War, with the Bomber Command of the RAF, where the twenty-year-old scientist, assigned to the general staff, is to carry out a statistical study to determine whether the operational experience of a crew diminishes the probability of being shot down. The evidence that Dyson collects is distressing: the German fighters succeed in shooting down the English bombers independently of whether the crews are well trained or novices; the English Lancasters—unlike the American bombers—are unable to defend themselves from enemy fire and are built in such a way that, once they're hit, it's very difficult for the crew to parachute to safety. But for the military hierarchies and their bureaucracy these results are a dead letter; the English airmen continue to fly over Berlin and die. Even the battle that a friend of Dyson's wages to promote a technical modification to the exit door of the Lancaster, which could have saved many lives, fails.

A still more important fact: Dyson realizes that the entire strategy of bombing cities is a mistake, given that the military results gained are minimal, and the losses maximum. The balance of the young Dyson's war experience couldn't be more negative: "At the beginning of the war I believed fiercely in the brotherhood of man, called myself a follower of Gandhi, and was morally opposed to all violence. After a year of war I retreated and said, Unfortunately nonviolent resistance against Hitler is impracticable, but I am still morally opposed to bombing. A few years later I said, Unfortunately it seems that bombing is necessary in order to win the war, and so I am willing to go to work for Bomber Command, but I am still morally opposed to bombing cities indiscriminately. After I arrived at Bomber Command I said, Unfortunately it turns out that we are after all bombing cities indiscriminately, but this is morally justified as it is helping to win the war. A year later I said, Unfortunately it seems that our bombing is not really helping to win the war, but at least I am morally justified in working to save the lives of the bomber crews. In the last spring of the war I could no longer find any excuses."

This direct verification of the facts carried out by the idealistic young scientist gives a necessary context to the judgment on dropping atomic bombs over Japan in 1945, a judgment that at that moment could be only positive militarily and also morally, because the American action seemed to finally be a "useful" bombing, in that it actually served to put an end to the war. (All other considerations are part of "hindsight.") And all this serves as well to frame the postwar discussions in the world of American physics, in which Dyson, summoned in 1947 to Cornell University to work with Hans Bethe, participates. In the United States he becomes friends with many of those who a few years earlier had worked on the Los Alamos project and recollects their enthusiasms as well as their doubts.

So when Oppenheimer declares in an interview in 1948 that "the physicists have known sin," a statement that at that moment is repudiated by almost all his colleagues (how could constructing a bomb in the conviction that it would help to defeat Hitler be considered a sin?), Dyson understands it, in the sense that their sin was not building the bomb but that "they enjoyed building it." (It's a judgment typical of Dyson, in whom the religion of conscience converges with the realistic logic of a theoretical and technological design that can change the facts of the situation.)

So Dyson is bound to Oppenheimer, who soon becomes the prophet (and scapegoat) of the crisis of conscience of American science in the atomic age. But shortly afterward he takes the side of Oppenheimer's declared enemy, Teller, opposing the suspension of atomic experiments. Why? It should be said that in the meantime Dyson had gone on to be involved in peaceful uses of nuclear power plants and was convinced that if military experimentation ended, research in a field that was important to him would be stifled.

(In fact the opposite happened: the technology of nuclear arms progressed; that of industrial uses marked time.)

On this subject, I recommend that readers looking for the essential turn to chapter 9, which leads us back to the industrial exploitation of nuclear energy, seen as the great hope of the postwar period. (This era, too, has been forgotten, buried by "hindsight.") If this research comes to a halt because of the limited reliability of the protections against the dangers of radioactivity, the reason, Dyson thinks, is the myopia of the industrial and government bureaucracies (always his bête noire) that cut off the planning of larger and more secure reactors.

The priority he gives the moral factor also emerges in the story of this experience, here with the positive value of his awareness of acting for the good: "The fundamental problem of the nuclear power industry is not reactor safety, not waste disposal, not the dangers of nuclear proliferation, real though all these problems are. The fundamental problem of the industry is that nobody any longer has any fun building reactors."

In 1958 Dyson moves on to work for Project Orion, constructing a nuclear spaceship. The future of humanity in space is another of the guiding themes of the book, but if I have to choose, I prefer to linger on the subject of atomic disarmament. Its most important developments are recounted in chapters 12 and 13, where Dyson describes his participation in the Agency for Arms Control and Disarmament, established by Kennedy in 1961. There, too, Dyson's positions when he arrived are very different from those when he departed: he starts off asserting that tests should be continued and disarmament should be gradual; and after a year, on the basis of all the American and Soviet documentation, he is convinced of the immediate necessity of imposing a total ban on tests and bomb making. He maintains that at that moment a ban would have been possible: if the Americans had taken the first step, Khrushchev would have easily been persuaded that it was not a good idea to start on the arms race in which we are now involved, with no sign of a realizable alternative.

In this encouraging direction, he tells of two battles led by scientists that were crowned with success: Ted Taylor's fight to sensitize the authorities to the danger of atomic theft (chapter 14) and (chapter 15) [Matthew] Meselson's to convince Nixon (and automatically Brezhnev) that it would be expedient to abandon germ warfare (1969: a historical fact that I would call one of the most important of the century; unfortunately Meselson has not yet succeeded in his campaign against chemical weapons).

Another chapter not to miss is 16, on the experiments with recombinant DNA (genetic engineering) seen from an unexpected observatory: the municipal committee entrusted by the town of Princeton with the job of deciding if the experiments of the university's biologists are legal or not; the ubiquitous Dyson is a member of this committee, along with other residents, ignorant of science but extremely conscientious.

I will not linger on the other themes: prospects of journeys into space and agricultural colonization of asteroids;

computers; cloning (to which Dyson opposes "clades," that is, the need for differences, especially regarding the cultural and linguistic specificities of peoples); "gray" technology and "green" (Dyson favors "gray" but admires his son, who, as an adept in "green," is a pioneer on an island in the Arctic, living only on what he can take from the environment).

I should also talk about the final visions, between dream and fable, with which Dyson represents the teleological horizons of his beliefs as a scientist. But to express the moral of this book I prefer to cite a remark of Einstein's that Dyson quotes (in a wonderful passage where he describes seeing for the first time, with amazement, an electron behave according to the predictions of his calculations): "One may say that the eternal mystery of the world is its comprehensibility."

[1981]

Giovanni Godoli, The Sun: Story of a Star

Even if we can't stare at it with the naked eye, we can know the sun well—better than the Earth, which we can't observe beyond a fairly superficial level. We can and *should* know the sun: What object deserves to be thoroughly known more than the sun? For this reason the little volume by Giovanni Godoli entitled *Il Sole* (*The Sun*), subtitle, *Storia di una stella* (*Story of a Star*) (Turin: Einaudi, 1982), which can be read in three hours and can be read by anyone, is an opportunity not to miss. Giovanni Godoli, professor of solar physics at Florence, gives all the essential facts without using a formula and communicates the pleasure of the precise terminology and the precise notion of what we know and what we don't yet know.

From the first pages, the book leads us into the sun as if into our irreplaceable habitat, for all the reasons we think we know and for those we've never thought of. Among the first is the fact that our whole existence depends on it, directly or indirectly, our food, vegetable or animal, the energy stored millions of years ago or only yesterday, and that is only a tiny part of the solar energy that strikes the Earth and that we still don't know how to use. ("Nuclear energy, on the other hand, is independent of the sun. But how much its use is discussed!") Among the second is the fact that we live *inside* the sun: "The Earth is practically submerged in the sun, or, rather, in the thinnest region of its atmosphere, which continuously flows into interplanetary space, constituting what in an evocative expression is called *solar wind.*"

That statement, contained in the first chapter, is then refined in the second, as the solar corona—which on the surface of the star has a density a thousand times lower than that of the Earth's atmosphere—is so much thinner at the distance we are that our atmosphere is ten billion times more dense; therefore, we are submerged in the sun but we are also separated by a compact, very hard armor: the air.

I've said that Godoli has a taste for terminology: I will say more, that he has a sense of the relationship between the lexicon of current language and scientific language, and I would say that he doesn't approach the second until he has explored all the potential of the first. As in this passage: "In current, nonscientific language, various terms are used, some as synonyms, to indicate the fact that a source emits electromagnetic radiation. We say, among other things, that a source sparkles, shines, illumines, radiates, is luminous, is radiant, is resplendent, glitters, and we say that one source is more or less sparkling, shining, luminous, shimmering, resplendent, glittering than another. In scientific language we tend instead to be orderly and to give a precise meaning to some of these terms, while abandoning others." After this sumptuous farewell to current language, the simplifying operation of science asserts itself in its drastic linguistic economy, establishing the precise definition of *power, luminosity, irradiation.* And then, beyond the splendor, brightness, et cetera, et cetera, of the dazzling sun, a new lexical wealth becomes accessible to us: facula, spiculae, solar flare, solar prominence, not to mention spots, which have a *shadow* (darker central area) and a *penumbra,* with radial filaments all around.

Thanks to these observations of phenomena (or to these words?), the sun acquires consistency, reveals its granular substance. ("Photospheric granulation is made up of brilliant elements, polygonal in shape. . . . The granules have a diameter of around 1000 km. . . . They form, reach maximum brilliance, and then dissolve within ten minutes.")

The ephemeral, the discontinuous, the changing, the polymorphous are qualities intrinsic to the sun's nature: thus it's much more permeable to our knowledge than a misplaced human respect supposed. Only very late, in the time of Galileo, did men understand that the sun wasn't an immutable and incorruptible absolute but a living body in continuous process, with its rhythms, its sleeps, its awakenings. The sun is ready to tell us much about itself and its interior, but not everything, at least so far: among the book's most evocative chapters are the ones that concern ongoing research, such as the mystery of neutrinos (in theory many more should arrive on Earth than do arrive) and, naturally, the future of the sun in five billion years: *red giant, white dwarf, black hole, neutron star?* Among all the futures the most difficult to imagine is the *white dwarf,* "in which matter, although it's not in the gas or liquid state, isn't in the solid state, either."

It's pointless to try to describe this book at greater length through my impressions as a lay reader: I will say only that a series of very clear photographs of the solar rays, taken during total eclipses, show them as not dissimilar from the ones in children's drawings, but distributed irregularly, the "polar" rays more prominent and the "equatorial" and the "plumes" oblique, as in certain bristly, unruly hairstyles.

One of the last chapters is on the solar wind, which hits us with a flow of spiraling particles that reach Pluto and beyond, where this wind collides with interplanetary gas: an image of space that demonstrates how the void is an idea to understand in a relative sense. Bombarded by the solar wind, the Earth is contained in the hollow of its magnetic field, the "magnetosphere." Our climate and our survival play on these frontiers that are the Van Allen radiation belt, where the aurora borealis and the aurora australis wave their colored drapery at the gusts of particles coming from the sun or the Earth. In 1962, before the blasts of nuclear bombs in space were banned, one of those experiments caused an alteration in that zone that lasted several years; next time we'd better pay attention.

[1982]

Essays on Love *by Ortega y Gasset*

Ortega y Gasset is one of those philosophers who talk happily about things that professional philosophers don't usually talk about, and say things that we don't expect to hear but that, once said, acquire the obviousness of what we thought we'd known forever.

Which doesn't mean that everything he says should be immediately accepted as true or condemned as false; but that's the last thing on my mind when I read the philosophers I like to read. I read Ortega y Gasset not to be convinced by his ideas but for the pleasure of seeing how the mechanism of his mind works. (The same thing happens to me with Valéry.) It's the spectacle of his philosophizing that attracts me; the true and the false I'll decide on my own some time, on the basis of many other things.

Ortega is a philosopher who can reason in everyday language and in a discursive and digressive tone on themes of experience, and then seals the argument with the peremptory logic of the philosopher who follows (or gives the impression of following) a rigorous method. (Completely the opposite of the existentialists—although he, too, is often given that label—who judge the words of experience in an aura of absoluteness.)

He was also generous with his inspiration in the newspapers: in the years 1926–1927 he wrote a series of essays on love, in installments, for the Madrid daily *El Sol*. He collected them, together with other, analogous articles, in the volume *Estudios sobre el amor*, published in 1939 during his exile in Argentina and later republished in Spain in a series of editions in which the number and choice of minor texts varies but which all are centered on three important essays: on "features of love"; on love in Stendhal; and on the role of choice in love.

The Italian edition (José Ortega y Gasset, *Saggi sull'amore*, preface by Francesco Alberoni [Milan: Sugarco, 1982]) presents the three major essays (the first as introduction), and as for the minor essays, justly reduces the selection to the minimum: a more careful translation would have been deserved, but luckily the mistakes are only marginal; what's lacking is a note with the essential information about the history of the individual essays and the volume. The dates in any case are there and are important both for filling in the more properly philosophical picture (the authors he refers to most are experts in Husserl's phenomenology, like Scheler and Pfänder) and, what's more important given the theme, for filling in the picture of tradition and sensibility. (Especially when he speaks about woman, and man in relation to woman, we shouldn't forget that we're in the Spain of some sixty years ago.) Anyway, the reader who wants to know more about it can turn to a recent Spanish reprinting in an easily available volume (Madrid: Alianza Editorial, 1981), in the paperback series of the complete works of Ortega y Gasset.

The first distinction that Ortega poses is between *loves* and *love*. The former are more or less accidents that happen to men and women, while in defining *love* he considers a broader and at the same time more essential field of meanings. "Not only does man love woman and woman man, but we love art or science, the mother loves her child, and the religious man loves God." Thus Ortega takes off from the word to define the deed. But at the same time he refers to the idealistic tradition of love, starting with Plato, for whom love is a movement of the soul toward "something we regard as perfect," recognition of the "excellence" of being loved, or at least an element of it. Here another fundamental distinction intervenes: Ortega separates love from desire, a stimulus that comes from the object, while love goes *toward* the object, that is, from the lover to the beloved, and makes us feel united to the object despite the distance: "Falling in love even once is an insistence that the beloved exists; a refusal to accept (since everything depends on that one thing) the possibility of a universe without it."

Given this priority of the subject, we might expect that Ortega agrees with Stendhal's theory in *On Love* (Stendhal said that the lover projects a "crystallization" of positive qualities onto the beloved person, such that even defects are transmuted into elements of perfection). Not at all: Ortega's essay on Stendhal is a refutation of the theory of crystallization, considered idealistic "because it makes the external object for which we live a mere projection of the individual." For Ortega, then, are the values toward which love is guided (perfection, excellence, beauty in the Platonic sense) something objective?

We can find an answer to that question in the essay "The Role of Choice in Love." Every individual has his system of values, and choosing the beloved person reveals his deepest essence. For Ortega there are no wrong choices (therefore there are no wrong couples): if a woman "of an eminent nature" loves a "vulgar" man, that can be explained in two ways: either the woman is less eminent than we think or the man is less vulgar than we think. The choice is therefore always determined by an encounter with values we aspire to consciously or not.

Choice in love is thus separate both from an act of will (it's not an intellectual operation, even if it responds to a necessary rationality), and from the sexual instinct (which, as an instinct, is not a movement toward perfection, like true love, which is *also* sexual; and here Ortega brings in the biological force of improvement of the species, which seems to me a rather abrupt simplification).

Ortega explains persuasively that Stendhal was "a man who never truly loved nor, above all, was ever truly loved. His life is filled with false love affairs." And to Stendhal, who was so busy inventing unhappy love affairs for himself, he compares Chateaubriand: "Always removed from the woman and wrapped in his cloak of melancholy," he never needed to court any woman, yet he inspired unconditional and long-lasting loves.

From this opposition Ortega draws the conclusion that the true Don Juan is not the man who courts women but the man whom women court. This, however, is merely a reversal of the terms of the matter (probably for his own purposes), leaving them as they are: the Don Juan replaces the femme fatale as a love object because of his implicit and perhaps hidden objective perfection, but if he doesn't want to be reduced to passivity, merely letting himself be loved, the modalities of his "movement of the soul" toward perfection, et cetera, remain to be clarified.

The fundamental point is that Ortega's anti-romantic spirit tends to banish from the picture of love precisely "movement," its dynamic and temporal aspect. (He never mentions that the act of loving can change or transform the lover.) And if for Stendhal true love is *l'amour-passion*, for Ortega that condition, just like the ecstasy of the mystic, is incompatible with his idea of a love that lives permanently, like a "continued emanation," and "forever."

The essay on Stendhal is thus transformed into an insistent polemic against falling in love. Falling in love is a limitation of our consciousness, as its attention is fixed on one object: hence it's an impoverishment, not an enrichment. "All love passes through the frantic zone of 'falling in love'; but, on the other hand, 'falling in love' is not always followed by genuine love. Let us not confuse, therefore, the part with the whole."

This tirade against falling in love arouses a reaction in Francesco Alberoni (author of the preface to the Italian edition), who on the sequence falling in love (as movement, revolution, nascent state) and love (as institution, routine, continuity) has based an analogy between collective history and individual history.

It has to be said that Ortega's starting point is very different (and closer to Alberoni's) in the two (earlier) essays on Constant's *Adolphe* (included in the Italian edition, while in Spanish they appear in the collection *El Espectador*), where he doesn't say much about *Adolphe* but discusses "eternal love." Ortega's thesis is that when love appears (and here falling in love is considered to be more than positive), it has to believe itself eternal and swear that it is so; but this is an illusion. We can't claim that the ideal norms are achieved in reality; as soon as they are established they become unsustainable. (And here, I think, Alberoni no longer agrees.) If one were to take sides, it should be observed that Ortega is contradictory while Alberoni is not, but the richness of Ortega lies precisely in the fact that when he claims to settle accounts, something always remains outside, because the phantom he pursues will never be captured.

Many pages of these essays are devoted to explaining what love is not: to find positive definitions one has to dig between the lines. I will remember a definition of the *couple* as an "individuality of two" (and a reference to the theories of the Saint-Simonians, for whom the authentic human individual is the man-woman couple); and a mention of the "cosmic" dimension of love, a feeling of being connected to the force of the elements and to the universe.

In explaining Ortega's ideas in their general outline I didn't want to dwell too long on the aspects that accentuate the more than half century that separates us from his pages. The most difficult to get past is a certain worldly tone ("of a man of the world") when he speaks of women and love, in part because, given that the customs of Spain at the time imposed a reticence on love life that obliges him to keep to generalities, the worldly tone ends up becoming the dominant note. This happens especially in the minor essays, which are absent from the Italian edition. But the last essay translated here (alas, very badly) is merely a document of Spanish literary worldliness of the twenties (a gallantry-filled review of a book on Dante by Victoria Ocampo): and here the image of the fashionable philosopher can't be redeemed either by the many intelligent observations or by the atmosphere of the era.

[1982]

The View from Afar
by Claude Lévi-Strauss

The View from Afar is the fine title that Claude Lévi-Strauss gives his new book (*Le regard éloigné* [Paris: Plon, 1983]), a collection of essays and miscellaneous writings of the past ten years. Two preceding collections by the French scholar bore the programmatic title *Structural Anthropology* (1958) and *Structural Anthropology Volume 2* (1973); for this third volume, whose unity lies in the method of investigation and, even more, in the mental attitude that informs this method, rather than in the subjects dealt with, Lévi-Strauss has chosen a different title, "expressing what I consider the essence and originality of the anthropological approach." The book has a richness and density of ideas and suggestions that go beyond anthropology and are offered to us as an example of a mind that is always open and free.

Now that we've moved away from the reverberations of the "cultural trendiness" that in the sixties accompanied everything that was labeled *structuralism*, it may be the right moment to properly read an author who was the most eminent figure of that complex of schools, but who has above all been a personality unto himself. At seventy-five, Lévi-Strauss is confirmed as one of the few teachers who try to instill not only the application of a method but also intellectual honesty, the need to start from the reality of the object to develop the most suitable tools of knowledge, and the gaze that, unencumbered by biases, always finds a new perspective in order to reach the essence of every concept and every problem.

To understand what most interested me in a book so varied, I will simply present my reading notes, without trying to combine them into a unified discourse.

RACE. The volume opens with a lecture given at UNESCO in 1971 on *Race and Culture* which serves as a sequel and in part corrects the one on *Race and History* of twenty years earlier, given at the same site (published in Italian by Einaudi), and which from then on was considered a kind of fundamental charter of UNESCO's ideology on matters of race. In the second lecture, rather than repeat the same concepts, Lévi-Strauss maintained that "today the struggle against racism requires a broad dialogue with population genetics, if only because geneticists are in a better position than we to demonstrate any incapacity of fact or of law to determine, in man, the role of nature and nurture. However, since the question is now asked in scientific rather than in philosophical terms, even the negative answers have lost their dogmatic character. Cultural anthropologists and physical anthropologists used to debate racism in a vacuum. When I pointed out that geneticists have blown a blast of fresh air into the discussion, I was accused of putting the fox in the sheepfold." Thus in the introduction L.-S. discusses the uneasiness not to say outrage that he provoked in his audience.

For L.-S. the optimal conditions for human survival are those which allow differentiations within small groups, with their cultural and also biological specificities. Today the population of the human race is increasing enormously—and this is certainly the sign of a cultural and biological development—but the number of existing cultures is contracting enormously, through a process of homogenization that could have disastrous results as much from the cultural point of view as the biological.

L.-S. is adamant about the improper use of the term *racism*. Faithfulness to certain values to the exclusion of or opposition to others characterizes every culture, and can be called *racism* only when it leads to oppression and destruction of others' values and those who identify with them. Aggression toward and intolerance of what is different constitutes the true social evil, whether they seek justification on the racial level or the cultural.

SOCIOBIOLOGY. L.-S. is very hard on Edward O. Wilson's ambition to explain even cultural facts with "inclusive fitness" (adaptation in favor of the carriers of a common genetic patrimony), pointing out the contradictions of the new determinism in which *Homo geneticus* succeeds *Homo oeconomicus*. A refutation that is not ideological but based on very simple facts, and for that reason, perhaps, the first that seems convincing to me.

FAMILY. The "conjugal family" based on monogamous marriage is not an exclusive characteristic of evolved societies, for it is also found in societies that have remained at a cultural level that we would judge rudimentary. This doesn't mean that it's a feature characteristic of all societies or something to which all tend, let alone an attribute of human nature. There are populations in which the "conjugal family" is recognized as one formula among others; populations that are ignorant of it and sanction polygyny or polyandry, or forms of sexual promiscuity that follow diverse rules, group marriage, lending women; military societies in which the men are always at war and the women do the agricultural work and procreate outside of any family structure (among the Nayar on the coasts of Malabar in India; Hitler was striving for the same thing). But family organization that revolves around the couple and child raising can be encountered in all eras, from the Paleolithic to today, and all latitudes, with a series of unvarying properties; and even in polygamous societies, the fact that the number of women corresponds more or less to the number of men and that the majority of the men don't have the material means or the social prestige to take more women means that the monogamous couple asserts itself there, too, as the most frequent solution.

According to L.-S. the "conjugal family" offers the best situation for taking advantage of natural resources, and thus we find it as the dominant form at the two extremes of social development: among the forest nomads, the hunter-gatherers, and in evolved societies; that is, in situations in which there is more awareness of the need to establish an equilibrium with nature. But society as such isn't modeled on nature and tends to choose formulas much more complicated than the family to reach its own ends, which are multiplication, exchange, continuous redistribution of roles.

EMPIRICISM AND MENTALISM. *The View from Afar* contains important passages clarifying the philosophy implicit in L.-S.'s method, which has two facets: cataloguing the physical and practical details of every environment in which the myths he studies originate (plants, animals, geography, tools, recipes, meteorology, constellations); and, second, systematically arranging logical, abstract, and universal operations.

The more recent developments of neurophysiology tell us that in sensation the empirical and mental aspects of a logical operation are as one at their origin: hearing is recognizing first of all not sounds but distinctive traits between sounds, seeing isn't photographing objects but codifying differences in color, outlines, movement. The fundamental opposition in linguistics between phonetic (empirical) and phonological (mental) is diminishing to the point of elimination, or at least the first term can no longer be considered as something *preceding* the second.

What L.-S. tries to establish, treating myths as logical-linguistic creations based on empirical combinations, is the interaction between the two kinds of determinism: the one imposed by the specifics of the environment that makes available to our thought process a vocabulary of objects and actions, those and not others; and the one drawn from the mental mechanisms of the speaking subject that cause the facts of experience to connect and oppose one another according to patterns that are always those and not others.

THE ARBITRARY. One of the great pleasures of reading L.-S. is seeing how he never stops before the inexplicable but always looks for a path of reasoning that will lead to a logical explanation. Examples of this sort are abundant here, whether it's a line from Apollinaire or the stranger myths of the American Indians.

The arbitrary nature of the linguistic sign (the fact that there is no reason that a given word means a given thing) is one of the cornerstones of Saussure's linguistics. But Jakobson (and before him Benveniste), although he never questions this principle, in a certain sense goes around it, postulating a phonetic symbolism; and L.-S. picks up the ball on the rebound.

Referring to Mallarmé, who deplored that in French one had to use the word *jour*, with a heavy sound more fitting to an image of darkness, and the word *nuit*, with a sharp sound more suitable for representing light, L.-S. writes: "I must confess that I have never perceived this as a divergence: it only makes me think of these periods of time in two ways. For me, the day is something that lasts, the night something that occurs or that happens unexpectedly, as in the expression 'night falls.' *Jour* denotes a state; *nuit*, an event. Rather than perceiving a contradiction between the signifieds and the phonic peculiarities of their respective signifiers, I unconsciously ascribe different natures to the signifieds. *Jour* represents a durative aspect, congruent with a grave vocalism; *nuit* a perfective aspect, congruent with an acute vocalism; all this, in its way, makes for a small mythology."

Another example is Lautréamont's famous image of the "chance encounter of a sewing machine and an umbrella on a dissecting table." In an essay on Max Ernst, L.-S. manages to demonstrate that the three objects are perfectly congruent, and on this track he continues analyzing "mythologically" the paintings of the surrealist painter.

PARSIFAL. One of the most interesting essays in the book (and most accessible to the reader ignorant of structural anthropology) is on the myth of Parsifal in its various literary versions and in Wagner. (L.-S. wrote it for the program of the Bayreuth Festival in 1975.) The most exciting moment is where L.-S. demonstrates that the myth of Parsifal is "symmetrical though inverted" with respect to the Oedipal myths. (It was especially exciting for me, because, in a book I published in 1973, I had arrived at almost the same conclusion, trying to tell the greatest number of myths possible with different arrangements of the same cards in a tarot deck.)

WAGNER. There are other Wagnerian pages in *The View from Afar*, which demonstrate that L.-S.'s identification with Wagner not only involves admiration for the music and for the mythological imagination of the dramaturge but touches the essence of the idealist conception that in itself informs both Wagner's music and his dramaturgy: the overcoming of a rupture "between the emotions and the intelligence, between suffering humanity and the other forms of life, between earthly and spiritual values. Thus, through Schopenhauer, Wagner joins Jean-Jacques Rousseau, who was the first to see in compassion and identification with others an original mode of communication, predating social life and articulate speech—a mode capable of uniting human beings with one another and with all other forms of life."

MUSIC. How much musical composition counts in L.-S.'s thought processes we already knew from the four volumes of the *Mythologiques*. Here, too, he resorts to musical examples to explain concepts that are hard to describe. In the variants of a myth, the series of transformations of elements from positive to negative and the way they neutralize each other remind him of "the formidable orchestral explosion at the end of the dispute in act 2 of *Die Meistersinger*, which, cutting off the tumult of voices, is perceived not as additional noise but as the triumph of re-established silence."

Elsewhere, on the other hand, L.-S. seems to attribute fixed meanings to musical motifs (the theme of renunciation, which he tracks through the entire Wagnerian Ring Cycle), and this to me appears to contradict the fundamental principle of his entire method (the meaning of every element is always given in terms of its relations with the other elements). But we can also recognize a fundamental trait of his temperament: the need to find a meaning for everything, because the great abstract mechanism that rules the human mind (in mythical thinking as in music) can never be idle, it always has to be loaded with sensory experience.

PAINTING. In painting, the same requirement leads to a demand for representation, content. Besides the essay on Max Ernst I've already cited, there's another that is a kind of tirade against all painting from Impressionism onward. For L.-S. painting lost what it had reached in the period of the Renaissance (which didn't last long) because it began to favor empirical sensation (which doesn't exist) or wanted to go "beyond the object" (and beyond painting). The weak point of these general tirades always emerges when he has to give positive examples: the occasion of the essay, the presentation of a German painter with a miniaturist style, appears disproportionately modest. But what's important is to identify L.-S.'s painterly ideal with a Nordic naturalist tradition of Gothic origin, based on attention to detail and technical elaboration, from which (according to Panofsky), the spheres of the "realistic" and the "fantastic" develop in Northern Europe.

FREEDOM. The writings on painting figure in a section of the book entitled, significantly, "Constraint and Freedom," which ends with a speech from 1976, "Reflections on Liberty," in the political and more broadly anthropological sense. The survival of small, differentiated groups, of "partial societies," is, as always for L.-S., the condition without which all progress is transformed into oppression and destruction. But the course of political thought in the last two centuries (including his adored Rousseau) leads in the opposite direction. For this reason L.-S.'s speech is bitterly pessimistic, and anti-conformist in every aspect. The basis of freedom for him lies in that dust of small inequalities, habits, beliefs that the planners of freedom have done all they can to eliminate.

To follow him in this defense of "partial societies" we should try to imagine for ourselves how they can be configured, not among the tribes of the forests of Amazonia but in our West; and the problem is that we immediately think of the Mafia and the Camorra. In the first essay in the book L.-S. had given as an example of a newly formed "partial society" the hippies (it was 1971), threatened by an intolerance similar to racial intolerance. We could then agree with him, saying that the world we should hope for is one in which new "partial societies" can come into being without constraints. But thinking of the followers of Sun Myung Moon and other sects of the type that took root in the metropolises of the West doesn't cheer us at all, nor can I have sympathy for many of the independence movements based on linguistic and religious differences; so that I am inclined to think that in the world we live in "partial societies" are at risk of reproducing and concentrating the negative aspects of society as a whole.

It should be said that for L.-S. the problem is set in a much vaster context than the relationships between minorities and power (or between private and public, individual and state, elite culture and mass culture); it concerns the "eco-logical" vision that for him is equivalent to a cosmic sense of existence, and means never forgetting to situate human beings among the other living species and assert the rights of the environment over man more than the rights of man over the environment.

The basic point of his arguments is this: Roman law inspired by the Stoics, great civilizations of the East and the Far East inspired by Hinduism and Buddhism, peoples without writing studied by ethnologists agree in consider-ing man a beneficiary and not a master of creation. Only if he again becomes conscious that his survival is conditioned by limits that he has to place on the consumption and de-struction of fauna, flora, geography, and resources—in short, on what was there before him—can acceptance of these limits on its own inform interhuman relations as well, restoring the freedoms of those "partial societies" the way L.-S. sees them, that is, as the ultimate resource "pro-viding ailing freedoms with a little health and vigor."

[1983]

Pietro Redondi, Galileo Heretic

A man on the beach in Capua observes the sunset. He's not looking for artistic or poetic inspiration but has a scientific intention: he wants to measure the speed of the sun. But he doesn't have any sort of measuring instruments. He has a single system for counting units of time whose precision is ensured by long habit: "As the sun disappeared on the horizon in a symphony of colors, he recited two *misereres*, truly a very brief fraction of time."

This man is the future cardinal and future saint Roberto Bellarmino, who in his youth had had a true passion for science, as he recalls, recounting this episode, in an ascetic book written in his old age; the seventeenth-century impulse toward the natural sciences and mathematical exactness had also involved the man who harshly restored Catholic doctrine at the Council of Trent, and who in 1616 summoned Galileo (although with all the regard due to the admired man of science) for the first official injunction against the Copernican theory.

Bellarmino is one of the main characters in Pietro Redondi's *Galileo Heretic* (Turin: Einaudi, 1983); another, perhaps the protagonist, in fact, is the Jesuit Orazio Grassi, who (under the fictitious name of Lotario Sarsi) was the object of Galileo's sarcasm in *The Assayer*, and whose vendetta (according to the thesis that this book proposes as extremely likely) was at the origin of Galileo's condemnation by the Holy Office in 1633.

As we know, on the specific question of the comets that triggered the Galilean polemic of *The Assayer*, it was Grassi-Sarsi who was right, when it came to the facts, and not Galileo. Grassi was not only an astronomer and mathematician but an architect, and he was entrusted with the design of Sant'Ignazio, the Society of Jesus's most important church. A character not at all to be taken too lightly, therefore, and Galileo spied on his moves from Florence through a network of faithful friends in Rome, who even managed to describe to him Grassi's reactions when the first copy of *The Assayer* appeared on the counter of a Roman bookshop.

But with a reversal of roles that gives rise to one of the most narratively enjoyable passages of this historical investigation, Father Grassi, who is as shrewd as the devil, is transformed from the spied on to the spy, using the same people who were spying on him. The faithful Galilean Guiducci, who had the job of looking out for the plots of the Jesuits in Rome and reporting them to the master, is such a candid soul that he is deceived by Grassi's offers of friendship and robbed of information on the *Dialogue Concerning the Two Chief World Systems*, which Galileo was still writing.

What I've said so far is enough to indicate that Redondi's book (the author is a young Milanese historian of science, currently at Princeton) portrays, even more than Galileo, the atmosphere surrounding the dispute on the new science (or "new philosophy," as it was called) during a crucial twenty years of the seventeenth century and beyond: with lively portraits of both the adversaries, as I said, and the staunch friends, beginning with Prince Federico Cesi, the founder of the Accademia dei Lincei and the promoter of an encyclopedic project, centered on his fabulous library, that would represent the triumph of the new knowledge. Among the most important of Galileo's friends we should mention Pope Urban VIII, that is, the literary Florentine Maffeo Barberini, whose papacy (sustained by the Francophile party headed by the cardinal and man of the world Maurizio di Savoia), starting in 1623, brought hopes of a new renaissance.

This is the same pope who ten years later condemned his former favorite, the most prestigious scientist of the time, to perpetual house arrest. How did such a radical change of direction happen? How do we move from the "marvelous conjuncture" of the start of the Barberini papacy to the dark climate of the great ideological trials of the Inquisition? This is what Redondi explains to us, in fact presents vividly. (And we see that there are two faces, rather than two phases, always present in that papacy. As early as 1624 there is a postmortem trial whose baroque funerary scene Redondi evokes: the trial that condemned the memory of [Marco Antonio] De Dominis, an adventurous theologian twice a fugitive and twice an abjurer, in Venice, London, and Rome.)

The book offers a rich and detailed portrait of a world in which scientific research at a moment of maximum intellectual tension is interwoven with the expectation of many who are not scientists but—in the world of culture or simply of worldly society—share these expectations, as well as the preoccupation with doctrine in the post-Tridentine Church that makes every question a barrier in the war against Protestantism and every suspicion of collusion with the enemy a weapon for the internal fights between religious orders and theological currents. There are also the political intrigues of the Curia regarding the fight between France and Spain, and to these elements are added, in baroque Rome, the favors of fashion, which in those years supports the "new philosophy" and Galileo above all.

The prestige of the innovators on the rise clashes with the authority of the Jesuits, who, with the arrival of a Francophile pope, are at first slightly on the defensive. Then (when the alliance of Richelieu with Gustavo Adolfo returns Spain to a privileged role in papal politics) they are increasingly on the counterattack. The reasons for this authority emerge clearly here: first, outstanding scientific expertise (we've seen that in the debates they turn out to be right about specific facts more than once); second, a forbidding dogmatic intransigence that would be battling with science if it weren't served by the art of constructing philosophical arguments in support of dogma; third, a very complex but firm idea of cultural politics, along with the ambition to manage modernity and the new by means of a difficult strategy of openings and closings. In addition, there is the proverbial persuasive and dissembling and diplomatic ability (thanks to which, as soon as one of the characters in this book gets sick, he inevitably ends up in the hands of the Jesuit directors of conscience, who make him play their game).

Redondi is a well-documented historian, but he loves to tell stories, and the narration of both the historical facts and his own research acquires the suspense of a thriller. Which condemnation provokes Galileo's trial? No one has ever known. Redondi is sure that he has succeeded in getting his hands on the crucial document in the archives of the Inquisition, a manuscript in which the tribunal is asked its opinion of Galileo's atomist theories. It certainly wasn't an anonymous letter, but the page with the signature has disappeared. Redondi recognizes the handwriting and the style and the arguments of the man who had been the victim of Galileo's sarcasms, Father Grassi.

Here we are, then, at the central thesis of Redondi's book. If Galileo was officially condemned as a Copernican, that was only a political expedient for, yes, getting him out of the game, but at the same time saving him from a much more serious accusation: heresy against the dogma of transubstantiation in the Eucharist. Astronomy, according to Redondi, was not—even then—the material of faith; certainly the literal interpretation of Scripture wants the sun to revolve around the Earth, and it was good discipline to keep to that; but a trial so sensational, of the era's most prestigious man of science, openly protected by the pope, can't be justified solely on the basis of Copernicanism. Physics, however, was a matter of faith, Redondi maintains, because it had to explain how the body of Christ was transformed into bread and His blood into wine, with nothing remaining (dogma of the Council of Trent) of the substance of the bread and the wine, but at the same time it would take on (another miracle of the miracle) the "color, taste, and smell" of bread and wine. The only physical theory capable of explaining this phenomenon was Aristotle's, which separated the substance from its sensory or "accident" qualities, and that is the reason—not cosmography—that Aristotle becomes unassailable. (Things then get even more complicated, because the Jesuits' "new theology" went beyond Aristotelianism, but it's better if I stop here.)

What did Galileo, who had never been concerned with the Eucharist, have to do with it? He had to do with it in that the physical theory asserted in *The Assayer* explained sensations in a way that left an opening for, on the one hand, subjectivity (the example of tickling), which had already been condemned in Occam, and, on the other, the atomism (the "indivisibles" that form light, the "tiny fires" of heat) of notoriously godless philosophers like Democritus and Lucretius.

The Jesuits, who are able to show that Galileo is an atomist, and therefore a heretic, can ask for his head from Urban VIII, who until then had been his great protector.

The pope protector of a heretic? The scandal would have been too great. The pope manages to avoid a trial at the tribunal of the Inquisition by taking over the case himself and having it heard by a special commission named by him: Galileo has to be condemned in any case, because at that moment the Jesuits are a threat to the pope, but the charge will be the less compromising one of Copernicanism. The severity and the publicity of the sentence will be enough to block any further impulse toward innovation.

The Jesuits accept the compromise and play the game: they no longer attack Galileo for his heretical physics but only for his imprudent astronomy. So much so that the principal creator of the charge of atomism, Father Orazio Grassi, has to break off his brilliant academic career at the Collegio Romano and his direction of the work at Sant'Ignazio and retire in obscurity to Savona, his native city, until the end of his days. Strange fate of this assiduous mathematician who, as we've seen, is mocked (unjustly) by someone more illustrious than he, then pretends resignation and humility, then plots a devious and poisonous revenge, and in the end is himself sacrificed on the altar of a reason of state.

Redondi thus overturns the historical picture that up to now has formed the background of all our ideas on the transition to the modern era: we've always believed that the crucial question was the movement of the Earth around the sun, and for good reason, because it put an end to the conception that man was at the center of creation. No: it turns out that in the seventeenth century the cosmological issue was secondary, whereas an issue that today we can consider only on the symbolic spiritual plane was of primary scientific importance. (And every symbolic interpretation was called "nominalist" and judged a heresy.)

One chapter of the book gives us the essential facts of the Eucharistic problem as it was reflected in philosophy and physics, pointing out that all those who, following Saint Augustine, emphasized the spiritual aspects of the mystery rather than its material mechanics (Occam, Wycliffe, Huss) were condemned by the Church. Raphael's fresco *The Dispute Concerning the Holy Sacrament* is analyzed by Redondi as the expression of Christian Neo-Platonism's dream of reconciliation, which by now, in the Rome of the Counter-Reformation, is distant.

The historical picture that Redondi has reconstructed detail by detail seems to me convincing, but from the perspective of various elements within the picture I think there is still something to discuss. We can't underestimate the fact that the Galilean theory that was solemnly condemned concerned the movement of the Earth; this was the message that the sentence conveyed to the world. The Jesuits' goal was to damage the reputation that the totality of the new science enjoyed with the pope, and all that that involved (and the theories of Copernicus were the most obvious element). The charge of Eucharistic heresy was a formidable tool for this, because it was difficult to prove that it was a pretext, even if everyone was convinced of that (Urban VIII and maybe also the accusers themselves), and so it functioned as a weapon for blackmail.

And there is still the "Galileo heretic" of the title to discuss. Heretic in that he was accused of a heresy that he was ignorant of? No, says Redondi, Galileo had to be aware that the words *color, odor, taste* that he used in his atomist arguments were the same as those used by the apologists of transubstantiation: therefore he not only intended scientific controversy but was advocating a change in religious dogma.

This, too, is a very possible hypothesis, but to demonstrate it we would have to be able to situate the Galilean vision of the book of nature written by God in mathematical language more precisely; that is, in the cultural context of theology and natural philosophy between the Neo-Platonic Renaissance and the new religious sensibility represented in the years immediately following by another anti-Jesuit mathematician, Pascal. In Redondi's study, which contains many valuable and new elements for understanding the story of Galileo and situating it in its time, Galileo himself is what we see least clearly. We're left with the desire to examine more closely some details about him (or maybe only about him as a young man) "adopting a speculative mysticism that had Augustinian accents and referring explicitly to the Neo-Platonism of Dionysius the Areopagite, a source which the new theology of St. John of the Cross rendered topical."

Among the characters who appear in the margins of the main action, I will mention two: Campanella, who in those years has the rare (for him) good luck to be at liberty in Rome, and whose irrepressible and inopportune enthusiasms are always on the point of causing trouble; and Descartes, whom Redondi spies in Rome among the crowd of pilgrims in the Holy Year 1625, and as, unnoticed, he buys a copy of *The Assayer* at a stall in Piazza Navona and frequents the same places as Galileo without anyone's noticing, and develops Galileo's ideas without ever citing him, and avoids the theological traps and troubles whose machinations he is perfectly aware of. The philosopher of the method shines with illuminated prudence just as the utopian from Calabria is a champion of illuminated imprudence, in a century when the courage to think could cost you very dearly.

[1983]

Ancient and Modern Ideas of
Fate *by Giorgio de Santillana*

"Five times in the span of eight years the star Venus rises at the moment before the sun rises (a solemn moment in many civilizations). Now, the five points thus marked on the arc of the constellations, connected according to the order of their succession, turn out to form a perfect pentagram (that is, the design of a five-pointed star). That truly seems a gift of the gods to men, a mode of revelation. Whence the Pythagoreans said: Aphrodite was revealed in the sign of the Five. And the sign became magical. But what concentration of attention and memory it must have taken to hold in the mind, over eight years, the positions of the five flashes of the planet that appears to get lost immediately in the morning light—to reconstruct with the intellect the diagram they suggested." Giorgio de Santillana, taking off from the extraordinary precision with which the ancients observed the vault of the sky, gives us a book as small in mass as it is dense and fascinating in content: *Fato antico e fato moderno (Ancient and Modern Ideas of Fate)*. It should be said right away what Santillana means by *ancient* and by *precision*. The *ancients* are those who in the fifth millennium BC in Chaldea, Egypt, and India elaborated "the colossal features of a true archaic astronomy, which fixed the course of the planets, gave names to the constellations of the zodiac, created the astronomical universe—and with it the cosmos—as we find it ready when writing begins, around 4000 BC."

Evidence of this knowledge of the calculation of astral time is found in the proportions of the ziggurats of Mesopotamia (the Tower of Babel of the vilified Memrod was one of these complicated models of the order of the cosmos), and in the arrangement of the megaliths of Stonehenge. It seems that when writing begins and, with it, what we mean by history, that identification of the human mind with celestial movements begins to fail. Plato is still "the last of the ancients and the first of the moderns"; with Aristotle cosmic knowledge has already dissolved.

As for *precision*, it is "a passion for measurement, which centers everything on numbers and timings . . . At the top are the pure numbers, then the orbits of the sky, farther down earthly measurements, geodetic facts, then astrological healing, scales and musical intervals, then units of measure, volume and weight, then geometry, magic squares." The Egyptians' symbol of precision was a very light feather that serves as a weight on the pan of the scale of souls. "That light feather has the name Maat, Goddess of the scales, Goddess of exactness and strict compliance, of that implacable justness that acts as justice in the division of good from evil . . . The hieroglyph of Maat indicated also the unit of length, the 33 centimeters of the standard brick and also the fundamental tone of the flute." This precision seems to Santillana much more essential than that of modern physics, to which he devotes this passage: "It's very true that physical reality on its own account kicks to take revenge on its experts, shooting in their faces a confusion of transient, hard-to-distinguish elementary particles, an insult to common sense, while the scientist wanders around like someone riddled with bullets in the night." (A quotation that should be included in an ideal anthology, evidence of the tone and style of Santillana the writer, and the causticness of his sarcasm; but it should be situated in the time when it was written, twenty years ago: before, that is, the new surge of euphoria that—if I understand it—has returned to gratify subatomic physics.)

Giorgio de Santillana (1901–1974), a Roman, lived for thirty-five years or more in the United States, where he was a professor at MIT. He was a historian of science (*The Crime of Galileo* is one of his best-known books) who in his studies of the history of thought, mainly mathematical and astronomical, gave a lot of space to myth ("the first scientific language") and to literary imagination.

His monumental *Hamlet's Mill*, written with a German ethnologist (a student of Frobenius), Herta von Dechend, has as its subtitle *An Essay on Myth and the Frame of Time* and is comparable to Frazer's *Golden Bough* in the boundless wealth of anthropological and literary sources that are woven into a dense network around a common theme. The key to all myths, which for Frazer was the ritual sacrifice of the king and vegetation cults, for Santillana-Dechend is the regularities of zodiac time and its irreversible changes in the very long term (precession of the equinoxes) due to the inclination of the ecliptic with respect to the equator. Humanity bears a distant memory of the heavenly shifts, so that all mythologies preserve the trace of events that are produced every 2,400 years, such as the change in the zodiac sign in which we find the sun at the equinox; almost equally ancient is the prediction that the constant, extremely slow movement of the firmament coalesces into an immense cycle, or Great Year (26,900 of ours).

The twilight of the gods recorded or predicted in various mythologies is connected to these astronomical recurrences; sagas and poems celebrate the end of times and the start of new eras, when "the children of the murdered gods will find in the grass all the golden chess pieces from the game that was interrupted by the catastrophe." Going back to the sources of the legend of Hamlet in the Danish chronicles and Nordic mythologies, and bringing in the African Dogon, Hinduism, Aztecs, Greek and Latin authors, Santillana and Dechend trace the emergence of a first philosophical problem: the idea of an ordered cosmos whose rules are overturned by a physical and moral catastrophe, and, in response to that, the aspiration to find harmony again.

Hamlet's Mill was translated into Italian and published by Adelphi last year (it came out in America in 1969); if it wasn't talked about then in these columns, that was—as sometimes happens—precisely because of the overenthusiasm of us reviewers, which made us first argue among ourselves about the book, then consume the five hundred pages too quickly, then left us stymied by the job of summarizing it. The publication of *Ancient and Modern Ideas of Fate* gives me the opportunity to make up for this at least in part, because the small volume just published is partly an introduction, a preliminary declaration of the themes of the larger work. In fact the text that opens the book and gives it its title is a lecture that Santillana gave for the Associazione Culturale Italiana (Italian Cultural Association) in various Italian cities in 1963, and later published in Nicola Chiaramonte's *Tempo presente* (at the time one of the best Italian journals). Listening to the lecture in 1963, I had a sort of revelation of a knot of ideas that were already perhaps buzzing confusedly in my mind but that were difficult for me to express; and they would have been difficult to express afterward as well, but from that moment I was conscious of a distance to bridge, of a something to "confront." (Santillana: "And is it insignificant that the very name of science in Greek, *epistéme*, means confront?") I mean the idea that no human story or thought is possible unless it is situated in relation to everything that exists independently of the human; the idea of a knowledge in which the world of modern science and that of ancient wisdom are reunited. Rereading the text now, I rediscover the emotion of the moment when Santillana came up with the unexpected example of Pierre Bezukhov in *War and Peace*, who, imprisoned and with his life in danger, looks at the stars and thinks that all that sky is in him, *is* him.

The common theme of the four essays in this small book is the connection between Fate and freedom, that is, the place of man in the universe as it was conceived by the ancients, or rather the archaic peoples (and those archaic peoples who remained as such up until the threshold of our time, that is, the so-called primitives): the Fate that looms over all, men and gods (the gods are identified with the planets, which command every change), and the freedom that can be gained only by those who understand and respect the laws and measurements of the Cosmic Clock.

Fate was therefore very different from that inscrutable power, obscurely connected to our sins, which it became from the time of Greek tragedy up to our own: on the contrary, the idea of Fate implied precise knowledge of physical reality, and the awareness of its necessary and unavoidable dominion over us. Thus the true representatives of a scientific spirit were the archaics, not we who believe we can use natural forces at our pleasure and so have a mentality closer to magic.

To be in tune with the rhythm of the universe was the secret of harmony, a Pythagorean "music" that still in Plato rules astronomy as it does poetry and ethics. But it is also the sense of necessity, which will rise again, in an altered form, with Kepler, Galileo, Bruno, "in whom the intellect opens to ends that are no longer limitedly human, and wants to embrace and include the whole in a splendid *amor*

Fati." Does Santillana therefore assert a strict determinism? Certainly in every speculation in this direction, from Plato's *Timaeus* to Calvinist predestination or Islamic renunciation, he finds supporting arguments ("the greatest free energies of history" were released by ideas that seem made purposely to repress them), but we see how he continuously contrasts two different attitudes that arise in every era in the face of the inexorable: on the one hand, a tragic sense of guilt, and on the other the classic serenity of those who—"primitive" or supercivilized—accepting necessity establish their own place in the world, harmony. And certainly Santillana's sympathies go to the latter—although he is able to evoke with equal sensitivity the values of both.

Silence, music, and mathematics: the Pythagorean program is contained in that trinomial; and this book offers in passing illuminating descriptions of the Pythagoreans— understandably loved by Santillana—as well as a broad and convincing interpretation of Parmenides. (These explanations add to what is said on both subjects in an earlier, very useful work of Santillana's, *The Origins of Scientific Thought*, 1966.) But it's hard to establish clearly where Santillana is for and where he is against. If he sometimes seems to exalt a preliterate golden age and give a bleak picture of today's technological culture, enslaved to the car, he is still always ready to dissolve every idyllic illusion concerning archaic civilizations, depicting all the horrors and psychic traumas of living in those times; similarly, he can highlight the values of every new situation and the possibilities that it achieves—along with the negative values and losses.

An extraordinary historical essay contained in this volume begins as a report to a cardiology conference on different types of stress that men in various societies were subjected to, an anti-history of civilizations that can't be used by supporters of progress or by their habitual antagonists: every era has its collective neuroses, and they were not necessarily all inevitable. "So let's forget the virtues of the good ancient time. Let's forget the *douceur de vivre*. The first clinical description of an insane asylum is that of Arthur Haslam, who was the chief doctor in Bedlam. There we see not only inconceivable conditions but cases of psychosis that have no comparison in our handbooks. Another world."

If the reader of Santillana seeks generalizations that are convincing on the spot (the spatial thinking that has dominated science in recent centuries is bad, while thinking based on time is good; or, conscience not yoked to individual thought gave us an advantage over our anxieties), he can also find them; but they will be refuted on the next page, if not in the same paragraph.

Santillana's writing follows the very movement of intelligence, which understands even more than it judges, and sometimes judges in order to understand, ready to judge differently when it's a question of understanding something different. This is a necessary attitude for the historian, provided he knows how to avoid every sort of dialectic mechanism and, similarly, every sort of moral relativism. He succeeds thanks to a sense of values that is always alert: objective truth and human empathy.

For example, all the benefits that psychiatrists and neurologists identify in the absence of doubt or choice can't let Santillana forget that that also means absence of a sense of humor: a loss that he would certainly never want to face.

[1985]

Source Notes

READING, WRITING, TRANSLATING
Good Intentions
L'Unità (Rome), August 12, 1952

Characters and Names
Epoca, September 27, 1952, 3 (answer to a survey with the title "Our Literary People Confess: We Writers as Baptizers Work Like This")

The Failure of the Italian Novel
"Unpublished. Answer to a RAI radio survey, I believe of 1953, which was never broadcast. The judgment of Manzoni I expressed then had time to change." Published for the first time in Italo Calvino, *Saggi: 1945–1985* (Milan: Mondadori, 1995), 1507–11. Typewritten text of three pages with scattered corrections by hand kept in a file titled "On the Novel." On the top right of the page that contains this editorial note is the marginal note "See in what year the radio broadcast was supposed to happen. 1953? 1951?"

Source Notes

The Fates of the Novel

Ulisse 4, nos. 24–25 (Fall/Winter 1956–1957): 948–50

Questions on Realism

Tempo presente 2 (1957): 881–82 (answers to questions from Franco Matacotta)

Answers to Nine Questions on the Novel

Nuovi Argomenti 38–39 (May–August 1959): 6–12. Giorgio Bassani, Carlo Cassola, Eugenio Montale, Elsa Morante, Alberto Moravia, Pier Paolo Pasolini, Guido Piovene, Sergio Solmi, and Elémire Zolla also responded to this survey.

Industrial Themes

Il Menabò 5 (1962): 18–21

Correspondence with Angelo Guglielmi Regarding "The Challenge to the Labyrinth"

I.C. and Angelo Guglielmi, "Correspondence with Postscript on 'The Challenge to the Labyrinth,'" *Il Menabò* 6 (1963): 268–71

On Translation

Paragone letteratura 168 (December 1963): 112–18

Letter from a "Minor" Writer

Letter to Guido Fink, June 24, 1968, published in *Paragone letteratura* 428 (October 1985): 7–9.

Sitting-Down Literature

Response to a survey by Guido Ceronetti on "sitting-down literature," *Il Caffè* 17, no. 3 (October [December] 1970): 133–34

Art Thefts (Conversation with Tullio Pericoli)

I.C. and Tullio Pericoli, "Art Thefts," conversation on the occasion of Pericoli's show *Stealing from Klee* (Milan: Edizioni della Galleria Il Milione, 1980).

Translating a Text Is the True Way of Reading It

Paper delivered at a conference on translation in Rome, June 4, 1982, *Bollettino d'informazioni* 32, no. 3 (September–December 1985): 59–63

Literature and Power (on an Essay by Alberto Asor Rosa)

"Il poeta e Machiavelli" ("The Poet and Machiavelli"), *Repubblica*, January 13, 1983

The Last Fires

Repubblica, October 9–10, 1983

Gian Carlo Ferretti, Bestseller Italian-Style

"Minos's Tail," *Repubblica*, March 10, 1983. The allusion to Fortini has to do with a negative review of *If on a winter's night a traveler* and Umberto Eco's *The Name of the Rose*, which appeared shortly before in *Corriere della Sera* ("Romanzi a mano e romanzi a macchina" ["Handwritten Novels and Typewritten Novels"], February 27, 1983), and was then collected in the volume *L'ospite ingrato I e II* (*The Ungrateful Guest I and II*), Casale Monferrato, Italy: Marietti, 1985.

The Written World and the Unwritten World

Paper read at New York University as the James Lecture at the Institute for the Humanities, March 30, 1983: "The Written and the Unwritten World," *New York Review of Books*, May 12, 1983 (in somewhat different form, translated by William Weaver), then in *Letteratura internazionale* 2, nos. 4–5 (Spring/Summer 1985): 16–18.

A Book, Books

Speech given at the Buenos Aires Book Fair and published in *Nuovi quaderni italiani* 10 (1984): 11–21.

Why Do You Write?

"I said that . . . ," *Repubblica*, March 31–April 1, 1985. Reworking of the answer to the survey "Pourquoi écrivez-vous? 400 écrivains répondent," *Libération*, March 22, 1985.

ON PUBLISHING
Notes for a Book Series on Moral Inquiry

Three-page typescript, entitled "Notes and General Ideas for a Small Series of Books of Moral Inquiry for the Modern Man"; at the bottom, "Chicago January 18, 1960." Published for the first time in Calvino, *Saggi*, 1705–9.

Plan for a Journal

Four-page typescript that can be dated 1970. Published for the first time in Calvino, *Saggi*, 1710–17. It's the same journal that Calvino talks about in the exergue to the essay "Lo sguardo dell'archeologo" ("The Archaeologist's Gaze"), in *Una pietra sopra* (*The Uses of Literature: Essays*), as well as in the interview with Fernando Camon collected in *Il mestiere di scrittore. Conversazioni critiche* (*The Writer's Craft. Critical Conversations*): "Journals, or things like them, yes, every so often we talk about them, conceive projects. With Gianni Celati, especially, who is a kind of volcano of ideas, the friend with whom I have the most fertile exchange of ideas. But we always end up with a journal of critical studies, of theory, we're in an era that is more speculative than creative, it seems to me. We'd be making something that hardly anyone would read, so we're better off making books. But I also dream of a completely different sort of journal, especially in terms of the audience: a journal of serial novels like the ones Dickens and Balzac wrote. Real writers should write for it, write on commission (I believe deeply in writing on commission), and through this journal discover the true functions of a relationship with the public: crying, laughing, fear, adventure, mystery . . . because it should be a kind of 'Peanuts' but not a comic strip, serial novels with a lot of illustrations, an attractive layout" (Calvino, *Saggi*, 2785–86).

Issue 14 of *Riga* is devoted to this project: *Alì Babà. Plan for a Journal 1968–1972*, edited by Mario Barenghi and Marco Belpoliti (Milan: Marcos y Marcos, 1998). Several copies of the text reproduced here are preserved among Calvino's papers, one in a file that holds papers from 1970, one in a red rigid cardboard file along with his correspondence with Gianni Celati, Guido Neri, and Carlo Ginzburg.

A New Series, Einaudi's Centopagine Series

Introduction to the series, a folder attached to the first four titles

The Mondadori Biblioteca Romantica

"La Romantica," in *Editoria e cultura a Milano tra le due guerre (1920–1940)* (*Publishing and Culture in Milan Between the Two Wars [1920–1940]*) (Milan: Fondazione Arnoldo and Alberto Mondadori, 1983), 172–78

ON THE FANTASTIC

The Knights of the Grail

"Una scodella chiamata Graal" ("A Cup Called the Grail"), *Repubblica*, May 31–June 1, 1981

Fantastic Tales of the Nineteenth Century

Introduction to *Racconti fantastici dell'Ottocento (Fantastic Tales of the Nineteenth Century*), vol. 1 (Milan: Oscar Mondadori, 1983), 5–14

Seven Flasks of Tears

Repubblica, January 24, 1984

The Fantastic in Italian Literature

"La literature fantastica y las letras italianas," in *Literatura fantastica* (Madrid: Siruela, 1985) 39–55 (paper given at the Menendez Pelayo International University in Seville in September 1984).

Notturno Italiano

"Benvenuti fantasmi" ("Welcome, Ghosts"), *Repubblica,* December 30–31, 1984

SCIENCE, HISTORY, ANTHROPOLOGY

The Genealogical Forest

Corriere della Sera, July 16, 1976 (preceded by "The Indian Gods Who Talk About Stone," later included in *Mr. Palomar*)

Cosmological Models

"Ultime notizie sul tempo. Collezionista d'universi" ("Latest News About Time: Collector of Universes"), *Corriere della Sera,* January 23, 1976

Montezuma and Cortés

"Montezuma and Cortés," in C. A. Burland, *Montezuma signore degli Aztechi* (*Montezuma Lord of the Aztecs*) (Turin: Einaudi, 1976), xiii-xxii (published first in *Corriere della Sera,* April 14 and 21, 1974). This essay appeared in the Italian edition of the book.

Cannibals and Kings *by Marvin Harris*

"Onore ai cannibali" ("Homage to Cannibals"), *Repubblica,* January 8, 1980

Carlo Ginzburg, *"Clues: Roots of an Evidential Paradigm"*

"L'orecchio, il cacciatore, il pettegolo" ("The Ear, the Hunter, Gossip"), *Repubblica,* January 20–21, 1980

Source Notes

Ilya Prigogine and Isabelle Stengers, La Nouvelle Alliance
"No, non saremo soli" ("No, We Won't Be Alone"), *Repubblica*,
May 3, 1980; published in English as *Order Out of Chaos: Man's
New Dialogue with Nature* (New York: Bantam, 1984)

Arnold van Gennep, The Rites of Passage
"Noi portatori di chiavi" ("Carriers of Keys"), *Repubblica*, July 28,
1981

Long Journey to the Center of the Brain
by Renato and Rosellina Balbi
"Che testa!" ("What a Head!"), *L'Espresso,* October 11, 1981

Disturbing the Universe *by Freeman Dyson*
"I disturbatori dell'universo" ("Disturbers of the Universe"), *Repubblica*, December 27–28, 1981

Giovanni Godoli, The Sun: Story of a Star
"Noi alunni del Sole" ("Students of the Sun"), *Repubblica,* May 15,
1982

Essays on Love *by Ortega y Gasset*
"Se amore non è desiderio" ("If Love Isn't Desire"), *Repubblica*,
June 13–14, 1982

The View from Afar *by Claude Lévi-Strauss*
"Sotto gli occhi di Lévi-Strauss" ("Under the Eyes of Lévi-
Strauss,"), *Repubblica,* July 15, 1983

Pietro Redondi, Galileo Heretic

"Forse è meglio parlare del sole" ("Maybe It's Better to Talk About the Sun"), *Repubblica,* October 13, 1983

Ancient and Modern Ideas of Fate *by Giorgio de Santillana*

"The Sky Is Me," *Repubblica,* July 10, 1985

ITALO CALVINO (1923–1985) attained worldwide renown as one of the twentieth century's greatest storytellers. Born in Cuba, he was raised in San Remo, Italy, and later lived in Turin, Paris, Rome, and elsewhere. Among his many works are *Invisible Cities, If on a winter's night a traveler, The Baron in the Trees,* and other novels, as well as numerous collections of fiction, folktales, criticism, and essays. His works have been translated into dozens of languages.